Democracy after Democratization:
The Korean Experience

DEMOCRACY

AFTER

DEMOCRATIZATION

The Korean

Experience

Jang-Jip Choi

SHORENSTEIN
APARC
STANFORD

THE WALTER H. SHORENSTEIN
ASIA-PACIFIC RESEARCH CENTER

The Walter H. Shorenstein Asia-Pacific Research Center
Freeman Spogli Institute for International Studies
Stanford University
Encina Hall
Stanford, CA 94305-6055
tel. 650-723-9741
fax 650-723-6530
http://APARC.stanford.edu

Democracy after Democratization: The Korean Experience
may be ordered from:
The Brookings Institution
c/o DFS, P.O. Box 50370, Baltimore, MD, USA
tel. 1-800-537-5487 or 410-516-6956
fax 410-516-6998
http://www.brookings.edu/press

Walter H. Shorenstein Asia-Pacific Research Center Books, 2012.
Copyright © 2012 by the Board of Trustees of the
Leland Stanford Junior University.

Library of Congress Cataloging-in-Publication Data
Ch'oe, Chang-jip.
Democracy after democratization : the Korean experience / Jang-Jip Choi.
    pages cm
Includes index.
ISBN 978-1-931368-26-1
1. Democratization—Korea (South) 2. Civil society—Korea (South) 3. Korea
(South)—Politics and government—1988–2002 I. Title.
JQ1729.A15C434 2012
320.95195—dc23

                                                                    2012042069

First printing, 2012.

Typeset by Classic Typography in 10.5/13 Sabon MT Pro

Contents

Tables and Figures   vii

Preface   ix

Acknowledgements   xi

PART I Problems

1 The Portrait of Democracy in Korea after Democratization   3

PART II The Origins of Conservative Democracy

2 State-building and Premature Democracy   23

3 Authoritarian Industrialization and Democratization by Mass Movement   53

4 The Conservative Outcome of the Democratic Transition and Regionalized Party System   81

PART III Korean Society after Democratization

5 The State after Democratization   113

6 The Market after Democratization   145

7 Civil Society after Democratization   167

PART IV Conclusion

8 Democratization of Democracy   187

Index   205

Tables and Figures

Tables

2.1 Chronology of Major Events, 1945–60   23

2.2 Percentage of Votes Received by Political Parties: First–Fourth General Elections   37

2.3 Establishment of Universal Suffrage by Country   46

3.1 Chronology of Major Events, 1961–80   53

4.1 Chronology of Major Events, 1987–2001   81

5.1 Degree of Concentration by Sector (1998, %)   141

6.1 Change in General Concentration of *Chaebŏl*, 1988–2006   150

6.2 Yearly Labor Disputes Under the Kim Dae-jung Government   156

6.3 The New Cleavage Structure in the IMF-led Globalization Period   158

8.1 Cleavage Structure in the Post–Cold War Neo-liberal Era   194

Figures

1.1 Declining Voter Turnout Since Democratization   4

1.2 Income Inequality Index   9

1.3 Ratio of Private Spending on Education Relative to GDP   11

2.1 Political Genealogy Immediately after Liberation   26

2.2 The Polarization of the Ideological Representation System in Korea   35

3.1 Change in Korean Industrial Structure (%)   59

4.1 Labor Dispute Incidence after 1980   90

8.1 Inter-party Conflicts   191

8.2 Party Competition, Voter Alignment, and the
        Conservative Party   193

8.3 Structural Mechanics after Democratization   201

Preface

This book examines the origins, characteristic features, and changes in Korean democracy, focusing on the politics of the country over the past fifty years. To understand the issues of Korean democracy today, one has to go beyond what meets the eye and look into the structural and historical restrictions of its early development and how the situation has changed since then. Instead of a chronological narrative or a formalistic structure used by most textbooks to teach Korean politics, this book takes an issue-oriented approach and narrative. I start out by identifying the central issues of democracy in Korea; I then examine their origins and structures. I must confess the examinations are more schematic than exhaustive. In this sense, this book is less of a precision drawing than a rough sketch of politics in Korea. It focuses on the structural core and its dynamics, leaving out other details, as in a painter's drawing of a torso.

This book is composed of four parts. Part One is a critique of the current situation of conservative complacency, in which democracy does not respond to the social demands and changes of the time. Part Two focuses on answering the following questions in terms of the historical and structural origins of democracy in Korea: Why does democracy in Korea not respond to social changes and demands? Why is it conservative even after democratization? Part Three of the book deals with the social issues that emerged after democratization, especially after the coming to power of opposition parties that had struggled for democratization. Why are democratic governments in Korea ineffectual? Is it right that they should pursue a stringently neo-liberal market economy as a matter of principal economic policy? What can and cannot be expected from civil society? Part Four is the conclusion of the book.

When I was preparing for this book, there was a recurring scene in my mind, from the musical *Les Misérables*. In the early part of the musical the people sing in a chorus, "Nothing changes, nothing ever will." This is in reference to the aftermath of the French Revolution, the backdrop of the original novel. Today, in Korea too, there is widespread skepticism and many ask, "What has changed after democratization?" But the questioning cannot stop there. This question must accompany the questions of how democracy must be understood and how it can further develop. I hope that we will once again face democracy with earnestness and passion.

Lastly, I dedicate this book to all citizens who have struggled for democratization and to those who still ardently wish for further development of democracy in Korea.

Jang-Jip Choi
Seoul, Korea
September 1, 2012

Acknowledgements

This book originally began with a public lecture series on Korean democracy, organized by the Asiatic Research Institute at Korea University. Thus, this book is not strictly for academic experts in the field of political science. Instead, it is written for general readers in mind, taking the 1987 June Struggle as its background, and discussing the experience of democratic transition in South Korea and some of the ensuing issues today. I tried to avoid using too much jargon and minimized the use of footnotes.

It would have been impossible to write this book without the sustained conversations I had with the researchers at the Institute, who were actually and deeply involved in the democratization movement in the 1980s, as well as with graduate research assistants. I am greatly indebted, in particular, for the insights I gained from the Friday Seminars, a discussion series on democracy that continued for a number of years at the Asiatic Research Institute.

The English translation of this book in its initial stage was supported by the Ministry of Culture and Tourism, South Korea. I am grateful to Kyunghee Lee who translated this book into English. And I also thank the staff at Humanitas, the publisher, whose assistance is beyond my reckoning in publishing both the Korean and English editions.

The publication of *Democracy After Democratization* by the Shorenstein Asia-Pacific Research Center (Shorenstein APARC) was made possible by a generous grant from the Academy of Korean Studies and the Ministry of Education, Science and Technology, South Korea (AKS-2007-CA-2001). Without the support of the Academy of Korea Studies, I would not have been able to conduct new research that enabled substantial revisions of the previous manuscript. During the 2009 spring quarter I was a visiting professor at Stanford University's Department of Sociology and was able to further the research that resulted in this publication. I engaged in invaluable scholarly collaborations during this period, and my teaching at Stanford University helped me in the final stages of writing. My appreciation goes out to the staff at Shorenstein APARC, and I especially wish to thank Professor Gi-Wook Shin for the support he has given to this book over several years.

Democracy after Democratization:
The Korean Experience

Part I

Problems

1 The Portrait of Democracy in Korea after Democratization

1. The Crisis of Participation and Representation

There is no better example that succinctly captures the portrait of democracy in Korea than the low voter turnout for a recent election. In the general election that took place in April 2008 to elect members of the 18th National Assembly, the voter turnout had dropped to less than 50 percent. The important question here is not which candidate or party should have been supported. Nor is it about who or which party benefits from such a situation. The real issue is the low voter turnout itself. Political participation and representation by political parties constitute the core of modern democracy. The fact that the majority of the voters refused to exercise the civic right bestowed by a democracy is not only proof in itself of the "crisis of participation," but it also highlights the "crisis of representation." It raises the following questions: Does democracy in Korea function as a legitimate process for coalescing the voice of the majority? Do political parties in Korea indeed legitimately represent the voice of the civil society in policy decisions and legislative processes that have a direct impact on civic life?

The low voter turnout shown in Figure 1.1 for the 2008 election is not an isolated incident. Since democratization in 1987, voter participation rates have continuously declined. In what can be called the "founding elections,"[1]

1 Founding election: An election that concludes a transition to a new political regime. This is a concept developed by O'Donnell and Schmitter. High voter turnout and strong competitiveness are characteristic features. The uncertainty of transition is eliminated through a founding election, and the pattern of competition and coalition among political parties in this election tend to repeat themselves in later elections. Guillermo A. O'Donnell and Philippe C. Schmitter, *Transitions from Authoritarian Rule: Tentative Conclusions about Uncertain Democracies* (Baltimore: Johns Hopkins University Press, 1986), 61–64.

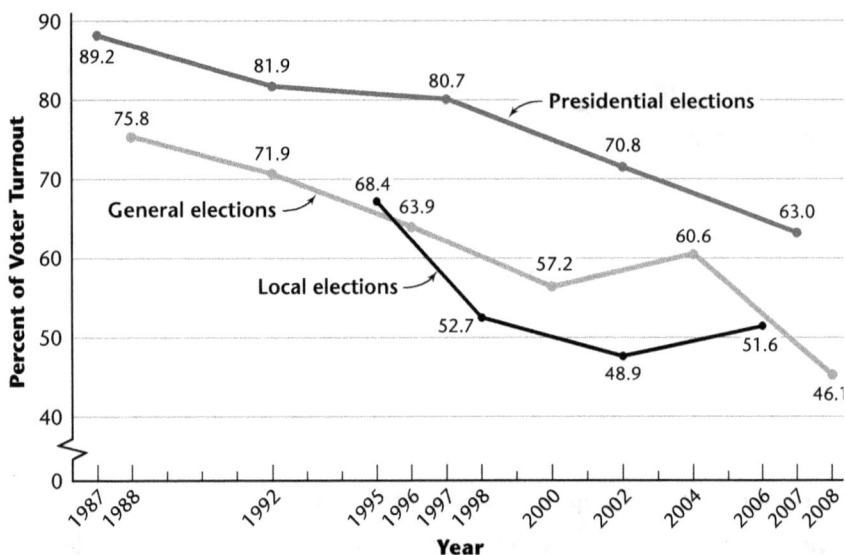

FIGURE I.I Declining Voter Turnout Since Democratization
Source: National Election Commission.

the 13th presidential election in 1987 and the 1988 general elections soon after democratization, the voting rates were 89.2 percent and 75.8 percent, respectively. In comparison, the voter turnout for the same elections in 2007 and 2008 was 62.9 percent and 46.0 percent, respectively. In the twenty years since democratization, close to 30 percent of the voters gave up their right to exercise this right of citizenship. Of course, the trend toward low voter turnout is a worldwide problem that is not confined to Korea. However, it is difficult to find another country where the turnout has declined so precipitously that it brings into question the very legitimacy of the election process.

The low voter turnout is not likely to change. More than anything else, the major cause of the declining voter turnout is the low participation of young voters. Accordingly, if the current trend continues, the voter turnout will decrease as the eligible young voter population increases. According to a study by the National Election Commission, for the 1996 general election of the 15th National Assembly, the voter turnout among those in their 20s was estimated to be 44 percent, which was 20 percent lower than that of the overall voter population. For the 2000 general election, the rate was estimated to be approximately 37 percent, and by the 2008 general election the turnout stopped at 29 percent. The wild enthusiasm of the 2002 World Cup fans, represented by the Red Devils, and the intensity of the "mad cow" candlelight vigils of 2008 were an explosion of a collective involvement that surprised not only Koreans but also the international community. The political meaning of this phenomenon has many possible interpretations, but what is certain is that there is a strong desire in the young generation to express and participate collectively. The fact that these young people, who turned the nation into a sea of candlelight, do not vote makes the future of Korea dark.

It is difficult to categorically criticize the young for not voting. Today, the government is ineffectual. Political parties refuse to formulate policy alternatives that are based on social demands. Members of the National Assembly, who purportedly represent the people, have shown more interest in accumulating personal political assets than in dedicating themselves to a greater political cause. It does not come as a surprise then that public hatred or antipathy toward politics is growing.

It is also logical that under such circumstances, voter decisions cannot be made rationally. For those who wish to hold the government accountable for its irresponsibility and incompetence, the rational choice would be to support a strong opposition party. In the context of actual Korean politics, such a choice would lead to another difficulty. In short, voters are not particularly inspired to reprimand today's incompetent government by way of casting a ballot for the party of yesterday's incompetent government.

Voters with a progressive inclination are also faced with a lack of alternatives from which they can make a positive choice. A voter who is critical of the two leading conservative parties—the ruling and the opposition parties—and who wishes to support a progressive party candidate, faces a difficulty in making such a choice, given that under the current electoral system any vote not cast for the winner becomes a wasted vote. In the past four general elections since democratization, the winning candidate received, on average, over 45 percent of the vote. There are few election districts in the nation where a progressive party would receive this level of votes.

Under the current condition, people who have a real alternative in Korea are those with vested interests in the status quo and voters with a conservative disposition. Considering that a large number of eligible voters with a different political inclination are boycotting the elections, the active voting behavior of the conservative voters is necessarily overrepresented. A party system that cannot provide eligible voters with an opportunity to make a rational choice cannot be expected to realize the equal rights of its citizens.

The most serious problem of democracy in Korea is the ideologically very narrow base of political representation, which in fact represents only conservatives. In substance, this structure of conservative bias has only become reinforced after democratization, despite changes in the overall political landscape. When a nation is ideologically fettered, that is to say, when Cold War anti-communism still functions as the dominant language of

the nation's politics, democracy does not become a mechanism for building consensus to solve the various problems that the nation faces as a society. Instead, it serves to justify vested interests and special privileges "in the
name of democracy."

There are many social ills attributable to the conservatively biased political representation, a system that is dominated by Cold War anti-communism. One such direct outcome is "democracy without labor," where the
interests and demands of the poor and the working class are not politically
represented. This also creates a social atmosphere where labor is regarded
with contempt, and the social value of dedication to work is undermined.
In the meantime, the whole country has been thrown into a whirlwind of
rent-seeking[2] activities, from real estate speculation to financial management, fund management, and other activities that do not involve productive
labor. Under these circumstances, the questions of social justice raised by
the democratization movement of the 1980s do not carry much weight any
more. Today, it would be rare to find a civic leader or a politician who takes
social justice as his or her guideline for making decisions. What dominates
their language is the logic of amoral technical rationality that only questions
what is efficient. In the end, such logic must inevitably be one that ignores
the communal issues of society.

Due to the heavy voter mobilization campaigns under the authoritarian
government, the voting pattern in Korea typically showed a high percentage
of participation from low-income, elderly, female, less-educated, and farming
populations, a rare phenomenon from the perspective of comparative politics. However, since democratization, what Korea finds is that the variation in
voting rate according to educational level, region, and gender is decreasing,
while the non-participation rate among the newly eligible voters in their 20s
has increased to an inexplicable level. There is an important fact that must be
added to this. The correlation between income- and class-level and the voting
participation rate has begun to change in a direction that is opposite to that of
the past. According to a survey[3] conducted by the Asiatic Research Center of
Korea University in 2001, a high correlation began to appear between subjective class category and voting rate, as well as between income level and voting
rate. Among the respondents categorizing themselves as belonging to the upper
class, the voting rate was 8.5 percent higher than among those who responded
as belonging to a lower class. The voting rate among those who identified

2 Rent-seeking: Refers to the non-productive activities of those private-sector actors
that try to make profit by improper appropriation of public resources or by influence
peddling rather than by productive activities.

3 Survey Data on the Quality of Life of Koreans (The Asiatic Research Center, Korea
University, 2001).

themselves as either upper class or upper-middle class was again 10 percent higher than among those identifying themselves as either lower class or lower-middle class. The voting rate among those responding that their monthly income was higher than 2.5 million won was 10 percent higher than among those responding that it was under 2.0 million. Research based on the 2006 census shows these characteristics more plainly. According to the study, the poorer an area, the lower the turnout rate—and this also applies in reverse.[4] It seems logical that dissatisfaction with the existing political parties is rapidly increasing among the poor and the low-income class, because the ideological conservatism of the political representation system and the deepening entrenchment of the class structure found in all spheres of society go hand in hand with the political demobilization that is exclusive of the lower strata of society. In fact, after democratization, the existing political parties made no effort to transform themselves into popular political parties by way of mobilizing and organizing the poor and the working class. In this way, the political parties in Korea have acquired some striking characteristics. First, they have become cadre parties[5] where officially less than 1 percent of their registered members pay membership dues to participate in regular party activities. Second, the political parties in Korea are electoral-professional parties[6] whose only purpose lies in winning elections rather than in advocating and disseminating any ideology or policies. Third, they are are colorless catch-all parties[7] seeking support from all strata of society and reflecting the interests and demands of no particular class or group. It is not difficult to understand the social consequences such political competition will bring when these characteristics of the political parties are combined with the conservatism of the ideological representative system.

4 Son Nak-ku, *Taehan min'guk chŏngch'i sahoe chido* (The Map of Politics and Society of Korea: The Greater Seoul Metropolitan Areas) (Seoul: Humanitas, 2010).

5 Cadre Party: A concept of Maurice Duverger. A type of political party in which nomination of candidates and decision-making on party policies are made by a small number of elites in contrast to a mass party. Maurice Duverger, *Political Parties* (New York: John Wiley, 1959).

6 Electoral-professional party: A concept developed by Angelo Panebianco. It is a party that aims at winning the election as an end in itself rather than seeking to realize its own platforms or ideologies. Election campaign professionals exercise a great influence in such a party. Angelo Panebianco, *Political Parties: Organization and Power* (Cambridge: Cambridge University Press, 1988).

7 Catch-all party: A concept used by Otto Kirchheimer. It is a new type of political party in Europe that appeals to the electorate of all social strata, beyond its traditional constituency based upon class. Otto Kirchheimer, "The Transformation of the Western European Party Systems," in *Political Parties and Political Development*, ed. Joseph LaPalombara and Myron Weiner (Princeton: Princeton University Press, 1966).

2. The Worsening of Social Conditions

The most striking social consequence brought on by Korean democracy, characterized by the conservative bias of its political parties, is the fact that class inequality has deepened precipitously. Politics based on the principles of democracy operates as an equalizing mechanism that mitigates the unequal effects of the market. The experience of Western welfare states with social democratic parties at the centers of their systems well illustrates this point. Korean democracy, however, stands on a structure of vested interests and a system of special privileges, and the market in Korea reflects the conservative bias of the nation's political structure. The routine real estate speculation and corruption of the upper class reflect the conservative Korean social structure. In the past, to make up for its lack of political legitimacy, the authoritarian state mitigated any excessive inequality among social classes, even as it kept a small group of specially privileged elite. On the other hand, after democratization, Korea has been gradually eliminating the existing market regulatory mechanisms without having developed the democratic role of the state to govern the inequality inherent in the structure of vested interests and the market system.

The outcome of this process over the years can be seen in the high measure for the Gini coefficient,[8] which measures income inequality. The average income difference between the top and bottom 20 percent income groups was: 4.74 times in 1996, 6.75 times in 2000, 7.75 in 2004, 8.22 times in 2005, 8.40 times in 2007, and 8.41 times in 2008. Despite the hype around the legislation of the *chaebŏl* (*jaebeol*)[9] reform policy in 1998, the concentration of the top *chaebŏl* groups in the Korean economy grew even further, and one cannot say that the situation of their monopoly and the market imbalance has improved. (South Korea's income inequality index is shown in Figure 1.2.)

Until the mid-1990s, Samsung was merely one of the top five *chaebŏl*. But by 2005, it became the *chaebŏl* of *chaebŏl*; it accounted for 50.8 percent of the combined assets of the top five *chaebŏl* groups, 45.9 percent of the combined market capitalization, 39.5 percent of the combined revenue, and 46.2 percent of the combined net profit for the year. Due to the job insecurity following massive layoffs during the 1997-98 financial crisis, and due to the rapid growth of the government-led knowledge information industry, polarization within the middle class is also becoming entrenched. At the

8 Gini coefficient: An index of income inequality presented by the Italian statistician Corrado Gini. On a scale of 0 to 1, the income distribution is more equal when it is closer to 0, while "the rich get richer and the poor get poorer" is more the case when closer to 1.

9 *Chaebŏl*: A major conglomerate in Korea owned by a single family.

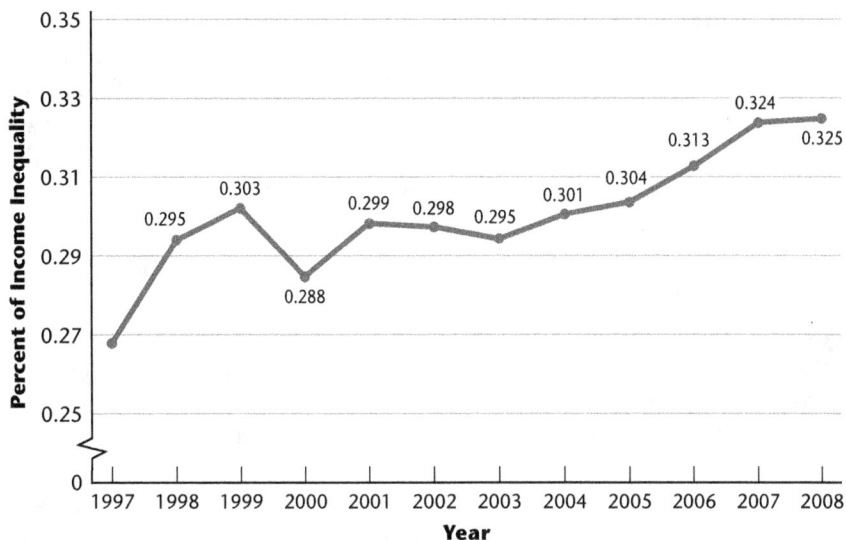

FIGURE 1.2 Income Inequality Index
Source: National Statistics Office.

same time, increasing unemployment and housing problems have made the lives of the working poor even poorer. With the percentage of temporary workers reaching above 50 percent of the total labor force, the labor market has been reorganized into a two-tier structure.

Poverty, thought to be an issue of bygone days, has reemerged. According to "The Trajectory of Poverty in Korea and Analysis of Its Factors" (Uri nara pin'gon pyŏnhwa chuŭi wa yoin punsŏk), a report published by the Korea Development Institute in July 2009, the percentage of low-income households below the 50-percentile median-level income increased twofold to 14.3 percent compared to the early 1990s. Looking at the figures between 2000 and 2008 only, the overall inequality level increased by 7.4 percent while the number of low-income households increased by 36.2 percent. Economic polarization is a serious problem in Korea, but poverty has become even more serious. There is no better example than the failure of public education in Korea to illustrate the problem of the widening class gap. There was a time in Korea when one could make an upward social move with only a diploma from one of the "top-notch" universities and thus, for the poor, education provided a viable channel for social mobility.

Over the years, one's bargaining power in the labor market was determined by the prestige of one's alma mater; now, the competition for college entrance has developed into a permanent class struggle. Since democratization, this struggle has become more pronounced than during the authoritarian period.

No family with school-aged children is free from the increasing pressure to spend more of its household income on educating its children. The biggest industry in any residential area is *hagwŏn* (*haegwon*),[10] the main source of after-school private education for children. In terms of the ratio of private spending on education relative to the national income, Korea by far leads the world. According to a study done by the Korean Educational Development Institute, Korea as a nation spent 3.4 percent of its national income on private education as of 2004; this figure is approximately three times higher than the average 1.3 percent spent by the Organisation for Economic Co-operation and Development (OECD) nations. In terms of private spending on education in comparison to the national household expenditure in Korea, the ratio is 12 percent for 2005, which means it has doubled since the early 1990s. Figure 1.3 illustrates the trend in South Korea for the ratio of private spending on education relative to gross domestic product (GDP).

In every household, the number one goal of the parents is to send their children to a high-ranking university, even if it means increasing household spending on education. Not surprisingly, the level of household income has now become the main variable determining educational opportunities and achievements. Education determines future income, while present income determines the education for the future. Accordingly, the class hierarchy and the university hierarchy now run parallel.

Since democratization, the main contribution of the government to the college entrance system has been to allow universities, in the name of allowing them more autonomy, to increase the number of students admitted per school class through various means and tactics. As a result, universities have now become oversized. Today, a college diploma in itself does not mean much, so that upward social mobility has become difficult with merely a diploma from a prestigious university. At about the same time, Korea also witnessed a wave of college students preparing for various government examinations. In the past, taking a government examination was limited mostly to law students or students of public administration. Today, it has become a routine practice for the general student population. The strange phenomenon of science majors from top-ranking universities, as well as PhD holders, taking the civil service examinations illustrates that for upward mobility one needs something more than a high level of education.

10 *Hagwŏn* (*haegwon*): Commercially operated private tutoring establishment(s) that can have anywhere from one instructor teaching one subject—such as a piano *hagwŏn*—to a large number of instructors teaching all major school subjects to various grade levels. There are also *hagwŏn* that specialize in tutoring students for the highly competitive college entrance examination. The preparation for the examination can start as early as before a child enters elementary school.

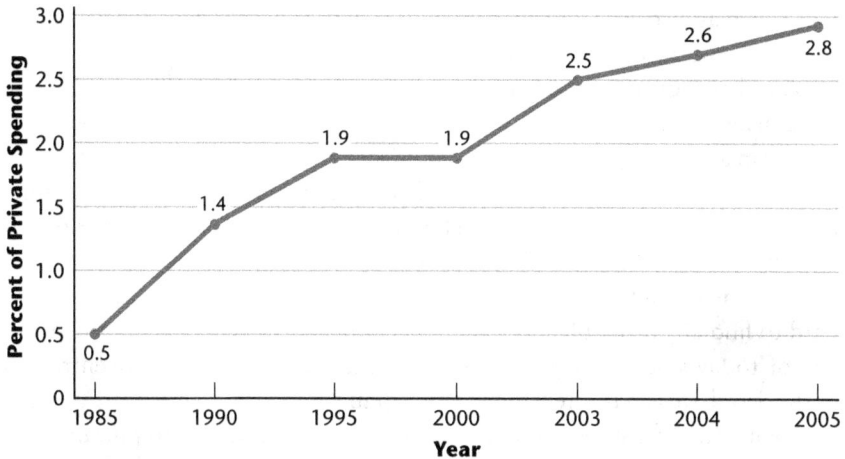

FIGURE 1.3 Ratio of Private Spending on Education Relative to GDP
Source: National Statistics Office.

The proverbial story of a poor lad, working by day and studying by night to pass a civil service examination because his family was too poor to send him to a university, has now become folklore of the distant past.

But the wave of taking civil service examinations did not last long. It was soon replaced by another wave, despite the fact that the government eased access to special privileges by greatly expanding the pool of those passing government-administered tests, including the national judiciary examination and the certified public accountants' examination. The students were in search of other channels for social mobility. With the International Monetary Fund (IMF) bailout crisis of 1997–98 as the starting point, new waves sweeping the nation, apart from neo-liberalism,[11] have included English education abroad and going to top-notch universities in the United States. Again, these phenomena show that the education system in the democratic era does not function as a mechanism to mitigate class inequality. Instead, they show that education is another system that is a function of class structure, not vice versa; they show

11 Neo-liberalism: The term neo-liberalism began to be used widely as a reference to the economic policy or the general policy line of President Ronald Reagan of the United States and Prime Minister Margaret Thatcher of the United Kingdom. Reagan (a Republican) and Thatcher (a Tory) came into power in 1980 and 1979, respectively. The core of neo-liberalism is to resurrect the basic ideas of the laissez-faire liberalism of the nineteenth century. The main goals of its economic policies are the control of inflation, downsizing the state and its costs, incentives for entrepreneurial activities, and removal of restrictions that hinder the operation of free market. Thus its policy goals are entirely focused on creating conditions for free enterprises to prosper.

that Korea as a society is neglecting to deal with the fact that market inequality and its effects are now encroaching upon the educational sphere.

Another indication pointing to the worsening social conditions in Korea since democratization is the fact that urban concentration in the Seoul metropolitan area has intensified. One could say that the problem of urban concentration in Seoul is not a new one; it has been a problem for a long time. Decades ago, Gregory Henderson stated that "Seoul was not simply Korea's largest town, it was Korea."[12] Certainly, urban concentration in the Seoul area is a problem that started long before democratization. However, it is hard to find any other phenomenon that more perfectly illustrates the problem of today's democracy in Korea than the fact that urban concentration in the Seoul areas has intensified rather than eased after democratization.

Democracy must be a power that develops the tendency to pluralize the center of society. One of the salient characteristics of a non-democratic society, such as an authoritarian, absolutist, or totalitarian society, is that political, economic, military, and cultural powers and influences are solidified around a single center. It would not be an overstatement to say that the very function of democratization is to break up the concentration of these power elements and to pluralize their sources. A subsequent question is how to reorganize the relations between multiple sites of power in accordance with the conditions and realities of various local communities so that the reorganization contributes to the development of each community. The reality in Korea is that, with only 0.6 percent of the nation's total land area, Seoul has more than 20 percent of its total population. Furthermore, like a black hole, it draws in all of the nation's political, economic, and cultural resources. This hyper-concentration, on one hand, and the absence of pluralistic values or the uniformity of the Korean society, on the other, are two sides of the same coin. Clearly, such hyper-concentration cannot occur in a balanced society. Under the present circumstances, diversity of ideologies and values, and free thinking are not possible.

I have always opposed the approach of understanding the "regional rivalry sentiment" in Korea as nothing more than an irrational emotion. I also do not agree with the explanation that the problem is the animosity and conflict between the Honam[13] and Yŏngnam (Yeongnam)[14] regions. Indeed,

12 Gregory Henderson, *Korea: The Politics of the Vortex* (Cambridge: Harvard University Press, 1968), 30.

13 Honam: The southwest region in Korea that comprises North and South Chŏlla (Jeolla) Provinces.

14 Yŏngnam (Yeongnam): The southeast region in Korea that comprises North and South Kyŏngsang (Gyeongsang) Provinces.

there are expressions of irrational emotions and false consciousness, but they are the surface symptoms not the causes of the problem. What is normally referred to as regional rivalry, or regional sentiment, is the side effect brought on by the particular type of urban concentration that took place in Korea and the subsequent imbalance in regional development, particularly during the period of rapid industrialization under the Park Chung-hee (Pak Chŏng-hŭi, Park Jeong-hui) rule. As such, the phenomenon of regional rivalry reflects deeper socio-economic and ideological cleavages.[15] The political propaganda inciting regional rivalry derives power from such cleavages.

The important fact is that, although the politics of regional rivalry has its roots in the urban hyper-concentration of the Seoul area and the consequent neglect of regional development, the political demarcation line of the conflict is expressed not in terms of center versus region but in terms of region

---

15 Cleavage: A concept that refers to a social distinction that causes or may cause conflicts and confrontations among social groups. In political science, it refers to the demarcation lines of social conflicts that shape the characteristics of one or another type of party system. The concept of cleavage came from the classical argument of Seymour Lipset and Stein Rokkan, whicth represents the sociological approach to the theory of party systems. According to Lipset and Rokkan, in the process of going through the Industrial Revolution and the transition to modern states, political systems in Western Europe were shaped based on the cleavages 1) between the center and the periphery, 2) between the state and the church, 3) between urban and rural, and 4) between capital and labor. These four cleavages overlapped and crosscut differently in different countries in Western Europe, and each country came to have a different party system, as the political weight of each cleavage and its hierarchical structure came to be formed differently from country to country. On the other hand, E. E. Schattschneider, who represents the political theory of cleavage in a different direction from Lipset and Rokkan, emphasizes political formation and mobilization of cleavages. In Schattschneider's view, party systems, or competition and confrontation among parties, do not represent political representation of social cleavages. Instead, political parties and the political elite selectively mobilize or exclude particular cleavages to shape a particular political system. Furthermore, voter alignments do not necessarily reflect social cleavages, because they can vary depending on what cleavage is made dominant by political parties and the political elite. Thus, according to this theory, the power and influence of a particular party, or a political elite, are derived from its ability to mobilize those cleavages that benefit its party and repress or exclude those that do not. In general, the theory of Lipset and Rokkan works well to explain party systems in Western Europe, while Schattschneider's theory explains better the case of the United States, which has a short history of social cleavages, or the cases of the Third World countries where the state's influence is overwhelmingly strong. Seymour M. Lipset and Stein Rokkan, "Cleavage Structures, Party Systems and Voter Alignments: An Introduction," in *Party Systems and Voter Alignments*, ed. Seymour M. Lipset and Stein Rokkan (New York: Macmillan, 1967); E. E. Schattschneider, *The Semisovereign People: A Realist's View of Democracy in America* (Hinsdale, IL: The Dryden Press, 1975).

versus region. Such a power to transpose the problem of hyper-concentration into that of a conflict between regions lies, once again, in the conservatism of Korean democracy. The current political and social conditions are marked by the ideological narrowness of the political representation system, the political party organizations that are neither class- nor ideology-based, the elite oligarchic system monopolized by the conservatives, and the powerful hegemony[16] of Cold War vested interests. Under these circumstances, political competition can only be expressed as one-dimensional conflict around the issue of seizing the national state power. In this conflict, the dividing lines for the competing parties are drawn according to the individual's ties to the regions and schools, the elemental ties that form an elite group.

Accordingly, if Korea is to overcome the problem of regional rivalry, a structural change in the party system must take place. The current structure is characterized by its conservative monopoly. It appropriates and distorts various elements of social conflicts according to the interest of the political elite. I insist on making an issue of the narrowness of the ideological representation system, not because I believe any progressive changes are to be expected soon, but because the ideological narrowness distorts the structure of conflicts in society. It turns conflicts into ideological battles, and it discourages rational thinking and free imagination for alternatives. The problem of the hyper-concentration at the center, and the exclusion of the provinces, has been transposed as a problem of irrational emotions, making a rational approach to the problem difficult. There is nothing that better illustrates the sinister effects of the ideologically narrow party system than this phenomenon.

3. The Structure of Political Conflicts: Who Is Represented and Who Is Not?

In a political representation system where Cold War anti-communism is hegemonic, the interests of the poor are not represented. This non-representation at the political level has consequences at the social level, where upper-class pride and discrimination against the working classes are reinforced, and overt disparagement of the poor made possible. Under such circumstances, the desire to move upward in social class and the effort to secure symbolic

---

16 Hegemony: A concept of the Italian Marxist Antonio Gramsci. It explains that a group dominates another group in society not only by coercive power, but also by moral and ideological power. In other words, to rule by hegemony is to rule by obtaining the consent of the ruled through institutions, social relations, ideologies, or moral power. Antonio Gramsci, *Selections from the Prison Notebooks* (New York: International Publishers, 1971).

objects of wealth become matters of life and death. The blind preference for name brands is but an example of such a phenomenon. Given the situation, the accelerating competition for survival and the extreme success-oriented behaviors that have become generalized are perhaps not surprising. That means that a poor person cannot expect to receive decent human treatment. Appearances are important, and individual differences are not tolerated much. The other side of this phenomenon is the absence of individual moral autonomy and the desolation of the internal lives of individuals.

I read a shocking newspaper report in *JoongAng Ilbo* (Chungang Ilbo, Jungang Ilbo, August 12, 2002). It was an article on how popular plastic surgery is in Korea. In the survey quoted by the newspaper, 68 percent of the respondents said that "Looks are important in determining success or failure in one's life," and 70 percent responded that "one can determine the living standard of a person by looking at the person's skin and the body shape." "Become rich!" has become a routine greeting. We now live in a society ruled by the supremacy of looks and by mammonism. This is the result of the labor-exclusive political system that looks down upon work; it is the pathological phenomenon of the Cold War anti-communism that created such a political system. As a dehumanizing ideology that promotes hate and exclusion, the Cold War anti-communism is being strengthened as it combines its forces with that of the extreme right-wing-dominated social structure it has created. The hatred of North Korea is often repeated, as it induces similar types of emotions and sentiments in different situations, for different matters, and at different levels. Examples of this can be found in the antagonistic language of the regional rivalry in which the people of the alienated region are described as if they are depraved by their hunger for political power; in the use of the culturally and politically loaded invectives such as "pro-north guerilla" or "pro-north partisan," by National Assembly members to attack their political rivals, and in the behavior of the mass media that gleefully report on such details ad nauseam.

One of the most significant facets of politics to emerge in Korea after democratization is that the role of the press in politics has become very important. It is said that politics in Japan is moved by bureaucrats. If anyone asks me who moves the politics in Korea, I would say it is the press.

The political agenda in Korea is set by the press, not initiated by political parties. It is also the press that determines policy issues and priorities. From the president to the members of the National Assembly, from cabinet ministers to political advisors to ranking bureaucrats, one could say with little exaggeration that their job every day is to adjust their role according to what is reported that day in the press. The most they do in terms of making any decisions is to anticipate how the press might evaluate such decisions. The political function of the press is thus powerful in evaluating the performance of the government, political parties, and individual politicians and bureaucrats. The press also functions as a quasi-judiciary agent. Judgments on ethical and legal matters in the political arena are first made in the press. Self-corrective mechanisms within political parties or in the National Assembly come into play afterwards, as do any formal judicial processes, and usually only as a matter of formality; conclusions are already drawn before the investigation has started. The power of the press does not stop here. In private spheres, it arbitrarily intervenes and defines a person's intellectual and emotional spheres, calling a person "ideologically suspicious" or "leftist" as it sees fit. The press freely conducts ideological inquisitions that one would credit to the Japanese colonial rulers or a totalitarian regime.

Who controls the press that has such mighty power? In the case of political parties and the government, their performances are evaluated, and they are held accountable for their actions or inactions; this is accomplished through regularly scheduled direct elections. The trust acquired through the support of the majority voters becomes the legitimate basis for the exercise of their public authority. In contrast, although the influence of the press is as strong as the government's, if not actually stronger, the various civic attempts to control it have been incapacitated by the giant mass media corporations waving the flag of "freedom of the press" as if it were their inalienable human right. In the nineteenth century, freedom of the press in a democracy meant the freedom to express opinions. I do not believe this is the same freedom the press speaks of today. The press has become a world of giant media corporations wielding more private power than was imaginable then.

Many intellectuals, among them John Keane and Anthony Giddens, have expressed their concerns about the press leading politics in the modern world.[17] It seems that the domination of politics by the press has become a generalized phenomenon in the world. I believe that the greatest threat to modern democracy is the powerful press that has become a world of giant conglomerates. In a democracy, public opinion is a forum for a variety of opinions and rational persuasion. But when the press becomes a series of giant corporations, it tends to control the public opinion market through monopoly.

The problem of the press monopoly and dominance in Korea is far more serious than the general world trend. Even in advanced democracies,

17 John Keane, *The Media and Democracy* (Cambridge: Blackwell, 1991); Anthony Giddens, *Where Now for New Labour?* (Cambridge: Polity, 2002).

the press tends to become giant corporations. However, the media markets in these countries support multiple opinions, multiple political tendencies, and multiple ideological viewpoints. In contrast, the public opinion market in Korea is monopolized by a few large newspapers that have very homogeneous political and ideological viewpoints. Needless to say, democracy cannot flourish under such circumstances.

The newspaper subscription market in Korea does not respond to the preferences and demands of the mass media consumers. The problem of unfair trade practices in the newspaper subscription market has a long history in Korea. The editorials of the mainstream newspapers like to emphasize the importance of following market principles. But when it comes to newspaper subscriptions, the newspaper market does not allow free competition. It is a thoroughly institutionalized monopoly market. Given the situation, it is false to assume that the subscription rate in any way reflects the preferences of the public. It is imperative to reform the monopolistic newspaper market. The "free citizen" does not exist when freedom of speech and freedom of ideas are restricted. As long as the press dominates the political agenda, democracy cannot address the various issues pertinent to the civic community free from the hegemony of vested interests.

Of course, the subordination of politics to the press is primarily a political problem, and only secondarily a problem of the press. The subordination of politicians and political parties to the press is more than a problem of their incompetence; it is a systemic problem that is deeply connected to the conservatism of the political representation system and the oligarchic elite system that has no popular basis. In a democracy, I believe the political structure in a sense follows certain laws of physics. Grassroots mobilization and participation are based on social cleavages, and they prevent the conservative complacency of the political elite; at the same time the competition between political parties operates as a mechanism to expand the scope of representation to correspond to social changes and demands. In this process, political parties and the political elite are given an impetus to be clear about the theoretical, ideological, and policy grounds of their political behaviors and are pressured to strengthen their self-awareness of the normative legitimacy of their behaviors. It would be difficult for competition among political parties to have social content unless social cleavages have political expression, the masses participate in politics, and ideological alternatives can freely compete.

Of the many problems Korean society faces today, the issues surrounding unemployment and job creation, social justice and welfare, income redistribution, political reform to further advance democracy, building in-ter-Korean relations based on peace and ending Cold War hostility, pub-lic education, and reducing centralization are the major ones. The social consensus on how we as a society should deal with these problems is that the answers cannot come from without but from within, through confronta-tion and conciliation among the various stakeholders in society. However, I have not seen different viewpoints and demands competing against one another either in policy debates of political parties or in the press. What I have seen are at best mobilizations of side issues engaging in wars of words whose only purpose is to inflict injury on the opponent. In the case where an important social issue becomes the focus of a public debate, it is often dif-ficult to distinguish how the positions of the various parties differ. All of the political parties agree that the social issues mentioned above are important. Their alternatives, however, are usually too abstract or too bogged down by bureaucratic technicalities.

Such phenomena also have their origin in the conservative homogeneity of the party system in Korea. In any society, it is not possible to have only a single perspective in understanding social problems. If that were possible, democracy would have no reason to exist. Democracy is a political system whose very *raison d'etre* lies in mediating conflicts. In a democracy, conflict-ing interests mutually compete with one another, compete and are organized by rational alternatives. In this way, the content of political discourse is en-riched and the social foundation of politics made stronger; certain compro-mises are made and a social consensus is reached in the process. Only then can democracy be called a meaningful decision-making structure. As Dankwart A. Rustow has said, democracy is a political system that has its foundation in conflicts.[18] Accordingly, Stuart Hampshire has stated that justice is conflict.[19] In a democracy, justice is not the discovery of what already exists as such; it is the formation of what is just, as various opinions and interests conflict and compete in a fair process. The conservatism of the party system in Korea im-pedes political competition among the various interests and opinions in soci-ety, and it operates as a cause for debasing the party system into an oligarchy of the political elite separated from any social foundation.

I do not believe that the greatest cleavage in our society exists between the ruling and opposition parties. It is difficult to see the conflicts and struggles between these parties as anything that has ideological and policy

18 Dankwart A. Rustow, "Transition to Democracy: Toward a Dynamic Model," *Comparative Politics* 2 (1970).

19 Stuart Hampshire, *Justice Is Conflict* (Princeton: Princeton University Press, 2000).

significance to the central issues confronting Korean society today. To any observer, their fights are nothing more than a power struggle that is isolated from the fundamental social issues and are focused on seizing state power itself. The result is that the number of voters rejecting the current party system has steadily been increasing. For each new election held, a new record is set in this regard. In the 16th general election of 2000, the top three parties combined received 41.7 percent of the total eligible votes, while non-voters accounted for 42.8 percent. In the general election of 2008, in which the 18th National Assembly members were elected, the number of non-voters increased by 11 percent to 54 percent. The leading political party in Korea has now in fact become the party of non-voters. Under such circumstances, it is difficult to recognize and accept election results as a democratically authoritative decision, regardless of their effect on the status of the ruling party, majority party, etc. In short, the greatest cleavage in politics in Korea today is that between the political representation system that does not have a social basis, and the non-voting eligible voters who are not represented in this system and are resisting it.

It is now time to proceed to the main section of this book. It will deal with two issues. One is the conservative origin of democracy in Korea. To understand a political system anywhere, it is best to start with the structural characteristics of the system's origin and its formative period. Thus the first part of the main section will deal with the question, Where did democracy in Korea come from, and where is it headed? To do so, we will examine the political and social framework shaped by Cold War anti-communism and its structural characteristics; the problems left behind by authoritarian industrial development; and how the transition to democracy culminated in conservative democracy.

The other main issue addressed is how the conservatism of democracy in Korea reproduces itself after democratization. I will examine this question from three levels, i.e., the state, the market, and civil society. Questions will include why democracy after democratization in Korea failed to meet the expectations of its initial period, what are the causes, and what are the new issues that have to be highlighted to better understand the changes that took place after democratization.

Part II

The Origins of Conservative Democracy

2 State-building and Premature Democracy

1. Society of Mass Mobilization and the Birth of a Strong State

Emergence of the "Liberation Space"

The younger generation of students of modern Korean history widely uses the term *"haebang konggan"* (*haebang gonggan*), or "liberation space." Here, "liberation" refers not only to the end of the Japanese colonial rule in Korea but also to the period immediately following liberation in 1945. In contrast, "space" is more complex, and has at least two meanings. First, it

TABLE 2.1

Chronology of Major Events, 1945–60

1945	August 15	National Liberation
	September 8	U.S. Army Military Government in Korea (USAMGIK) inaugurated
1946	October 1	October People's Uprising
1948	April	Cheju Island Rebellion ("April 3rd incident")
	May 10	May 10 South Korea–exclusive election
	August 15	Inauguration of the Republic of Korea
	October 19	Yŏsu and Sunch'ŏn Rebellion
1949	May 20	National Assembly "spy" incident
1950	June 25	Korean War begins
1952	May 25	"Selected amendment" (first constitutional amendment)
1953	July 27	Armisitice signed
1954	November 29	The "round-off" amendment (second constitutional amendment)
1958	January 13	Progressive Party incident
1960	March 15	March 15 election fraud
	April 19	April Student Uprising (April 19 Revolution)

Source: Author.

refers to the absence of a state power following the sudden collapse of the colonial rule, when a new center of power or a new form of government had not yet appeared to replace the old. Second, in a very positive and active sense, "space" also refers to the political realm of possibilities, where various forces and powers within Korea could have competed with one another and created an order by themselves. In other words, it refers to the possibility given to Koreans to autonomously create a new order in their society. One could compare it to the notion of "state of nature," a primordial condition, or a starting point, for building a nation-state, political society,[1] or civil society.

More than anything else, the liberation space was marked by voluntary and explosive bottom-up mobilization of the masses. It was an eruption of joy at national liberation and of a desire to create a self-reliant and independent nation-state. Perhaps the mood and circumstances of the liberation space can be compared with that of the 1987 June uprising and the 2002 World Cup combined. The comparison can be made from both a political and non-political perspective. Politically, the 1945 situation had the goal of eliminating the remnants of colonial rule and creating a new social order. From a non-political perspective, the whole nation came together to enjoy national liberation in an outburst of excitement.

The Advent of the Cold War

Under these circumstances, the Cold War stormed through the Korean Peninsula, and the axes of conflict shifted violently. First, the major axis of political conflict and confrontation in the period immediately following the national liberation can be summarized as that between the Japanese colonial forces and the national independence movement forces. Conflict and confrontation were inevitable products of the colonial period, and as the axis of conflict developed, so did a strong and defiant nationalist movement. It was under Japanese colonial rule that Koreans first discovered a modern collective

---

1 Political society: A concept of Gramsci and Tocqueville, referring to the middle stratum that mediates the state and civil society. According to the definition of Jean L. Cohen, Andrew Arato, Juan J. Linz, and Alfred Stepan, political society is composed of the political forces that make up public power, such as political parties and other political organizations. Its core institutions are political parties, elections, electoral rules, party coalitions, and the parliament. Political society is the realm in which members of a political system organize themselves in a particular manner for political competitions in order to achieve control over public power and the state apparatus. Antonio Gramsci, *Selections from the Prison Notebooks* (New York: International Publishers, 1971); Alexis de Tocqueville, *Democracy in America*, ed. J. P. Mayer (Garden City, NY: Anchor Books, 1969).

ego as a "nation." In content, nationalism in Korea basically consisted of anti-Japanese and anti-imperialist struggle for national sovereignty. In other words, it made its mark as a resistance movement in Korea, whereas in Japan and Germany, aggressive nationalism played the role of an ideological flagpole for imperialist expansion. Accordingly, at an early stage of the liberation space immediately following the collapse of the colonial rule, it was natural that the leaders of the independence movement rose to the top in the political world. Complications, however, also arose in this regard. The independence movement during colonial rule had been divided in two directions. One was led by the revolutionary ideology of socialism or communism, and the other was led by the conservative ideology of cultural and educational reform. Of course, between these forces, there were socialists who were not revolutionaries, and anti- and non-socialist moderates who remained unwavering moderates without compromising any nationalist interest under the highly pressurized circumstances of colonial rule. In any case, at the beginning of the liberation space, the leftist nationalist forces had the lead and secured a dominant position in the political competition and popular mobilization. With the onslaught of the Cold War soon afterwards, a new axis of confrontation materialized rapidly between pro- and anti-communists.

The emergence of the new axis of confrontation would have caused enough complications. What made the situation even more complex and amplified the conflicts even further was the fact that there had not been a center of gravity to the Korean independence movement during the colonial period. In contrast to the independence movements in India, Indonesia, and Vietnam, each of which developed an integrated alternative government,[2] the Korean independence movement did not. For example, Syngman Rhee (Yi Sŭng-man, Lee Seung-man) in the United States, Kim Ku (Kim Gu) in China, Yŏ Un-hyŏng (Yeo Un-hyeong), Kim Sŏng-su (Kim Seong-su), and Pak Hŏn-yŏng (Park Heon-yeong) in Korea all had different geographical bases for their movements. As for Kim Sŏng-su, Yŏ Un-hyŏng, and Pak Hŏn-yŏng, who were based in Korea, there were big gaps in their ideological commitments. Add to this Kim Il Sung of the north, who was mostly active in Manchuria during the colonial period, and the Independence Alliance group, also of the north and active in China, and the situation becomes even more complex.

2 Alternative government: A government established as an alternative by people who do not approve of the current ruling regime or accept its legitimacy. During the colonial period, it existed in the forms of an underground government, provisional government, or government in exile. After independence, an alternative government generally becomes the center for a new modern political system. The most prominent examples of alternative government are the Indian National Congress of India led by Mohandas K. Gandhi and Jawaharlal Nehru, and the Viet Minh of Vietnam led by Ho Chi Minh.

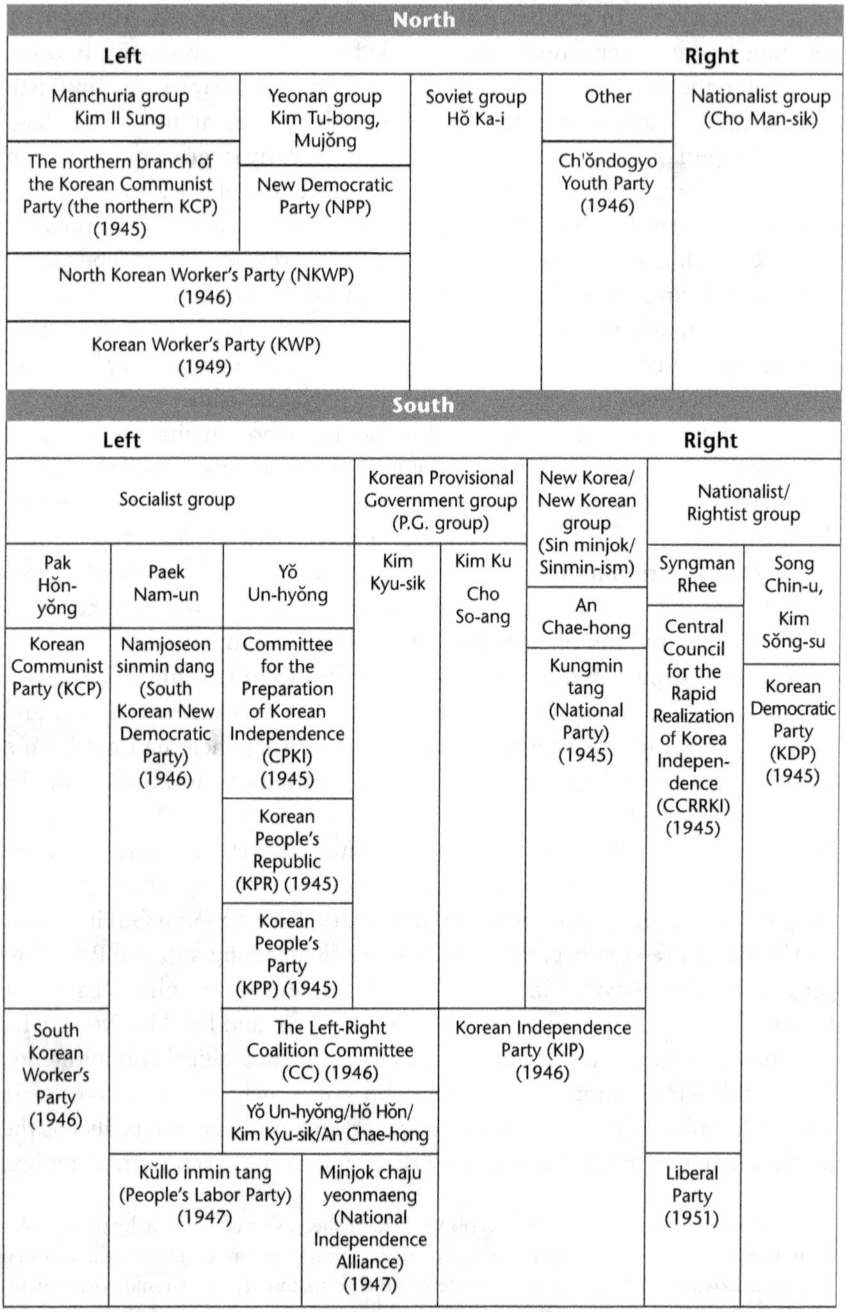

North

Left			Right	
Manchuria group Kim Il Sung	Yeonan group Kim Tu-bong, Mujŏng	Soviet group Hŏ Ka-i	Other	Nationalist group (Cho Man-sik)
The northern branch of the Korean Communist Party (the northern KCP) (1945)	New Democratic Party (NPP)		Ch'ŏndogyo Youth Party (1946)	
North Korean Worker's Party (NKWP) (1946)				
Korean Worker's Party (KWP) (1949)				

South

Left						Right	
Socialist group			Korean Provisional Government group (P.G. group)		New Korea/ New Korean group (Sin minjok/ Sinmin-ism)	Nationalist/ Rightist group	
Pak Hŏn-yŏng	Paek Nam-un	Yŏ Un-hyŏng	Kim Kyu-sik	Kim Ku Cho So-ang	An Chae-hong	Syngman Rhee	Song Chin-u, Kim Sŏng-su
Korean Communist Party (KCP)	Namjoseon sinmin dang (South Korean New Democratic Party) (1946)	Committee for the Preparation of Korean Independence (CPKI) (1945)			Kungmin tang (National Party) (1945)	Central Council for the Rapid Realization of Korea Independence (CCRRKI) (1945)	Korean Democratic Party (KDP) (1945)
		Korean People's Republic (KPR) (1945)					
		Korean People's Party (KPP) (1945)					
South Korean Worker's Party (1946)		The Left-Right Coalition Committee (CC) (1946)	Korean Independence Party (KIP) (1946)				
		Yŏ Un-hyŏng/Hŏ Hŏn/ Kim Kyu-sik/An Chae-hong					
	Kŭllo inmin tang (People's Labor Party) (1947)	Minjok chaju yeonmaeng (National Independence Alliance) (1947)				Liberal Party (1951)	

FIGURE 2.1 Political Geneology Immediately after Liberation

Source: Author.

In the case of India, it was quite natural that Gandhi and Nehru, who were the leaders of the Indian National Congress during the British colonial rule, become the leaders of the new Indian government after its independence. The question in Korea was, who should be the leader of the nation's new government? Should there be a coalition body in the manner of the coalition party in Italy that was formed by six major parties that participated in the anti-fascist movement? Thus, when the Cold War arrived in Korea and a new axis of conflict began to appear, some very basic issues had not yet been resolved, and the situation became exacerbated and insoluble.

The Process of Cold War Taking Root in Korea

In the beginning, immediately after the Second World War, the 38th parallel was a temporary demarcation line between two Allied Powers, the United States and the Soviet Union. The United States would be in charge of disarming the retreating Japanese military units south of the line, while the Soviet Union would be in charge of the task in the north. However, when the United States and the Soviet Union each set up a military government in the south and the north, respectively, the 38th parallel became a political and ideological demarcation line. The U.S. military government (known as USAMGIK, United States Army Military Government in Korea) quickly began to consolidate its alliances with the native forces in the conservative independence movement. Syngman Rhee, who was active in the United States, and Kim Sŏng-su and Song Chin-u were the military government's main contact points. In the process, far-left groups such as the Korean Communist Party (KCP)[3] were suppressed and excluded. Figures such as Yŏ Un-hyŏng and groups such as Committee for the Preparation of Korean Independence (CPKI),[4] which were either socialist-democratic or moderately left, were also suppressed and excluded in the process. The conflicts and confrontations between the left and the right, and the subsequent confusion, reached the utmost limits as the north and south each set up a separate government a few months apart from each other in 1948. At the time, there were many ordinary people who were not communists but who resisted the

---

3 Korean Communist Party (KCP): The KCP was the first communist party in Korea organized in Seoul in April 1925. Reorganized after the independence by Pak Hŏn-yŏng (Park Heon-yeong). Incorporated in November 1946 into the South Korean Workers' Party along with the South Korean New Democratic Party and the Korean People's Party, for the purpose of uniting all the communist forces in South Korea.

4 Committee for the Preparation of Korean Independence (CPKI): The first organization for the preparation of Korean independence, established by Yŏ Un-hyŏng (Yeo Un-hyeong) after the liberation of Korea on August 15, 1945.

institutionalization of the division and aspired to a single independent nation. A large number of these lives were sacrificed during this period.

The political confusion during this period was experienced in three stages as the Cold War began to take institutional shape in Korea.

The first stage was the early period of the liberation space. The left was the dominant force. The second stage was the period from the end of 1945 to early 1946. In December 1945, the foreign ministers of the United States, the Soviet Union, and the United Kingdom met in Moscow. In the ensuing debate on the trusteeship issue, the right and left clashed violently. When the left was losing momentum to the right in this process, the two sides were still engaged in a contest for hegemony. The third stage is the period after the October uprisings[5] of 1946, the largest bottom-up mobilization of masses since national liberation. In the aftermath of the October uprisings, the left was clearly weakened while the right gained a clear upper hand. Then, after the breakdown of the U.S.-USSR Joint Committee[6] talks in July 1947, control was held exclusively by the right. The left-right confrontation in the south thus ended with a monopoly of power by the right. This led to the simplification of the ideological confrontation on the peninsula, into that between North and South Korea only. The institutionalization of the division of the nation followed, which was then followed by a war. Thus, the Cold War on the Korean Peninsula had the effect of establishing the most anti-communist regime in the south, and the most radical socialist regime in the north.

The Cold War and the Overdeveloped State

One of the results of the extreme confrontation between the left and right ideologies was the creation of a strong state. A strong state in this case had at its center authoritarian institutions such as the military and the police, and the prosecutorial and the counterintelligence agencies. The

5 September general strike and October uprising: The September general strike broke out when more than 8,000 railroad workers began a walkout in Pusan (Busan) on September 23, 1946, followed by the walkouts of more than 250,000 workers in the major industries. The subsequent October uprising broke out with a street demonstration in Taegu (Daegu) on October 1. The angry mob attacked police stations and prisons to release prisoners, and also attacked the residences of bureaucrats and police officers. The uprising spread out to neighboring areas and lasted for about three months.

6 U.S.-USSR Joint Committee: A committee for the resolution of the Korean issue, constituted in December 1945 by the representatives of the United States and the USSR, according to the Agreement of the Moscow Summit of the foreign ministers of the United States, the USSR, and the United Kingdom. They held a preliminary meeting on the resolution of general problems, such as the trusteeship of Korea and the establishment of a provisional government. The first meeting was held on March 20, 1946.

expansion of these authoritarian institutions was inevitable to exclude and demobilize the leftists and the popular forces that had become politicized and mobilized during the period of the liberation space.

However, the creation of a strong state in Korea was not the result of only the Cold War and the division of the nation. The Chosŏn (Joseon) dynasty was a Confucian state, and as such it had the tradition of a strongly centralized bureaucratic state. Also, during the colonial period, the Japanese developed strong authoritarian institutions in Korea to rule the country. After liberation, the historical and structural conditions for creating a strong state were right again.

Of course, this is not to say that a strong state was created as a matter of course after liberation because Korea had the political and cultural legacy of a strong state. On the contrary, it should be emphasized that a series of events after the national liberation reintroduced the legacy from the past. It would thus be misleading to argue that a strong state existed continuously in Korea and that it existed as a matter of tradition.

Although I have not recently used it frequently, I have in the past used the concept of an "overdeveloped state" to define the characteristics of the state in Korea after liberation. This was a concept originally used by Hamza Alavi, a Pakistani political economist, to analyze post-colonial states. Alavi observed that the colonial powers transplanted their well-developed state mechanisms to their colonies.[7] As a result, he further observed, even after independence, the state in former colonies is excessively strong in comparison to its economic foundation and social infrastructure, and it is the dominant institution in society. This can be seen in Korea in the unfolding of the Cold War and the ideological polarization in the liberation space, and in the demobilization of the masses during the establishment of the separate North and South Korean government. This historical development goes hand in hand with the appearance of the overdeveloped state in which the role of colonial state institutions is revived.

2. The Transposition of the Axes of Political Confrontation Resulting from Ideological Polarization

From Pro-Japan vs. Anti-Japan, to the Right vs. the Left

The development of the resistance movement under Japanese colonial rule saw the advent of nationalist ideology and attendant social movements for the first time in Korea. However, after the March First Independence Movement (1919), the influence of the Soviet revolution and socialist

---

7 Hamza Alavi, "The State in Post-Colonial Societies," *New Left Review* 74 (1972).

ideology on Korean activists grew rapidly. This has a lot to do with the fact that the Korean diaspora grew under colonial rule, and the independence movement expanded geographically. The Korean independence activists in the maritime province of Siberia and the Irkutsk area of the Soviet Union and on the Chinese mainland were strongly influenced by revolutionary socialism. While a revolutionary nationalist movement was unfolding abroad, in Korea a different kind of nationalist movement was developing. The latter was focused on education and culture. Methodologically, the nationalists in this category preferred peaceful approaches and a cultural orientation, and ideologically they were conservative; they came mostly from the landed class. After liberation, they come together under the banner of the Korean Democratic Party (KDP, 1945).[8] The left-right bifurcation of the nationalist movement was the first modern split of its kind in Korea; it was the first modern split in competing political ideologies and social movements.

With the arrival of liberation, the issue of establishing an independent nation became an urgent political issue, and the question of who should lead the new independent nation became a cause for potential conflict. In this context, the Cold War arrived and stormed across the nation. The issue of establishing an independent nation and the left-right ideological confrontation were enmeshed together, and in the process the right and the left forces clashed violently. It is wrong to categorically identify all those who opposed the north-south division as having been leftists or having harbored leftist ideology. The majority of the ordinary people at the time opposed the division of the nation. Thus, it could be said that people opposed the U.S. military government and the conservative Korean political forces and individuals in alliance with the military government, because the military government was pursuing division, not because the critics were all communists. For the same reason, there were many people who opposed Syngman Rhee when the separate government in the south was established and he became president. Once again, their opposition to Rhee did not mean they were all north sympathizers. In reality the demarcation lines were blurred. Accordingly, massive chaos and sacrifices followed as the axes of political confrontation reconfigured rapidly.

From the Right vs. the Left, to South vs. North

The establishment of the separate government in the south took place by way of a thorough expulsion of communists. There was an all-out demobilization of the masses. In the process, many people were wrongly victimized.

---

8 Korean Democratic Party: A conservative party organized in September 1945, led by Song Chin-u and Kim Sŏng-su.

One must emphasize that such a phenomenon was not limited to the situation in the south. In North Korea, all issues were handled from the class perspective; in March 1946, in only three weeks, it completed land reform[9] in the most radical manner and expelled the landlords and wealthy farmers from their land. The ruling forces in the north may boast of it as a model of proletarian revolution to be emulated by the world, but it was a revolution accomplished in the most violent manner. It destroyed communities instantly by excluding and expelling the landed class; there was no room for them in this revolution. Many of the victims of the exclusion and violence fled to the south to form the most hardened and far-right anti-communist force.

With the establishment of the first Republic of Korea in 1948, the left-right ideological conflict in the south was resolved with the complete demise of the left, and Cold War anti-communist system was firmly established. At this point, the left-right conflict in the south went through a metastasis, and it reappeared in the form of a north-south conflict. North and South Korea came to represent the polar ends of an opposing ideological spectrum. On the far right side of the Cold War ideology, the south had the monopoly as its "spokesnation," while the north had this status on the far left. Thus, the geographical division between South and North Korea was enmeshed with the ideological division between the right and the left.

From South vs. North, to the Internalization of the Conflict

The word "commie" in the south, the phrase "U.S. imperialist spy," and the word "reactionary" in the north do not simply refer to the concept of the enemy in their respective societies. They are powerful discursive jargons that have the power of turning the mode of control and the frame of thinking in their respective societies into dichotomous and simple diagrammatic structures; they also have the power of continuously reproducing the same discourse. In other words, the hostile relationship between South and North Korea is now reproduced within its respective societies. This topic will be covered in further detail later on. Here I will only mention that political parties, too, have been institutionalized in this structure. In other words, the rhetoric and the pattern of competition between political parties have

9 Land reform in North Korea: The North Korean Provisional People's Committee enacted the Law on Land Reform on March 5, 1946, and dissolved the landowner system overall by the end of March. The basic principle of the land reform was the confiscation and redistribution of land without compensation. Poor peasants supported it, while landowners resisted it; many landowners decided to move to the south because of it.

a likeness to the hostile Cold War relationship of North and South Korea. However, a divided nation engaged in severe ideological conflict with its other half-nation still has its own conflicts arising from economic and other spheres, as does any other society. As such, the country needs political parties with ideological commitments to speak on behalf of the different interests and passions they represent, i.e., to function as political organizations. This is why in a democracy, the party system does and must develop into a competitive system organized on the basis of ideological and spatial spectrums as wide as that of the different conflicts, cleavages, and passions that the society has. Under the Cold War anti-communist conditions, however, parties with different ideologies and support bases could not emerge in Korea. Whether it was a ruling party or an opposition party—unless it had conservative ideologies like Rhee or the KDP, the two founding forces of the divided nation—a third party, a different kind of political party, could not be maintained. As soon as a new political force entered the scene, it would be called a communist or a pro-north organization, and it would be easy to ostracize it. In North Korea where only one party exists, the situation is perhaps even more self-evident. A single-party system and democracy cannot coexist.

3. Centralization of Power and the Bureaucratic State

Hyper-centralization and the Concentric Elite Structure

The centralization of political power brought centralization in other spheres of society. That is to say, resources in the economic, social, educational, and cultural sectors were graphically and spatially concentrated in Seoul. This geographic and spatial concentration is accompanied by functional concentration in other spheres of society; the spatial concentration and functional integration therefore taking place simultaneously. Thus, to understand the problem realistically, one has to look at it as a hyper-centralization, not a simple centralization. As a result of this hyper-centralization, the social structure in Korea is now nearly perfectly concentric, where the elite in one sphere are also the elite in other spheres of society. On the one hand, this concentric structure brought stability to the elite structure, but on the other hand, it also created a fierce competition among the less privileged in society to move up to the elite class.

Why did hyper-centralization take place in Korea? We can delineate the following four historical conditions that contributed to its facilitation and maintenance: 1) the Confucian bureaucratic state and culture of the Chosŏn dynasty had already sown the seeds for nurturing the structure and culture of centralization in traditional Korean society; 2) the institutions and the system of Japanese colonial rule further strengthened centralization; 3) after liberation, the dynamics for centralization became stronger with the advent of the Cold War and as the left-right ideological struggles and the north-south confrontations became entrenched; and 4) in the 1960s and 1970s, the military authoritarian regime and government-led industrialization further strengthened centralization in Korea. Already in 1960, Gregory Henderson, a U.S. political scientist, emphasized the phenomenon of centralization as the most distinct characteristic of politics in Korea.[10] He had used the term "politics of vortex" to describe the phenomenon where all social resources and values are concentrated in Seoul and at the apex of power. Henderson's thesis on centralization, however, has the problem of emphasizing the Confucian bureaucratic culture as the paramount cause of the phenomenon.

The Dynamics of Centralization

Gregory Henderson explains the Korean situation with Alex de Tocqueville's *L'Ancien Régime et la Révolution* as his theoretical model. According to Tocqueville, the weakness or absence of autonomous intermediary groups leads to the acceleration of centralization.[11] This theory can find great applicability in Korea. But despite the structural similarity, France and Korea have fundamental differences in history and culture. In particular, it is important to examine the mechanism through which centralization has been strengthened. As can be seen in the four historical conditions mentioned above, it is not the continuation of the Confucian culture that caused the continuation of centralization in Korea. Instead, new conditions appeared in mutually exclusive historical situations and moments, and the changes led to accelerated centralization in Korea. In Tocqueville's France and in Henderson's Korea, the biggest dynamic for centralization is the state bureaucracy. However, there are fundamental differences between the two systems.

According to Tocqueville, by destroying the aristocracy and simultaneously eliminating the intermediary link that connected the individual to society, the French revolution atomized the individual, which then led to the strengthening of the state bureaucracy. Unlike in revolutionary France, centralization in Korea is the result of elite-centered social governance in which the channels of popular political participation are bottlenecked or blocked. Cold War anti-communism was established in Korea following

10 Gregory Henderson, *Korea: The Politics of the Vortex* (Cambridge: Harvard University Press, 1968).

11 Alexis de Tocqueville, *The Old Regime and the French Revolution* (Oxford: Blackwell, [1856] 1947).

the violent left-right ideological confrontation. This created an ideological uniformity in society, and at the same time, strengthened the state bureaucracy that monopolized the allocation of resources; and in turn the centralization process was accelerated. Under such conditions, competition among different elite groups on a wider ideological horizon is impossible, and the extremely simplified and homogenous elite structure, or the concentric structure as mentioned above, was fortified. As a result of a small number of the elite controlling nation-building, the concentration of power was inevitable. In sum, an overdeveloped state is another word for a centralized state bureaucracy.

4. The Development of an Ideologically Narrow Party System

The Emergence of a Conservative Two-Party System

A strong state bureaucracy is one that is based on a weak representative, or parliamentary, system, and the two go hand in hand. In the meantime, at the core of a weak representative system, there is an ideologically narrow party system that does not have strong roots in society. Major political forces from the era of liberation space include the Central Council for the Rapid Realization of Korean Independence (CRRKI) led by Syngman Rhee; KDP led by Kim Sŏng-su and Song Chin-u; the Shanghai-based Korean Provisional Government (KPG, the predecessor of the Korean Independence Party [KIP] led by Kim Ku); the moderates led by Kim Kyu-sik and the National Independence Alliance;[12] the Committee for the Preparation of Korean Independence (CPKI) of Yŏ Un-hyŏng (CPKI later became the Korean People's Party and the Labor People's Party); and the Korean Communist Party (KCP) of Pak Hŏn-yŏng, which later became the South Korean Worker's Party (SKWP). Pak Hŏn-yŏng went to the north. The south and north were already divided along an ideological fault line, and it was difficult for any communist or socialist forces in the south to avoid exclusion. While the separate governments were being established in the north and the south, Kim Ku, Kim Kyu-sik, and other rightist nationalist forces and the moderate leftist groups, represented by such figures as

12 National Independence Alliance: Organized on December 20, 1947, as the center for all moderate political groups after the Committee for Left-Right Cooperation, led by Kim Kyu-sik and Yŏ Un-hyŏng, had been dissolved. After the assassination of Yŏ Un-hyŏng, Kim Kyu-sik organized the National Independence Alliance by incorporating into it such moderate groups as the People's Alliance, the New Progressive Party, and the Socialist Democratic Party. Its platform was against left or right prejudices, and it advocated the principle of self-determination for the Korean people.

North

NKWP (Kim Il Sung) Went to the North	Cho Man-sik	Repression
	Exclusion of the moderates	
Annihilation **SKWP** (Pak Hŏn-yŏng)	Yŏ Un-hyng, Kim Kyu-sik, Kim Ku, Young activists	Fled to the South **LP, KDP**

Left   **Right**

South

☐ Closed indeological space   **NKWP** = North Korea Worker's Party
☐ Open indeological space   **SKWP** = South Korea Worker's Party
                                                    LP = Liberal Party
                                                  KDP = Korean Democratic Party

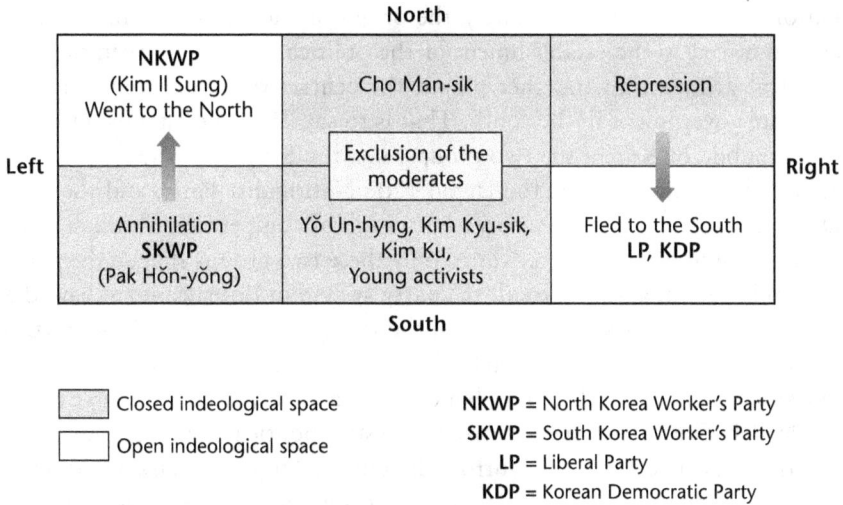

FIGURE 2.2 The Polarization of the Ideological Representation System in Korea
Source: Author.

Yŏ Un-hyŏng, also opposed the division; they either boycotted or were excluded from the political process. How the influence of these different political forces changed in the process of the ideological polarization is summarized in Figure 2.2.

Among the many political forces, only the groups led by Syngman Rhee and KDP participated in the election campaigns that institutionalized the north-south division. They were the two axial coordinates of political forces that established a separate state in the south. The wide spectrum of the remaining non-ultra-right groups participated, as independent candidates, in the first two elections for the National Assembly seats, the second of which was held on May 30, 1950. By the end of the Korean War, most of them ceased to exist, and the two-party system of the Liberal Party vs. the KDP became entrenched. An exception may have been the emergence of the Progressive Party[13] in the mid-1950s, led by Cho Pong-am (Jo Bong-am). Except for its emergence, the Progressive Party did not leave any significant mark on the

13 The Progressive Party incident: In January 1958, Cho Pong-am (Jo Bong-am) and other leaders of the Progressive Party, who stood for the peaceful reunification of Korea, were arrested on charges of secretly communicating with the enemy and promoting the North Korean way for reunification. In the final decision of the Supreme Court on February 27, 1959, Cho Pong-am was sentenced to death and executed on July 31. After this incident, public debate on reunification policies became frozen, and the activities of progressive movements became severely limited.

nation's party system. Ultimately, the origin of the party system in Korea can be traced to the establishment of the political rivalry between the two political groups that together played the central role in establishing the separate government in the south. That is to say, after the establishment of the Republic of Korea, the two groups, i.e., the Syngman Rhee group and KDP (which later became the Democratic Nationalist Party, and then the Democratic Party) entered into a relationship of competition, through a political division of labor. Afterwards, only these two groups shaped the party system in Korea, and as a result the party system in Korea came to have the following characteristics. First, both the ruling and the opposition parties compete on the same ideological horizon. Second, neither party has a base in grassroots interests or demands, but each has a "boss," a highly visible political leader. The parties are organized with such political bosses at the center, and the respective elite forces surrounding them. Third, the class, vocational, and professional interests of society cannot organize themselves for political representation. Fourth, despite these conditions, both parties claim the just and righteous cause of representing the entire society, the entire nation, and the entire people; they tend to be catch-all parties.

The Founding Election and the Freezing of the Conservative Two-party System

In examining the origin of the party system in Korea, it is necessary to review the characteristics of the "founding election." The term was originally suggested by Guillermo A. O'Donnell and Philippe C. Schmitter as a concept to explain a democratization process.[14] Specifically, they were interested in examining the voting patterns of the public when democratic liberalization[15] makes free competition between political parties possible. The term refers to an election that literally "founds" the pattern that would have

14 Guillermo A. O'Donnell and Philippe C. Schmitter, *Transitions from Authoritarian Rule: Tentative Conclusions about Uncertain Democracies* (Baltimore: Johns Hopkins University Press, 1986), 61–64.

15 Liberalization: This concept has been used by scholars of democratization, such as Guillermo A. O'Donnell, Philippe C. Schmitter, and Adam Przeworski. An authoritarian regime allows voluntary organization of civil society in the early stage of its transition from authoritarianism. Such an authoritarian regime opens the controlled political space with intent to broaden the support base of authoritarianism. In reality, however, such measures for liberalization bring about unintended results in the process, which play a crucial role in the coming process of democratization. Guillermo A. O'Donnell and Philippe C. Schmitter, *Transitions from Authoritarian Rule: Tentative Conclusions about Uncertain Democracies* (Baltimore: Johns Hopkins University Press, 1986).

TABLE 2.2

Percentage of Votes Received by Political Parties: First–Fourth General Elections

Election year	1st (May 10, 1948)	2nd (May 30, 1950)	3rd (May 20, 1954)	4th (May 2, 1958)
Percentage of votes received by political parties	NSRRKI 24.6	Korean National Party 9.7	Liberal Party 36.8	Liberal Party 42.1
	Korean Democratic Party (KDP) 12.7	Democratic National Party (DNP) 9.8	Democratic National Party (DNP) 7.9	Democratic Party (DP) 34.2
	Taedong Youth 9.1	Kungminhoe (National Association) 6.8	Kungminhoe (National Association) 2.6	Unification Party 0.6
	Chosŏn National Youth Party 2.1	Taehan Youth Corps 3.3	Korean National Party 1.0	Kungminhoe (National Association) 0.6
	Taehan Youth Corps 1.5	Taehan Youth Corps 1.7		
	Miscellaneous 12.0	Miscellaneous 5.5	Miscellaneous 3.8	Miscellaneous 1.1
	Independents 38.0	Independents 62.9	Independents 47.9	Independents 21.5
Voting rate	95.5	91.9	91.1	90.7

Source: National Election Commission, Republic of Korea, *Past Parliamentary Election Results* (Seoul: NEC, 1989).

a great impact on all the elections to follow from then on; it is an election that has a certain "freezing effect"[16] on the reorganization of the political map and on the pattern of voter alignment. However, in Korea, the first election in the post-liberation period was different from the 1987 founding election for democratization, which was accompanied by an explosion of civic passion. The election in 1948 took place in a somewhat oppressive, rather than a completely democratic, atmosphere, because there had been a forced demobilization of the masses in the process of violent clashes between those

16 Freezing effect: A concept used by Lipset and Rokkan on the formation of party systems in Western Europe. Refers to the fact that the party systems established in the 1920s, the transition period to mass politics, were sustained for a long time thereafter. Seymour M. Lipset and Stein Rokkan, "Cleavage Structures, Party Systems and Voter Alignments: An Introduction," in *Party Systems and Voter Alignments,* ed. Seymour M. Lipset and Stein Rokkan (New York: Macmillan, 1967).

who supported the establishment of separate governments in the south and north, and those who did not. Also, as can be seen from the over-90 percent voting rate (see Table 2.2), the election had strong characteristics of being mobilized top-down. In any case, the 1948 election had a decisive effect on the pattern of the party system in South Korea for a long time after the First Republic was established.

Which election in South Korea, then, is the founding election? Is it the Constitutional Assembly election of May 10, 1948, which was the first election ever to be held? The assembly members elected through this election established the Constitution of the Republic of Korea, elected the president, and were given the responsibility to establish the Republic. The election of these assembly members had effects on the future political system and voting patterns in South Korea in two ways. The first point is that the National Society for the Rapid Realization of Korean Independence (NSRRKI),[17] the president's political organization, received the greatest number of votes. The second is that the political parties and organizations that received any meaningful number of votes were all right-wing groups. This, however, was an election result of an "inchoate party system." The system had not been institutionalized yet, and the fact that the independent candidates in this election received a high percentage of the votes illustrates this point. By the time of the fourth National Assembly election in 1958, the pattern of the party system became clear, and that pattern would subsequently continue. Through this election, the institutionalization of the political parties gained strength to the extent that the number of independent candidates was conspicuously reduced. Also, the ruling party and the opposition party reached a certain balance with the 42 percent and 34 percent of the votes received, respectively, solidifying a conservative two-party system. To the extent that this characteristic of the two-party system has continued to the present, the fourth general election of May 1958, not the first election of May 10, 1948, was more the "founding election" that serves as the origin of the party system in Korea.

5. Korean Caesarism and the Japanese 1955 System

Cold War and Personalized Authoritarianism

To examine the effects of the Cold War and the U.S. hegemony in Korea, it is interesting to compare the Korean case with that of Japan. Both Korea and

---

17 National Society for the Rapid Realization of Korean Independence: A political association organized by nationalist political parties on February 8, 1946. Its activities were opposed to trusteeship, the activities of the U.S.-USSR Joint Committee, and the leftist movement. It was a rightist political association and most feared by the left.

Japan are part of East Asia where the United States built an anti-communist defense network after World War II. The two nations were both strongly influenced by the Cold War, and the influence of U.S. policies and the occupying military governments were dominant in both countries. In this regard, the two countries share more similarities with one another than with any other country. Upon comparison, however, one sees that the degree of Cold War impact was different in the two countries. The difference may come from the fact that geopolitically, Korea was in the foremost frontline of the ideological confrontation between the United States and the USSR. It may also come from the fact that Korea experienced an extreme ideological confrontation, national division, and war. To see the difference between the Cold War impacts on the two countries, let us now compare the political systems that developed in each country as the post-war social orders also took shape in each society.

First, perhaps we can call the First Republic of Korea under Syngman Rhee a Caesarean republic, in the sense that the power of the state came from the personal authority of the president. Rhee's government was in the beginning very weak, but it quickly turned into a strong president-centered system. Soon, power was concentrated singularly on the president who was at the apex of the power structure, and thus strong power became personalized or personified. The power monopoly of the president under Rhee's system went far beyond what political scientists would normally criticize as a "winner-take-all" system. The power monopoly was itself potentially authoritarian, and in fact Rhee's government became authoritarian immediately after taking power. The president monopolized executive power; reigning above the power of the National Assembly, the president exercised omnipotence. The president, in the meantime, created the Liberal Party, his own political party, from the top down, according to his own will. On the other hand, the president weakened the power of the opposition party so that it could function only in the most minimum capacity.

Inside Rhee's institutionalized government structure there was no power that could check the presidential power. Under such circumstances, the opposition party could only remain the "loyal opposition" of the authoritarian government. Thus, a structure arose where a meaningful opposition party could only come in the form of a movement from civil society, outside of institutionalized politics. When popular support for the government weakens, or when the popular attitude becomes critical of the government, such a system cannot be maintained without authoritarianism, i.e., without a mechanism that raises the level of oppression. This created in Korea a peculiar combination of democracy and authoritarianism, where the political system was democratic but its practice was authoritarian. From the perspective that the opposition party and the National Assembly had the power to check presidential power when the First Republic was established in 1948, one could say that at the beginning the democratic institutions and authoritarian practice formed a balance. However, through the Korean War, after which Rhee's government stabilized, the balance tilted quickly toward authoritarianism.

Many causes can be cited for leading the situation to this state of Caesarism.[18] For example, one can point to the delay in modernization because the authoritarian and patriarchal elements of traditional society were still strong in the social structure, its values and culture. What was critical in forming the Syngman Rhee Caesarism was the Cold War. The extreme ideological confrontation, the experience of the subsequent war, and the permanent state of semi-warfare were enough to make the threat from the north very real. This condition provided the president with many resources for power, and the president used the situation as a basis to justify his authoritarianism. To a political leader in office, this cannot but be an enormously tempting power to exercise. Political conflicts and competition under Rhee's authoritarian government could easily be repressed because any of the conflicts could easily be transposed as a confrontation between South and North Korea. In fact, politics in Korea did not involve competition between parties for political alternatives. Instead, politics was reduced to eliminating conflicts and promoting unity in the south for the exclusive purpose of winning the war against the north. When the opposition party went beyond the limits of a "loyal opposition," it was colored by the authoritarian government not as an opposition party but as a party that represented the interest of something that came from beyond the barbed wire of the demilitarized zone. This was the mechanism of political oppression of opposition parties. There are countless examples of this mechanism at work. The 1949 National Assembly "spy infiltration" incident,[19] and the 1958 Progressive Party inci-

18 Caesarism: A type of political dictatorship. Refers to an autocracy with a unitary leadership. Originated from the name of the great politician Gaius Julius Caesar in the late period of the Roman Republic. In 47 BCE, Caesar destroyed the triumvirate and seized power to become a lifetime dictator, which marked the end of the Roman Republic and the beginning of the Empire.

19 The National Assembly "spy infiltration" incident: In April 1949, the Vice Chairman of the National Assembly, Kim Yak-su, and other young progressive members of the Assembly presented the "Seven Principles of the Way to Peaceful Reunification." Their major propositions were total withdrawal of the foreign armed forces, and a north-south political meeting constituted by the representatives of political parties and associations

dent are two most prominent examples of this kind. Furthermore, attempts were made to justify incidents such as the 1952 "selected Amendment to the Constitution" [20]and the 1954 "round-off Amendment to the Constitution"[21] by utilizing the same ideological argument.

The Cold War and the 1955 System in Japan

The party system in Japan that was maintained for approximately forty years after World War II is generally referred to as the 1955 system. It refers to a political system in which the hegemony of the ruling Liberal Democratic Party and the role of the Socialist Party, as a force that held the ruling party in check, formed a partnership. But this was not a system in which a single presidency monopolized and personalized power and subjugated all politics into the personal will of the president, as in the case of the Syngman Rhee regime. The 55-year system refers to a party system that is a product of an open political competition. Furthermore, free factional competitions were allowed within the political parties that operated under this system. In other words, power was dominated by neither a one-person monopoly nor a winner-take-all logic. The prime minister was also the head of a leading

---

in North and South Korea. The Syngman Rhee regime, whose goal was the reunification of Korea by military conquest of the north, had them arrested on charges of communicating with spies from the South Korean Workers' Party in order to stir up the political situation. This was the first case in which the National Security Law was abused as a means to eliminate political opponents.

20 Selected Amendment to the Constitution: In the General Election on May 30, 1950, the opposition party won by a landslide and the reelection of President Syngman Rhee seemed impossible. On May 25, 1952, the president declared martial law in the 23 districts in and around Pusan, which was serving as the temporary capital of Korea. About 50 members of the opposition party in the National Assembly were arrested by the military police on charges of receiving funds from international communist parties. On July 4, the bill for amending the Constitution was passed by standing vote under siege by the police. The core of the change was in the presidential election system, which was changed to direct election. Minor adjustments were made based on certain aspects of the parliamentary system. This is called the Pusan Political Upheaval.

21 Round-Off Amendment to the Constitution: On November 29, 1954, a bill for amending the Constitution was illegally passed, which removed the restriction on president Syngman Rhee serving three terms. The bill was initially voted down; among 203 votes on the register, 135 were in favor, 60 were against, and 7 were blank ballots. As the votes in favor were 1 vote short of the quorum of 136, the bill was rejected. Then the ruling Liberal Party insisted on their forced interpretation. According to their argument, two-thirds of 203 votes is 135.333; a number less than 1 cannot count as 1 person; therefore, if rounded off the number is 135. As a result, the rejection was overruled, and the bill was passed.

faction within a ruling party, where many other coexisting factions could share power. In this way, the power of the prime minister was limited to the role of arbitrating various conflicts of interests within the party and to speaking on behalf of the party consensus.

It was a system that was created through ideologically open competition between political parties and free elections even as they were realized under the dominating influence of the Cold War anti-communist ideology. In other words, it was a party system developed in a process through which the masses themselves made choices. The Liberal Democratic Party, the hegemonic party, is not a highly integrated party but a coalition composed of five or eight different factions. The different factions represent conflicting interests within the ruling bloc, and they bring together conflicts and different demands of society by building consensus through compromises. For this reason, during the first half of the 1955 system, the factions within LDP were able to play the role of "political parties within a party." The transfer of power from one faction to another within the ruling LDP had similar characteristics to a power transfer from one party to another. Because the different factions within the party represented a variety of social conflicts and demands, the consensus formed in this manner was not greatly estranged from what the general public understood as being in the best interest of the country. One could criticize the 55-year system for dividing power among the members of the upper elite of society. However, since power was not monopolized by a single individual, it was a political system that differed greatly from that of the Syngman Rhee government.

The long life of the LDP rule in Japan has been criticized both within Japan and without, as a conservative single-party ruling system. To a large degree, the critics are right. What is important is that in Japanese society, LDP rule is not only grounded in procedural legitimacy but it also has hegemony. What made this possible? The answer is simple. Through elections that are completely open and free across the ideological spectrum and through competition among political parties, the LDP secured its position as the dominant party. Even political parties whose party platforms were based on Marxist revolutionary theories, such as the Communist Party and the Leftist Socialist Party before it joined the Socialist Party, could participate in electoral competitions without limitation. The U.S. policy on Japan took a "reverse course"[22] at the end of the

22 Reverse course: A term referring to the fact that, after the occupation of Japan at the end of World War II, the occupation policy of MacArthur's headquarters in Japan

1940s, and the U.S. military government and the Japanese government may have placed various forms of restrictions on leftist political parties. But in comparison to the situation in Korea, politics in Japan was much more free and open.

According to the political scientist Gieuseppe di Palma,[23] "maximal inclusion of parties in the game, even of avowedly 'extremist' parties, can overcome their resistance to democracy." The very formation of LDP was the result of political competitions based on such a premise in Japan. The 1955 system was created when the Democratic Party led by Hatoyama Ichiro and the Liberal Party led by Yoshida Shigeru came together to form a single party. Although the parties were both conservative, they each had a distinct foreign policy. If in Japan the ideological spectrum was narrow and only conservative political parties were allowed to compete in elections, as in the case of Korea, the 55-year system would not have started in the first place. The two conservative Japanese political parties that formed the LDP, instead of becoming a coalition party, would have become something similar to the Liberal Party led by Syngman Rhee and the KDP in Korea; they would have been engaged in fierce political confrontations while still maintaining a conservative monopolistic two-party system. In short, even under the same Cold War conditions, the results were very different in Japan and Korea, depending on how open and liberal the ideological spectrum was.

6. The Effects of Premature Democracy

Democracy as an Institutional Partner of the Cold War

It can be said the democracy introduced and practiced in Korea after the end of World War II was a "premature democracy." By "premature," it is not meant here that democracy came too early to Korea, or that its people were not historically, culturally, and mentally ready for it. Rather, it is meant

---

switched to anti-reform. In order to prevent the resurgence of Japanese imperialism, the Allied Forces initially took actions for democratic reform, such as the declaration of the Emperor as a human being, the purge of war criminals, land and zaibatsu reform, and tolerance of the freedom of labor union activities. With the advent of the Cold War, however, they withdrew from these reform policies in 1948 and began to strongly repress labor unions and leftist movements in order to build an anti-communist fortress in East Asia.

23 Giuseppe di Palma, "Party Government and Democratic Reproducibility: the Dilemma of New Democracies" (Working Paper no. 18, European University Institute, Florence, September 1982); Guillermo A. O'Donnell and Philippe C. Schmitter, *Transitions from Authoritarian Rule: Tentative Conclusions about Uncertain Democracies* (Baltimore: Johns Hopkins University Press, 1986), 60.

to emphasize that the first introduction of democracy was not led by political forces from within. In Korea, democracy was introduced as a part of an institutional set; it came as a part of the process of dividing the nation. In other words, democracy was the institutional framework for establishing separate states.

As the Cold War swept through the Korean Peninsula, the question was whether to establish a single unified independent state or to establish separate states, dividing the ideological forces that cannot coexist in a single society into two states. At the time, there was no other issue that was more important. The situation ended with the divided nation, but the number of people supporting the division at the time was a minority. Under such circumstances, the institutionalization of democracy was less likely to function as a competitive framework that brought coexistence and social integration among groups with different interests, ideologies, and passions, but more likely to function as a framework for exclusion.

Dankwart Rustow's thesis that a democracy cannot succeed without achieving national unity is applicable in the case of Korea.[24] There are many examples where a democratic framework failed to resolve an ethnic conflict and the situation turned into a war. The ethnic conflicts and civil wars that many East European countries experienced after the collapse of state socialism at the end of the 1980s are prime examples. In Korea after liberation, the masses revolted and resisted U.S. military policy. The mass actions represented an eruption of the demand to bring justice to the colonial collaborators; they also represented the popular passion against the division. They cannot, however, be regarded as anything that represented a democratic revolution. Democracy in Korea was introduced, lacking its value or commitment, in the absence of national integrity. This fact could not but be a continuous cause for institutional instability and practical problems that arose in the process of practicing democracy.

Universal Suffrage Comes at a Single Stroke

When speaking of a premature democracy, it helps to look at when the essential democratic institution of universal suffrage was introduced, and the circumstances of the May 10, 1948 election, the first election of its kind. This is very important in understanding the characteristics of Korean democracy. In the case of the West, the introduction of universal suffrage, which became the basis of the parliamentary system, generally followed the

24 Dankwart A. Rustow, "Transition to Democracy: Toward a Dynamic Model," *Comparative Politics* 2 (1970).

régime censitaire.[25] In the case of Great Britain and Italy, universal suffrage was introduced over a long period of time. In these countries, voting rights were initially given only to male property owners who could pay above a certain level of property taxes. Subsequently, voting rights expanded to include the middle class, working men of high rank, working men in general, all adult males, and finally all adult females. In the case of granting voting rights to all adult males, the practice was generally introduced after the First World War. In the case of women's suffrage, in France, Italy, Belgium and other European countries, it was not introduced until after the end of World War II. In the case of the United States, it was not until the end of the 1960s and the Civil Rights Movement that African Americans in the South could vote. Considering these facts, the introduction of democracy in Korea was not at all late, at least not in terms of institutional introduction. This, however, is not the end of the story. In the West, when voting rights were given to workers, workers' parties had been organized and were active in representing the interests of the working class. By the 1920s and 1930s, after the end of the First World War, most of these workers' parties had emerged as ruling parties in their respective countries. This was the result of the expansion of voting rights and a rapid transition of the party structure from those that were elite-centered into those that were mass-oriented. In short, the process of expanding voting rights in the West was accompanied by the expansion of political participation by a wide spectrum of social groups and classes.

In Korea, universal suffrage was granted in a single stroke with the May 10, 1948, election. Except for the introduction of the system itself, no changes such as those that occurred in the West took place in Korea. The political system in Korea did not reflect the social class structure and its functional interests with a wide ideological spectrum, nor did the parties establish a mass base. The May 10, 1948, election was the first election to be held after the introduction of universal suffrage, and the political situation surrounding the election illustrates how democracy was first implemented in Korea. At the time, most of the people understood that the establishment of a democratic republic meant

25 *Régime censitaire*: A system in which suffrage is limited to taxpayers who pay a certain amount of taxes. This had been enforced in Europe and in the United States until universal suffrage was granted. For example, during the Restoration period of 1815-30 in France, suffrage and eligibility for election to the lower house of the parliament were limited to taxpayers who paid more than 300 francs of direct tax. Consequently, the French electorate consisted of less than 1 percent of the national population until universal suffrage for men was granted in 1848. In England, a modern parliamentary system was established through an electoral reform in 1832, but the number of eligible voters was then only about 650,000. Such limited suffrage systems brought about the Chartist Movement that demanded the expansion of political representation.

TABLE 2.3

Establishment of Universal Suffrage by Country

Country	Belgium	France	Italy	Germany	Great Britain	Switzerland	New Zealand	United States	Korea
Universal suffrage (males only)	1894	1848	1913	1871	1918	1848	1879	1860	1948
Universal suffrage (all adults)	1948	1945	1946	1919	1928	1971	1893	1920	1948

Source: Thomas T. Mackie & Richard Rose, *The International Almanac of Electoral History* (London: Macmillan, 1991); Daniele Caramani, *Elections in Western Europe since 1815* (New York: Palgrave Macmillan, 2000).

the institutionalization of the north-south division, and for this reason not only the leftist activists but also students and much of the general public boycotted the election. Nationwide general strikes and strikes in solidarity, conducted by students followed. Agitation and riots led to casualties, and political chaos ensued. Under these circumstances, Hyangbodan[26] was organized. This was a civilian organization that was led by the police; it was a de facto public organization. Its role in the election was to mobilize voters and to control the ballot boxes. The fact that a civil agitation on Cheju (Jeju) Island to boycott the election turned into what we now know as the 4.3 Incident[27] was directly related to these election circumstances. In the meantime, under these circumstances, the voter turnout hovered above 95 percent. The high turnout rate in this election was not the result of a voluntary participation by the general population but a passive participation mobilized from the top.

A Constitution Removed from Its Own Social Reality

Examining the constitution, the institutional foundation of a democracy, is meaningful and important in understanding the characteristics of

26 Hyangbodan (Homeland Protection Group): A militia organized by the U.S. military regime to supplement police activities in preparation for the General Election of May 10, 1948. It was disbanded after the General Election was over, because of backlashes and repercussions against it. However, on Cheju (Jeju) Island, it was resurrected under the name of Minbodan (People's Protection Group) after the April 3 Rebellion broke out, and lasted for a very long time.

27 The April 3 Rebellion of Cheju Island: A popular uprising that broke out on Cheju Island on April 3, 1948. The U.S. military government in Korea, the Syngman Rhee government, and the extreme rightist youth organizations tried to suppress the insurrection during 1948-49, and roughly 30,000 civilians were killed.

a premature democracy in Korea. As can easily be assumed, the content of the Korean constitution was borrowed from those of liberal democratic nations in the West, including the United States. The fact that it came from without, and that its content was isolated from the social reality of the country, has the following significance. First, when the institutions of liberal democracy were introduced in Korea in a single historical stroke, they came without the historical experiences and the theoretical or ideological developments that gave rise to those institutions. Second, the constitution was less meaningful as a fundamental law that regulates and institutionalizes real politics, and more meaningful as a kind of desire, based on the assumption of a unified nation. The focus was more on identifying what a would-be-unified state should do, and what norms should be set forth for such a state.

In general, a constitution is prepared by a particular political force in society, or as a product of compromises among such groups. It is written to respond to the most urgent real issues of the time. Thus adopting a constitution inevitably becomes a matter of national interest and the subject of great public discussion. In the case of Korea, however, the constitution came from without. It stirred no national interest, and no discussion or controversy occurred in the parliament among different political factions or their representatives. Thus, the constitution was quite unrelated to realities in Korea. People neither carefully studied nor respected it, leading to the long-lasting syndrome of neglecting the constitution.

In this regard, a look at the constitutional process in the United States and in France provides a basis for comparison. The framers of the U.S. constitution worked together in order to build a sound framework for building a nation. It still remains today one of the most widely read political texts in the United States. While the U.S. constitution was written by political leaders with contributions from the civic sector, this would have not been enough to make the constitution respected and observed. The constitution would have become nothing more than pieces of paper if the American people did not follow the republican principles laid out in it, and if they did not actually rule themselves according to those principles. In the case of France, the Declaration of the Rights of Man and of the Citizen was announced in the midst of the 1789 French Revolution, and the constitution of the republic was established in 1791. These were two of the greatest achievements of the revolution. One cannot help marveling that the articles of the Declaration went through such penetrating philosophical debates as those one might expect from an academic conference, when the French National Assembly at the time was in the throes of explosive popular revolution and a tremendous political crisis. The

Declaration begins with the now famous sentence, "Men are born and remain free and equal in rights." It spells out the natural and inalienable human rights and continues to be cited today by all people who aspire to democracy.

In Korea, the articles of the constitution that dealt with the government structure might have interested and spurred debates among the political groups and leaders who were involved in setting up the separate government. This possibility, however, was far from reality. Who drafted the constitution? Why the presidential system and not the parliamentary system? And as the first article of the constitution spells out, why is Korea not simply a democracy but a "democratic republic?" These and countless other questions were unknown to the general public, and they were not the object of popular interest. The Korean constitution adopted the presidential system. Was it because the drafters of the constitution believed in the strength of the system, or did it have more to do with an attempt to give more power to President Syngman Rhee? We do not know. Nor do we know where the content of the constitution is from, whether it is based on that of the United States, Japan, the Weimar Republic, or a combination of different countries. The discussion and debate on important issues that are a natural part of establishing a constitution were left out, and it would not be an exaggeration to say that the constitution was written by the most competent constitutional scholars of the time, no doubt, but as if it were an academic thesis. If there were any public interest in the constitution, it had to do with issues such as who should be the president, how the president should be elected, and how long the president should serve. In other words, the public interest was limited to issues of presidential power. There have been a total of nine constitutional amendments since 1948. The first was in 1952, introducing a direct presidential election. In 1954, a two-term limit on presidency was abolished. All other amendments centered also on the issue of presidential power.

The Korean constitution is a document that strongly reveals the gap between a democratic institution and the authoritarian practice of it. At the least, the institutions and principles of democracy were consistently maintained according to the constitution even under authoritarian rule. The fact that the constitution is no more than an ornament, or merely something that defines the ideals to be achieved in the future, indicates that the constitution does not have real regulatory power in practice and that it debases its own authority as the highest law in the country.

Regarding the practical limitations of the constitution, we need to consider the issues of anti-communism. In reality, the ideological foundation of South Korea was anti-communist first and foremost. However, the constitution does not spell this out in its text. Thus the law that contains the ideological foundation and practical guidelines in South Korea is not the constitution but Legislation #10, or the National Security Law. The National Security Law (NSL) was passed in the legislature in December 1948 despite a strong opposition by junior members of the Assembly. This law is the higher normative law that supersedes all other law in South Korea; this was true under authoritarian rule, and it is true today.

7. Cold War Anti-communism and Democracy in Korea

In the past half-century, from the time of national liberation to the present, the divisive and hostile relations hardened between North and South Korea. Internally, it was a period when the conservative anti-communist order, which I have often referred to as a "domestic Cold War," was strengthened. At the same time, the Cold War was also the strongest force for organizing a political framework, and for narrowly restricting the scope of political practices and ideologies within that framework. I say that Cold War anti-communism resulted in conservative democracy in Korea. This is not to point out simply that Cold War anti-communism is a conservative ideology. That it is, but it is more; it is hostile to political and social organizations that smack of having any ideological content. In particular, if the organizational attempt involved suggesting labor-related problems, class-based complaints, or policies, programs, and thoughts that were linked to an adjustment of the capitalist system, such an attempt became the target of an ideological attack. The only political power that can survive under such conditions is right-wing power.

In Korea, it was fatal to the development of democracy that the early period of democratic institutions in the country overlapped with that of deepening the Cold War confrontation in general and violent internal conflicts of the post-liberation Korea. It was also fatal that these circumstances led to an extreme ideological polarization. As is well known, nationalism is a political thought and a movement that gives priority to the historical and communal experience of a people. It emphasizes the commonality and oneness of a people over any other value, such as individuality, and it is centered on strong collective sentiments and solidarity consciousness. The strong nationalism in Korea has as its foundation the common historical experience of the Japanese colonial rule. The greatest irony of the Cold War period in Korea is that the strong nationalism, which values the oneness of the Korean people more than anything else, was the very cause of the national division and war. Accordingly, the nationalism in the south and the north each competed to absorb the other, and within their respective societies each developed a political structure that thoroughly excluded the other's ideology.

The political structure thus shaped by the Cold War had two negative effects on the development of democracy. The first was the denial of the vast middle ground, owing to the effects of extreme ideological polarization. Political conflicts became fierce ideological polemics, and political competitions turned into extremely hostile relationships; opposition and criticism were excluded. The ruler could monopolize powerful political resources, and it was easy to utilize anti-communism as a weapon to repress those who opposed or criticized the government. The topography of political competition and the hegemony of anti-communism in Korea made it impossible to have any kind of political debate within a broad ideological spectrum. Politics was reduced to a choice between black or white. Democracy is hard to develop in such a structure, and it is not possible for ruling and opposition parties to compete openly and freely. Naturally, the Cold War anti-communism made it difficult to link the representative system of politics horizontally with civil society.

The other negative effect of the Cold War anti-communism was that it made the use of proper terms for common political concepts difficult, concepts such as "the left" or "the right," or "people" in English, *peuple* in French, and *popolo* in Italian, etc. Everyday political words could easily be colored ideologically. For example, it was difficult to use the words *inmin* (people), *minjung* (people), and *kyegŭp* (class), because their use was associated with the left, and one immediately became ideologically suspect upon using them. In fact, through such "ideological interpellation"[28] the use of certain words in Korea would associate one with communism in North Korea. Where there is no political language and discourse, there is no political practice. Under such circumstances, the ruling and the opposition parties could compete only within an ideologically very narrow spectrum; in other words, the competition was structurally, or systematically, limited in political society. It was also difficult for social forces to organize horizontal and functional conflicts in civil society and to organize a political movement or an alternative discourse that would represent the voices of the weak in society. When functional and class interests become diversified in society, and they enter into conflicts among themselves, the different interest groups—for example,

---

28 Ideological interpellation: Refers to the notion that a fact or a phenomenon is given a social meaning through mobilization and association of ideological factors. Louis Althusser conceptualized this term in order to emphasize that ideology interpellates individuals as subordinate subjects and dominates them. According to Althusser, the dominant structure or system in a society preserves itself not as a simple result of class structure in the relations of production. Rather, the multi-layered determination of the superstructure, such as the state and ideology, plays an important role in it. Louis Althusser, *Ideology and the State, Lenin and Philosophy and Other Essays* (London: New Left Books, 1977).

the workers, farmers, teachers, small- and medium-size business owners, and the self-employed—cannot but employ certain ideological and discursive language to politically organize and represent their special interests. Also, debate and mass mobilization can occur in various public spheres.[29] In this process collision and conflict with the political interests of the government in power and its ruling discourse would be unavoidable. Functional and class diversification and conflicts are natural, and the need for the ideology and language to express them is also natural. The Cold War anti-communism, however, does not allow such ideological or discursive freedom.

It is in this context that one asks, "Can anti-communist hegemony and democracy coexist?" The answer is, it is not impossible for the two to co-exist, but anti-communism greatly obstructs democracy by seriously re-stricting the development of the political representation system or the party system. Democracy is not only a political system that should be understood from the perspective of the "minimalist conception of democracy,"[30] which is based on conformity to procedural standards and on whether or not certain institutions and rules exist. Democracy also should be understood as a social ideal where a broad spectrum of the members of society would participate in its rule. It would require that the members experience the values of democracy through political participation, on the one hand, and political institutions and procedures that are supported by popular political culture, on the other hand. Accordingly, as long as democracy in Korea is rooted in the Cold War anti-communism, it would be difficult for it to develop into a high-quality democracy.

29 Public sphere: The public sphere, or the forum for public discussions, originally conceptualized by Jürgen Habermas, is a sphere where citizens as political subjects raise social issues and build public opinion through means of communication such as mass media. The process would influence the state's or government's policy decisions and executions. The idea was based upon the fundamental principles of modern democracy, i.e., liberty, equality, and justice. Habermas' concept has been criticized, however, since the ideal of a single united public sphere and the consensus of society on public virtue are hard to achieve. The public sphere is divided by different powers and interests, and can become a sphere of hegemony of the power and interests of strong interest groups. Jürgen Habermas, *The Structural Transformation of the Public Sphere: An Inquiry into a Category of Bourgeois Society* (Cambridge, MA: MIT Press, 1991).

30 Minimalist conception of democracy: A view that defines and understands democracy in terms of its procedural minimum. This is the view of the theory of democratic transition that has dominated political science since the mid-1980s. It inherits the traditional view of Joseph A. Schumpeter. According to Schumpeter, democracy is a system of competition among elites who wish to win majority votes. It is distinguished from authoritarianism by its establishment of procedural requirements for electoral competition. Joseph A. Schumpeter, *Capitalism, Socialism, and Democracy* (New York: Harper, 1942).

3 Authoritarian Industrialization and Democratization by Mass Movement

1. What are the Characteristics of the Park Chung-hee Model of Development?

The Self-contradiction of the Park Chung-hee Regime

What did the Park Chung-hee regime and its model of development, led by the authoritarian government and *chaebŏl*, leave behind for democracy? The Park Chung-hee regime did not directly produce a democracy. That is

TABLE 3.1

Chronology of Major Events, 1961–80

1961	May 16	May 16 military coup d'état
1962–66		The 1st Five-Year Economic Development Period
1963	December 17	Inauguration of the Third Republic (Park Chung-hee assumes presidency)
1964	June 3	Demonstrations against the Korea-Japan normalization talks
1967–71		The 2nd Five-Year Economic Development Period
1970	November 13	Chŏn T'ae-il self-immolation
1972–76		The 3rd Five-Year Economic Development Period
1972	October 17	"Extraordinary martial law decree" issued (Yushin Constitution passed)
1974	January 8	Emergency decree nos. 1 and 2 issued
1975	May 13	Emergency decree no. 9 issued
1977–81		The 4th Five-Year Economic Development Period
1979	August 11	YH incident
	October 16	Pusan-Masan Uprising
	October 26	Park Chung-hee assassination
	December 12	12.12 Incident (Chŏng Sŭng-hwa, the martial law commander, is arrested)
1980	May 18	5.18 Kwangju Uprising

Source: Author.

to say, it was only after the Fifth Republic of the Chun Doo-hwan (Chŏn Tu-hwan, Jeon Du-hwan) regime that transition to democracy was possible. However, there is no doubt that, when it collapsed, Park's regime left behind a momentum for eventual democratization in Korea. Professor Han Pae-ho asks an important question, "Why did authoritarianism fail to institutionalize in Korea?"[1] In short, by failing to institutionalize authoritarianism, Park's regime opened a pathway to democracy. But from the perspective that democratization in Korea was possible as a result of the success, not failure, of the authoritarian regime's economic policy, it is markedly different from the democratization that took place in most of the Latin American countries. The modernization project in Korea, led top-down by Park Chung-hee, was seen as a successful development model for industrialization of underdeveloped countries around the world, as it earned the title of "the Park Chung-hee model of development."

Why then, despite successful economic development and industrialization, did Park's regime fail to achieve the institutionalization of authoritarianism? This question illustrates the self-contradictory nature of the Park Chung-hee regime. That is to say, Park's regime created a modernization "success myth" on the one hand, while on the other hand it allowed an escape route to democracy by failing to make authoritarianism a sustainable system. We can define a state on two different levels. One as an infrastructure and the other as a government—this issue will be further discussed in Part III of this book. From this perspective, the industrialization led by Park Chung-hee contributed decidedly to the strengthening of the nation's physical foundation and state hegemony. But on the state-as-government level, Park's regime, like the Syngman Rhee regime before it, could not maintain its system because of the legacy of premature democracy and the effects of successful industrialization.

The Functional Relationship between Industrialization and the Political System: Three Theories

To better understand the issues involved in discussing the political effects of industrialization, let us take a look at three different theories, each taking a different point of view. The first is the concept of bureaucratic authoritarianism put forth by Guillermo O'Donnnell. The second is the modernization theory of Seymour Lipset and Adam Przeworski. The third is Barrington Moore's theory of the social origins of dictatorship and democracy.

1 Han Pae-ho, *Han'guk ŭi chŏngch'i kwajŏng kwa pyŏnhwa* (The Political Process and Changes in Korea) (Seoul: Pŏmmunsa, 1993).

First, let us take a look at O'Donnell's concept.[2] In the mid- to late-1980s, there was an active debate in Korea as to whether or not O'Donnell's concept of bureaucratic authoritarianism, which is based on the studies of the origins of military dictatorships in Latin America from the late 1960s to mid-1970s, could be applied to the 1972 establishment of the Yushin system in Korea. O'Donnell's theory explains the establishment of authoritarian regimes through economic variables, i.e., the exhaustion of import substitution industrialization and the "deepening" of industrialization. In other words, according to this theory, import substitution industrialization spurred a growth in the domestic market and this growth gave rise to a populist alliance that embraced a broad spectrum of social classes. This alliance was dissolved when the industrial structure became entrenched. In this process, to repress the politically activated and militant masses, a coup d'état was executed in an alliance with the private sector, military technocrats, and multinational companies as the major players. The result was the rise of the authoritarian states. However, the Yushin system in Korea was not a case in which a change in socio-economic conditions brought about a change in the political system. The Korean case can be better explained by the theory of the overdeveloped state.

The state in Korea had at its disposal the Cold War anti-communist system with which it could suppress the labor movement without having to change its system. The labor movement in Korea was weak before the institution of the Yusin system, and the movement grew rapidly under it. Also, unlike in Latin America, the economy in Korea grew continuously and quickly. This rapid growth co-opted the labor force into the economic establishment; repression was presented as the price of growth. It was possible for the state to exchange repression for growth. That is to say, the socio-economic condition that O'Donnell presents as the independent variable in bureaucratic authoritarianism did not exist in Korea. Of course, there did exist a correlation between labor movement suppression and the Yushin system. The president in Korea ran a strong state and invoked the threat of a crisis as a pretext to extend his presidential term, and he used repressive state apparatuses to do so. To compensate for the loss of the regime's legitimacy after the Yushin system, growth had to be accelerated. With rapid economic growth, the labor movement grew just as rapidly in terms of both the workers' consciousness and organizational strength, and the regime needed ever-stronger means to repress the movement. Thus, the theory of

2 Guillermo A. O'Donnell, *Modernization and Bureaucratic Authoritarianism* (Berkeley: University of California Press, 1973).

bureaucratic authoritarianism is more persuasive as an explanation of how the Yushin system ruled the country rather than as an explanation of the system's cause.

The second theory to examine is that of modernization, best represented by Lipset.[3] In short, it argues that industrialization and economic growth bring about modernization. According to this theory, economic development gives rise to the growth of a middle class; the spread of public education and civic attitudes instill democratic values and bring wider public participation in politics; and economic development institutionalizes social conflicts and makes the dialectic of conflict and integration possible. At one point, modernization theory and its implications for the linear interpretation of historical developments and functionalist theory were much criticized.

More recently, Przeworski and Limongi have suggested what could be called a "neo-modernization theory."[4] They argue that there is a close correlation between the level of economic development and the establishment of a democratic system; while it is difficult to discover a direct cause and effect between the two, it is empirically valid to hypothesize that the more prosperous an economy, the more stable democracy will be. They further argue that once the per capita income passes the threshold of US$6,000, it is difficult to reverse the course of democracy. It is interesting to observe, considering that O'Donnell's theory of bureaucratic authoritarianism came out in the early 1970s and Przeworski's neo-modernization theory in the late 1990s, that within the span of about a quarter-century, two completely opposite conclusions about the consequence of modernization had been drawn. The former states that modernization brings not democracy but authoritarianism, while the latter states that, in line with Lipset's tradition, it does bring democracy. From the perspective of neo-modernization theory, it seems that an authoritarian regime is no more than an episodic speck in the long historical march toward democracy.

The third is the theory of social origins of specific political systems, and it is best represented by Moore's work.[5] According to Moore, the type of a political system—a democracy, fascism or other types of dictatorship, or a revolutionary communist regime—is mostly decided by the early

---

3 Seymour M. Lipset, *Political Man: The Social Bases of Politics* (Garden City, N.Y.: Doubleday, 1960).

4 Neo-modernization theory: Przeworski and Limongi argue that democracy is closely interrelated with economic prosperity, based upon their data analysis of 135 countries from the period of 1950–90. Adam Przeworski and Ferdinando Limongi, "Modernization: Theories and Facts," *World Politics* 49, no. 2 (1997).

5 Barrington Moore, Jr., *Social Origins of Dictatorship and Democracy: Lord and Peasant in the Making of the Modern World* (Boston: Beacon Press, 1966).

development patterns of modernization. The question centers on the pattern of how the society moves from an agricultural society to an industrial society. In other words, the important question here is what kind of relationship does the landed aristocracy have with the tenant farmers who actually work the land; with the urban bourgeoisie, the newly emerging social class; and with the monarchy that represents the established state power. In particular, an important variable here is the degree of the use of brute force in the relationship between landlords and peasants, which is related to how agricultural surplus is acquired by the landed aristocracy from agricultural production. The Junkers in Prussia used slave labor to harvest crops; the French aristocracy forced feudal taxation upon farmers; in England, farmers were expelled from the common land, and the wool industry prospered on what used to be farming land. Under these different circumstances, the landed aristocracy formed an alliance with the state power in the case of Prussia, with the urban bourgeoisie in the case of England, and with both in France. In other words, each country had a different pattern of modernization, and each resulted in a different kind of political system. In the case of Prussia, it led to a dictatorship; in England to democracy; and in France to revolution. In terms of forming an alliance with the state in England, the landed aristocracy and the industrial bourgeoisie formed an alliance to check the power of the monarchy. In Japan and Germany, the agricultural landowners in alliance with the state weakened the bourgeoisie, so that while the bourgeoisie was strong economically it could not wield any political influence. In Russia and China, it is argued, the underdevelopment of the bourgeoisie led to an alliance between the state bureaucracy and agricultural landowners, which in turn led to the farmers' revolt.

The Korean Experience: Reinterpretation through Theories

Now let us shift our focus back to Korea. We are attempting to assess the effects of the Park Chung-hee era industrialization on today's democracy in Korea. In other words, what we are doing is looking at the historical status of the Park Chung-hee regime, not from the point of view where authoritarianism has become institutionalized or permanent, but from the perspective where one could say that democracy has become consolidated. We reviewed three different political theories above, dealing with countries in Latin America and Europe, all of which have very different historical experiences and political conditions from Korea. Now, let us take a look at the Park Chung-hee regime through the comparative perspectives of these theories.

First, in the bureaucratic authoritarianism theory, the pivotal variable for regime change was the explosive class conflict arising from change in the nature and level of industrialization. A bureaucratic authoritarian state emerges when a politically activated popular sector cannot be controlled except by high-level and massive state violence. In this theory, the socio-economic factor is the primary variable. In terms of cause and effect, the existence of strong popular sectors—including a labor sector that has been organized and is aware of itself as the central agent of a political system—and the activation of those forces that threaten the existing regime are important.

In the case of the modernization theory, the focus is on a long-term shift in the value orientation and attitudes of society and the individual, regardless of whether such changes take place at a microscopic or macroscopic scale. However, the theory pays less attention to the questions of by whom and how democratization is achieved. Equally problematic in this theory is that the focus of the analysis is limited to a single country; its viewpoint is limited by the experience of a single country. As a result, in understanding political changes in Korea, it would overlook the fact that the international politics of the Cold War, the division of the peninsula, and the strategic role of Korea under these circumstances were just as important as the socio-economic conditions and power relations within the country. The same problem of the single-nation perspective can also be found in Moore's theory, which roots causes for regime changes in social origins.

The theory of bureaucratic authoritarianism implies that the military authoritarian government installed in the aftermath of a bureaucratic authoritarian coup d'état is a risk management system for guaranteeing the interests of foreign capital, which is mainly composed of multinational corporations. The theory also implies that when the authoritarian system, accompanied by a high level of state violence, cannot guarantee the interests of the coup d'état alliance, the alliance dissolves, the government collapses, and an opportunity for democratization arises. Accordingly, democratization is a last-stage phenomenon that appears when the governments in these countries become unable to rule. Here, the government is violent but completely ineffective, and its support base itself largely comes from foreign capital. Now, from the perspective of the social origin theory, the alliance between major social classes, such as between the landowners and tenant farmers, and between landowners and the bourgeoisie, is of primary importance. The state functions only as a dependent variable here, and it takes a back seat in the cause-and-effect equation.

As we review these three theories, we can see how the experiences of the countries in which they have their empirical foundations are different from the Park Chung-hee era industrialization in Korea. First and foremost, we must pay attention to the timing of industrialization. The bulk of industrialization in Korea took place during the 1960s–70s under authoritarian rule.

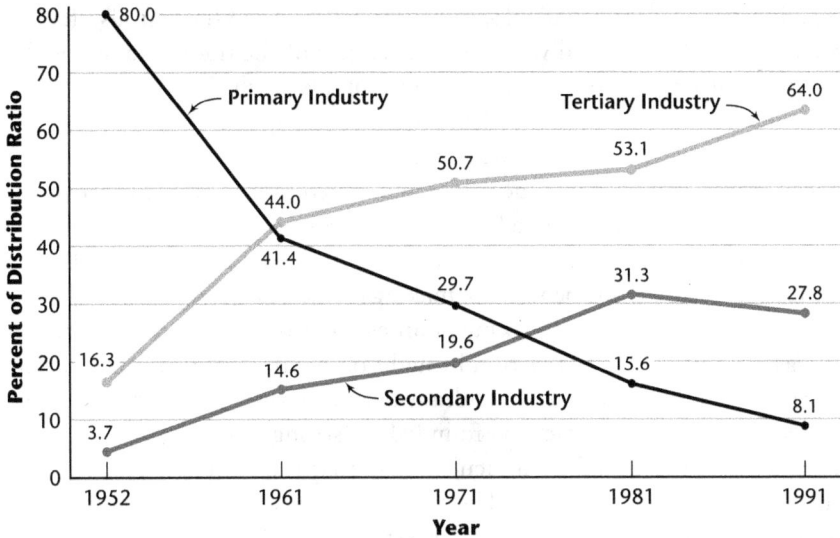

FIGURE 3.1 Change in Korean Industrial Structure (%)
Source: Bank of Korea.

The timing of industrialization in Korea is an important variable in distinguishing the characteristics of democratization in Korea before and after this period. The democratization attempt after the collapse of the Syngman Rhee regime held out for less than a year; its fate overlapped with the short-lived rule of KDP, the perennial opposition party in the same ideological league as the ruling party. However, the democratization attempt after 1987 had a different result. In this regard, we do need to distinguish "a democracy without industrialization," as in the case of the Second Republic (the failed KDP rule of 1960–1961), from "a democracy with industrialization," or a democracy supported by industrialization (as in the case of the post-1987 democratization in Korea). Such a distinction is very meaningful in analyzing the effects of the Park Chung-hee regime, and of the industrialization that took place under the regime, on the democratization of Korean society after industrialization.

The Syngman Rhee regime had been established in the divided nation with Cold War anti-communism as its ideological foundation. Its establishment was greatly aided by authoritarian state apparatuses that demobilized society. In the process of establishing separate governments in the south and north, and of the subsequent Korean War, the society Syngman Rhee faced became completely demobilized, politically and ideologically. Economically, it was a very poor county with a relatively high degree of equality. The effect of land reform was the most important contributing factor to economic equality, but the extreme ideological confrontation and the war also had an effect of equalizing social values and structures of the traditional hierarchical order. Strong centralization was an inevitable result. That is to say, Cold War anti-communism had the ideological hegemony, and the political power backed by this hegemony wielded enormous power of influence. Given such social circumstances, when the values and structures of social equality came together, centralization seemed inevitable. Tocqueville had understood early on that a strong political-cultural tendency toward equality in the United States was the dynamic behind the making of the U.S. democracy.[6] However, in Korea, equality was not so much an element of the political culture as it was a result of the destruction brought on by ideological confrontation, territorial division, war, and resultant overall poverty in society. In short, the Syngman Rhee regime was founded on strong authoritarian state apparatuses, but it would be difficult to say that the regime had hegemony throughout the whole society. The success of the student overthrow of the government on April 19, 1960, attests to this point. The subsequent military coup d'état of May 16, 1961, was also the result of a weak society. There was no other strong organization at either the state or the civil-society level that was as well organized and strong as the military, the strong authoritarian state apparatus. The bloodless coup d'état in 1961 was possible because none could fight against it. This situation contrasts with the May 17, 1980, coup d'état, in which case the new military junta faced an enormous resistance in Kwangju (Gwangju).

Who then supported the Syngman Rhee regime? Some political scientists have argued, borrowing from Karl Marx's argument in *The Eighteenth Brumaire of Louis Bonaparte*,[7] that Rhee's supporters were the farmers who benefited from land reform. They argue that the situation in Korea can be compared to that of France after the French Revolution. The French tenant farmers became autonomous through land reform, and the 1848 election of Louis Napoleon as the president depended on their votes. More specifically, the argument points to the election results in which the overwhelming support for Rhee came from the farmers. As indicated by the term *yŏch'on yado*,[8] a voting pattern in which the dominant support for the ruling and

6 Alexis de Tocqueville, *Democracy in America*, ed. J. P. Mayer (Garden City, NY: Anchor Books, 1969).

7 Karl Marx, *The Eighteenth Brumaire of Louis Bonaparte* (New York: International Publishers, 1963).

8 *Yŏch'on yado*: This Korean acronym refers to a voting pattern in which the ruling party (*yŏdang*) was strong in the rural area (*nongch'on*) while the opposition party (*yadang*) was strong in the urban areas (*tosi*).

opposition party came from the rural and urban areas, respectively. With regards to the changing economy, there could be much comparative similarity between the French farmers of 1840s and the Korean farmers of the 1950s. However, it must be emphasized that the farming population in Korea during this period had been demobilized and passively mobilized top-down by a well-developed administrative network. It must also be pointed out that the elections in the 1950s were characterized by a nationwide administrative mobilization and election fraud; the election fraud was the direct cause of the April 19 student revolution. In other words, the Syngman Rhee regime had always suffered from lack of legitimacy and weak support.

The Park Chung-hee regime was fundamentally different in this regard. Park's regime modernized the government in terms of both its structure and mode of operation, and it actively organized its support base. In these respects, I believe it was the first modern government in the history of Korea. On the other hand, it became an authoritarian system, both in the political aspect and in how it pursued industrialization; in this regard, it became a system that could not but pay an enormous price. After the coup d'état, the military junta plunged into an ambitious industrialization project by announcing the first Five-Year Economic Development Plan. At the time, in 1962, there was no strong force whatsoever in Korean society to stop their modernization plan. This was a situation that was different from Latin America or Europe. Unlike in many Latin American countries, Park's regime did not face strong agricultural interests resisting the modernization project. The land reform that abolished the old landed class, the material base of KDP, was a decisively important factor. This situation explains why conservative forces in Korea developed around the newly emerged industrial elite and not around the landed class as is typically the case in other countries.

Moreover, the military elites also had no strong bourgeoisie to face down. The government-led industrialization and the active government market intervention through economic planning were adopted after the French model of "indicative planning."[9] This would not have been possible if there were a strong urban merchant bourgeoisie. In this regard, we can consider

9 Indicative planning: A concept referring to the economic development model of France after the 1950s. In this model, high-level economic decision-makers in the government suggest a reasonable goal for private enterprises, instead of ordering them what to achieve. This is an economic system in between the socialist planned economy and the free market economy. The substance of indicative planning is the voluntary collusion between high-level government officials and entrepreneurs of large corporations. Politicians and representatives of organized labor are excluded from this process. Andrew Shonfield, *Modern Capitalism: The Changing Balance of Public and Private Power* (London: Oxford University Press, 1969).

the democratic government policy and the future of Korean society. From my perspective, the *chaebŏl* reform of the Kim Dae-jung (Kim Tae-jung) government is closer to failure than to success. Moreover, what success this weak government was able to achieve in this regard came not from the strength of the government but from the external impact of the 1997–98 financial crisis. The result suggests that any *chaebŏl* reform in the future, whatever its form, will be difficult to achieve unless the government has strong leadership, a broad social consensus, and a well-coordinated and planned reform program. The military elites of the early 1960s were in fact given a free hand for social mobilization to establish and implement its plans. The state in Korea during the industrialization period did not face strong opposition forces such as a politically activated popular sector including the working class, as the bureaucratic authoritarianism theorists would have it; nor did Park's regime face, as those who advocate the social origins theory would argue, any other strong forces such as the landed class or the urban industrial bourgeoisie. The rapid, government-led industrialization under Park's regime was possible under these circumstances.

Unlike the Syngman Rhee regime, the military elites of Park's government actively mobilized support. The central means to do that was industrialization through rapid growth. There were two issues that dominated Korean society after it experienced chaos, instability, and war during and after the division of the nation. One was democratization, and the other was economic independence, or escape from poverty. Economic independence here does not mean "autarky" or a self-sufficient economy isolated from the international economy. Rather, it refers to a sustainable, self-reliant, self-supporting economy. This was because, in the period after U.S. military rule, and particularly after the Korean War, the Korean economy and the lives of the people became impoverished. Korea was one of the poorest countries in the world as indicated by the per capita income index, and the nation's financial and economic survival was not possible without U.S. aid.

After the Korean War and through the 1950s, there were two major social groups that began to grow. The first was the student group, the leading force of the April 19 revolution, and the other was the military elite, the leading force of the May 16 coup d'état. In regard to their attitudes toward democratization, these two groups were polar opposites. The military elite came to the forefront of politics with the slogan of fighting poverty. The students represented the democratic aspiration. These two groups took on, albeit each a different one, the two major issues that Korean society had to solve after the Korean War. In this regard they were both "children of the 1950s." To the extent that the military elite promoted the establishment of a self-sustaining economy and a fight against the corruption that had been rampant in the previous government as their code of conduct, their sense of the problem had popular appeal. Perhaps these military elites took as their models the Young Turks who led the nation's modernization in the early twentieth century, or Gamel Abdel Nasser, the leader of the Egyptian coup d'état in the mid-1950s, to justify their actions. The problem was that democratization and industrialization were not united; they stood in opposition to each other in a confrontational relationship. In short, the military elite took as their central issue the problem of economic development, which the students and the intellectuals had not fully addressed in the discourses of their movement. When the military elite seized power, in order to achieve their goal, on the one hand they mobilized every social resource available for economic growth. On the other hand, they attempted to seal off the possibility of mobilizing any potential resources to bring democracy.

How then did the Park regime's elite carry out their ambitious plans for modernization? The pivotal answer to this question lies in the massive reform of the state bureaucratic system. They reorganized the bureaucracies involving economic policies, a process that included the establishment of the Economic Planning Board (EPB). They also newly established the Korea Central Intelligence Agency (KCIA), strengthening the authoritarian national security organization. These state vessels formed the two pillars of the government reorganization. The functional integration of national security and economic policies paved the way for the government to lead the economy, and to create and intervene in markets at will. The legitimacy of an authoritarian government lies in its performance and efficiency as a government. It is probably not an exaggeration to say that this was the basic guiding principle of the government led by the military elite. Growth, efficiency, and target achievement were their aims. Rapid growth was the top target objective, and thus development became a national doctrine and ideology. Thus, within the period of the first Five-Year Economic Development Plan (1962–66) to the fourth Five-year Plan (1977–81), an unprecedented growth rate in the world history of industrialization was achieved in Korea. In 1973–76 alone, Korea recorded an annual average growth rate of 15 percent; export of industrial products increased on average 25.7 percent annually; and the annual average GDP increased 10.3 percent. It was the result of a military-like operation of setting targets, taking charge of national organizations, and intensely developing and mobilizing all social resources to achieve the targets faster, on an ever-greater scale, and with even more efficiency.

Comparison with the Developmental State Model of Japan

With regards to the high performance of the Park Chung-hee regime, it is necessary to take a look at the "developmental state" theory. Many scholars both in Korea and abroad have referred to Park's regime as a developmental state. This concept was developed originally by Chalmers Johnson in research on the economic development of Japan, the result of which was published as *MITI and the Japanese Miracle*.[10] Using the Ministry of International Trade and Industry (MITI) from the 1920s to 1970s as a model, the book argues that socially autonomous and competent bureaucrats in Japan were the driving forces behind the economic development of Japan today. Taking Max Weber's theory of bureaucracy as his reference point, Johnson suggests a unique market-intervention or government-led development model, a model for a rationally planned capitalist developmental state that is neither socialist nor free-market based. Studies on the application of Johnson's developmental state model to Korea can be seen in an excellent book edited by Meredith Woo-Cumings,[11] a Korean American political scientist. Here the Japanese experience is expanded and applied as a general theory to explain the brilliant development of the late capitalist states, the "four Asian dragons." Even before this book, Alice Amsden applied the developmental state theory to Korea's economic development.[12] In fact, from the mid-1980s to the mid-1990s, studies that applied this theory were prolific, and the theory in fact dominated the field of political economy.

The developmental state model focuses its attention on the capability of the socially autonomous and competent economic bureaucracy to lead the economy and create and intervene in markets. In the developmental state, the role of the bureaucratic elite is crucial in defining national goals and in determining policy priorities. Political power in this case supports the bureaucracy to guarantee its autonomy from social forces. The elite of the economic policy bureaucracy commands and directs policy decisions and implementation at the apex of bureaucratic structure, and they perform the function of planning, implementing, and coordinating the overall economic policy.

10 Chalmers Johnson, *MITI and the Japanese Miracle* (Stanford: Stanford University Press, 1982).

11 Meredith Woo-Cumings, *The Developmental State* (Ithaca: Cornell University Press, 1999).

12 Alice Amsden, *Asia's Next Giant: South Korea and Late Industrialization* (New York: Oxford University Press, 1989).

Could the developmental state theory, based on the Japanese MITI model, be readily applied to the Park Chung-hee development model? The two models indeed show high relevance. But when we examine the similarities and the differences between the two, we may be able to better focus on the uniqueness of the Park Chung-hee development model. To say that there is a great similarity between the two models is significant. Many comparative political scientists in Korea and abroad do not hesitate to define Park's government as a military authoritarian regime; progressive scholars define it as a military dictatorship. These terms implicitly refer to Latin American military regimes as their bases to compare with the Park Chung-hee regime. Such comparisons do have the merit of explaining some phenomena, but fundamentally they obscure a correct understanding of the characteristics and the historical role of the Park Chung-hee regime.

To apply the developmental state model of the Japanese experience to the Park Chung-hee development model is to recognize that similarities do exist between the two models, and that there was much similarity between the Korean military authoritarianism and the Japanese development model, in particular pre-war Japanese authoritarianism. Albert Hirschman categorized the periods of "late industrialization" and "late-late industrialization."[13] According to Alexander Gerschenkron, late industrialization countries include Germany, Italy, and Russia, those that industrialized a step behind England, the first country to begin industrialization.[14] The late-late industrialization countries refer to Latin American and Third World countries. In terms of timing, Korea certainly belongs to the late-late category. In terms of how the political system and the means of industrialization were combined, however, it had strong similarities to late-industrialization countries. Korea was at a crossroads; depending on how Park Chung-hee implemented industrialization, the country could have gone the way of either late- or late-late industrialization. From the present vantage point, if we are to evaluate any historical contribution that Park's development model made, it is that it played a decisive role in preventing Korea from taking the course of the Latin American countries. In short, although Park's government began in much the same way as the military governments in Latin America, Park's military regime was closer to the pre-war Japanese authoritarian regime than to the Latin American military regimes.

13 Albert O. Hirschman, "The Political Economy of Import-Substituting Industrialization in Latin America," *The Quarterly Journal of Economics* 82, no. 1 (1968).

14 Alexander Gerschenkron, *Economic Backwardness in Historical Perspective* (Cambridge, MA: Harvard University Press, 1962).

At the same time, we cannot overlook the differences between the Park Chung-hee model and the developmental state model of Japan. Surely, the economic policy bureaucracy under Park Chung-hee, as represented by the Economic Planning Board, had much similarity to that of the Japanese MITI from the 1920s to the 1970s. Despite the similarity, one cannot say that in Korea the influence of the bureaucrats was dominant in planning and implementing the nation's macro-economic policies. In other words, the economic bureaucrats did not enjoy enough autonomy to act in the interests of long-term benefit to the national economy, free from the vicissitude of political lives. The president's political objectives and vision, his interests, and the means to sustain his power were more decisive than the autonomy and expertise of the bureaucrats. The logic of politics, that is, power, superseded that of the techno-rationality of economic bureaucrats. In addition, it must also be noted that the national security organizations were also as important in making economic policy decisions as they were in deciding policy matters in general in Korea. In fact, in Park's regime, the role of the national security organizations was as absolute in the economic policy area as it was in other policy areas. The authoritarian state security organizations did more than simply play the role of watching and suppressing labor and anti-government activities in the name of economic stability. They were the core decision-makers in major policy decisions. It was the national security agents who controlled the vast set of bureaucratic rules and regulations instituted by the regime; they became an extension of the president, allowing him to rule effectively as the chief commander of state authority. Furthermore, as Korean companies expanded their businesses overseas, the security agencies provided information on overseas investment conditions to individual companies, prepared in advance the terms of investments, and supported these business activities. In this way, they played a broad spectrum of economic roles. Thus, the Park Chung-hee development model was characterized by absolute service to the policy objectives of the authoritarian power with closed-circuit and technocratic decision-making and implementation. It was a development model that could only function within an authoritarian system.

One important characteristic of the Park Chung-hee model that we cannot overlook is its militarism.[15] Today, as a legacy from the authoritarian era,

15 Militarism: An ideology or a value that adopts the principles of military organization as the principles of social organization and mobilization, such as hierarchy, discipline, command, obedience to orders, selfless devotion to one's country, planning of national goals, and efficiency in achieving them. It also adopts the ethos of military organization as the dominant culture of society. In *Social Origins of Dictatorship and*

it has penetrated deeply into the far corners of Korean social fabric. The Park-era militarism is the origin of the military culture today in Korean society. One can say that the combination of developmentalism and militarism epitomizes the behavioral principles, moral precepts, and ethos of the Park Chung-hee model of development. It deserves special mention that the combination of militarism and developmentalism created significant dynamics within the framework of north-south Korea confrontation and competition. The development dictatorship led by Park Chung-hee has come to be recognized as the Korean model of the developmental state. The difference of the Korean experience from that of Latin American countries contributed to this recognition. In Korea, the economic developmentalism that united with militarism was also joined by a popular phenomenon. The collective desire of the Korean people to escape from poverty is captured in a slogan from the 1960s and 1970s, "Chal sara pose" ("Jal sara bose," "Let us live well!"). This slogan came top-down from the government. But there is no other slogan whose popularity exemplifies better the overwhelming response of the people. Albert Hirschman has pointed out that, unlike in the late-industrialization countries of Europe, the late-late industrializations countries, such as those in Latin America, lacked a certain élan, a certain passionate collective will.[16] In this regard, even among the late-late-industrialization countries, Korea is rare in that the government successfully drew out such a passion from the people.

There were, however, great negative effects of the union of militarism and developmentalism, particularly in the area of democratization efforts. The top-down delivery of target orders, primacy of target achievements with the implicit and explicit assumption of "no questions asked," bulldozer-style orderliness, and "*ppalli-ppalli*" ("hurry, hurry") are some examples of the behavioral codes that have infiltrated deeply into Korean society today. Just as in the authoritarian and hierarchical relationship between a commanding officer who gives an order and a soldier who must absolutely obey that order, one finds an authoritarian structure in the relationship between the president and the people, between the owner of a company and the workers, and

---

Democracy, Barrington Moore presents Japan and Germany as exemplary cases in which militarism mobilized the modernization process from above, ending in fascism. They built up an atmosphere of international conflict, united their upper classes through this, and made economic development the absolute goal of their nations. Barrington Moore, Jr., *Social Origins of Dictatorship and Democracy: Lord and Peasant in the Making of the Modern World* (Boston: Beacon Press, 1966).

16 Albert O. Hirschman, "The Political Economy of Import-Substituting Industrialization in Latin America," *The Quarterly Journal of Economics* 82, no. 1 (1968).

between an organization's head and its employees. In general, such a structure is deeply related to the military culture of the society. The control of the laborers and employees in production plants and in offices, respectively, is similarly patterned after the military barracks. Although democracy is institutionalized at the higher levels of politics, military culture still operates as a factor that restricts the spread of democratic values and norms in various sectors of society at the lower levels and in individual behavior.

2. What Was the Social Support Base of the Park Chung-hee Regime?

The Social Support Base of the Authoritarian Industrialization

Who supported the Park Chung-hee regime? This question is important not only in studying changing voting patterns during the authoritarian industrialization period but also in understanding the political system. One of the important characteristics of the Park Chung-hee regime is the fact that through an authoritarian industrialization, it created a broad support base for industrialization. In this regard, Park's regime differs from the previous Syngman Rhee regime.

First and foremost, Park's regime created *chaebŏl*. Of course, it was not during this regime that *chaebŏl* were created for the first time. The primitive forms of *chaebŏl* had emerged in two stages before the 1960s. The seeds of *chaebŏl* were sown first in the aftermath of national liberation, during the U.S. military occupation period, in the disposal process of vested property,[17] or the property that formerly belonged to the Japanese. The second stage of the early *chaebŏl* formation came after the Korean War. *Chaebŏl* were created through the rapid growth of the import substitution economy centered on the "three whites" industry,[18] and through the U.S. food aid distributed

17 Vested property: Refers to the property that had belonged to Japanese individuals prior to the liberation of Korea and was handed over to the Korean government, according to Article 5 of the First Agreement on Finance and Property signed by the Korean government and the U.S. government on September 11, 1948 (Act on Disposition of Vested Property, Article 2, Paragraph 1).

18 Three whites industry: As U.S. economic aid came to Korea on a massive scale in the 1950s, *chaebŏl* began to emerge as monopolistic capital closely interrelated with political power. The most prominent *chaebŏl* in this period were Samsung (Samsŏng, Samseong, Yi Pyŏng-ch'ŏl, Lee Byeong'cheol), Samho (Chŏng Chae-ho, Jeong Jae-ho), Lucky (Ku In-hoe, Gu In-hoe), Daehan (Taehan, Sŏl Kyŏng-dong, Seoul Gyeong-dong), Gaepung (Kaep'ung, Yi Chŏng-lim, Lee Jeong-lim, Yi Hoe-rim, Lee Hoe-rim), Dong Yang (Tongyang, Dongyang, Yi Sang-gu, Lee Sang-gu), and Keumsung (Kŭmsŏng, Geumsong, Kim Sŏng-gon, Kim Seong-gon). They grew rapidly in the consumer goods industry, nicknamed "three whites industry" because they manufactured products made of cotton, flour, and sugar.

in Korea. What is important here is that *chaebŏl* in Korea were formed by a political power and also access to the productive resources controlled by the government. Also, the government mobilized *chaebŏl* to implement the five-year economic development plans on a full scale. To achieve rapid growth, the government made unilateral and concentrated injections of financial investment loans to *chaebŏl* and mobilized all socio-economic resources for them. The government planned and promoted economic policies, but it was the *chaebŏl* that implemented these policies of rapid growth in their factories in the 1960s-70s. *Chaebŏl* were the consignees consigned with the national goal, and they were the civilian agents implementing the national economic plan. That is to say, it was a state-*chaebŏl* alliance, with the state on top and *chaebŏl* at the bottom, that led the rapid mercantilist growth. In fact, collusion between politics and business does not fully portray the nature of the relationship. Political power and *chaebŏl* were merged in a structural relationship in which the two are difficult to separate. Thus, *chaebŏl* emerged as a new ruling class in Korea, filling the gap left by the demise of the traditional landed class. Certainly the new ruling class was of the private sector, and of the civil society. But this Korean bourgeois class lacked autonomy from the state power, and whether this class can become a force for democratization that leads the civil society, as was the case in the West, is highly questionable.

How about the urban middle class? The growth of this class was the result of industrialization. One cannot say that the middle class did not exist at all in 1950s, but its size was limited. The social changes following industrialization divided the middle class into the "new middle class," whose members were employed by large corporations in cities, and the traditional self-employed or the petit-bourgeoisie. Their exact political attitudes are not simple to describe. The political attitude of the middle class educated in the 1950s under the Syngman Rhee regime was mostly democratic, and in the latter half of the 1950s, when the regime's authoritarianism accelerated, many became anti-government. It is possible that this political attitude of the middle class was the central vulnerability of Rhee's regime. We cannot say, however, that the middle-class attitude of the 1960s–70s was the same. Let us come back to this issue in the next chapter.

What about the farmers and laborers? Farmers were the strongest supporters of the Park Chung-hee regime. It was in the farming villages, more than anywhere else, where the changes from the effects of industrialization were most directly experienced. The villages were the reservoir of the labor force needed for rapid and full-scale urban industrialization. The villages changed rapidly in two aspects. One was the rapid reduction of the farming population. The surplus farm-labor force and the high unemployment rate in rural areas pushed the younger generation en masse to secondary industrial jobs in urban areas. Another change was that through government-sponsored investment programs, such as the "New Village Movement" (Saemaŭl undong), the government sought to improve life in farming villages and mobilized the rural population. The voting patterns of the period show that farmers were supporters of the ruling party. This pattern shows no change from the 1950s. The difference, however, is that farmers in the 1960s and 1970s were very active supporters of the government and were actively mobilized by the government.

The political attitude of the workers took a different direction from that of the farmers. The increase in the number of workers was the flip side of the young people leaving villages en masse. It could be that these young migrants were one of the beneficiary groups of industrialization. Because they came from poor farming families, the move to an urban area and a job in the city meant a chance to live an urban life and an improvement of income. Unlike farmers, however, workers in the 1970s gradually began to organize and to participate in the labor movement. As they began to form a collective self-identity and to challenge the growth policy of the government supported by the repressive labor policy, they began to become a pro-democracy force in this period.

Elections in Two Very Contrasting Periods: The 1967 Election and the 1971 Election

The election results from the period before the 1972 Yushin Constitution reveal political conditions described above. There were the 5th, 6th, and 7th presidential elections in 1963, 1967, and 1971, respectively. During the same period, the 6th, 7th, and 8th general elections were also held. During this period, a new pattern of voter alignment can be observed. In the 1963 presidential election, Park Chung-hee won by a narrow margin of 400,000 votes. In the 1967 election, however, after the national experience of rapid growth, voters gave Park Chung-hee and the ruling party more solid and widespread support than ever. In the 1963 election, Park won the presidency by a slim margin of 1.1 percentage points. But in 1967, he received 51.4 percent of the votes and won the election by 10.5 percentage points. The increase in support came mostly from urban areas. In large cities, support increased by 15.2 percentage points, while in small- and medium-size cities, it increased by 14.5 percentage points. In the 7th general election that took place a month after the 1967 presidential election, the ruling Republican Party received 50.6 percent of the votes, an increase of 17.1 percentage points. It was the only election in which the leading political party in the National Assembly received more than half the vote.

In the 7th presidential election and the 8th general election that took place in 1971, the gap in the support rate between the ruling Republican Party and the leading opposition party, the New Democratic Party (formerly KDP) sharply decreased. In the presidential election, the gap was reduced to 7.9 percentage points, and Kim Dae-jung of the New Democratic Party received 45.3 percent of the vote, the highest number of votes received by an opposition candidate in Korea. This percentage is higher than the 40.3 percent Kim received in his victorious 1997 election. In the 1971 general election, the gap narrowed from 17.1 to 4.4 percentage points. The 44.4 percent support that the opposition party received in this election is also the highest rate that an opposition party has ever received. Needless to say, the overwhelming support for the ruling party in 1967 was the direct result of rapid economic growth and competence of the government that pursued the policy, while the 1971 election outcome was the result of the negative impact of the ruling party turning authoritarian with the unpopular 1969 constitutional amendment that allowed a three-term presidency. The elections, only four years apart, brought dramatically reversed results.

We discover an important fact through this historic voting data. There are two values coexisting in Korea that receive widespread popular support. One is the value associated with democracy and the other is the value attached to the competence of a government. The sweeping support that the Park Chung-hee regime received in the presidential and general elections of 1967 shows the strong effect of industrialization in Korea. The phenomenon of the 1950s, i.e., strong support for the ruling party in rural areas and for the opposition party in urban areas, ended with the 1967 election; the gap in the electoral support rate between the rural and urban populations narrowed afterward. This demonstrates the fact that through industrialization, the Park Chung-hee regime secured a firm and strong base of support. In fact, the 1967 election results are important from the perspective of studying the history of politics or elections in Korea. Park's government showed a great competence that was unprecedented in any other government before him, and this led the regime to receive overwhelming support from the people. Looking back from today's standpoint, there has never been an election in Korea, except in 1967, when the incumbent government won a reelection based on a positive evaluation of its performance from the electorate.

The message of the 1971 election results is also clear. In terms of changes in political system, the 1969 constitutional amendment was a turning point, because henceforth the Park regime took a clearly authoritarian path. Thus the 1971 election results show that no matter how great the regime's achievements were, the voters opposed the regime when the regime's industrialization project could not coexist with democratic values, and when it became clear that it was an authoritarian development plan. The voting behaviors of the middle class most acutely reflected such a trend. The middle class was a direct supporter and beneficiary of the rapid economic growth. They became firm supporters of industrialization. They were the central force that dismantled the voting patterns of the 1950s, in which the urban population typically supported the opposition, and gave a sweeping victory to Park and his regime in 1967. However, the 1971 elections showed that when the regime veered away from democratic values and institutions, the same middle class began turning into a pro-democracy force.

3. The Opening of Spaces for Democracy

Democratization by a Mass Movement

Earlier I have noted that democratization in Korea resulted, not from a failure, but from the success of the authoritarian regime before it. In other words, Park's modernization efforts, marked by the combination of economic growth and political authoritarianism, were to a great extent a success. One does not have to borrow from the theory of Barrington Moore, Jr.; there is no country that can avoid modernization. What we can learn from Moore is that, under the circumstances, the question is not whether or not to choose modernization; rather, it is how to minimize the cost of transition, in particular the burden that falls on the shoulders of farmers, workers, and other grassroots populations. The fact that the cost was relatively low and the process very short can be seen as a positive aspect of the Park regime's modernization program. This positive evaluation, however, is applicable to the early period of industrialization, when it was still in a formative stage. The same evaluation could not be applied once industrialization took off and entered a stable period. In other words, the industrial structure went through a change in the early 1970s in Korea to one of heavy and chemical industrialization, and there was no reason for this change to result in the establishment of the Yushin system, i.e., a strengthening of authoritarianism.

The reality, however, was moving in the opposite direction. All forms of power were already concentrated in the president, and he could mobilize the massive resources—the fruits of tremendous economic growth—at his disposal. Under the circumstances, it was unrealistic to expect the president to voluntarily relinquish power. That is to say, in the process of pursuing rapid economic growth, the state bureaucracy expanded; power was hyper-concentrated with the bureaucracy as its basis; and a relationship of intimate cooperation between state authority and big businesses developed. The structural conditions were established for political authoritarianism and rapid economic growth to produce synergy between them. In this regard, it seems that Park's regime was a closed system with no exit. The regime had a positive role to play for a given period of time, but it was a regime with a fatal defect in that it did not have the political ability to self-transform into a different system. It was doomed to be scrapped by an external force.

The Park Chung-hee regime contributed to democratization in two ways that it did not intend. One way was through its success, and the other was through its failure. Its success contributed to democratization, because without capitalist industrialization, democracy cannot exist. The civil society that developed and expanded through the 1960s and 1970s exploded in the 1980s, and the demand for democracy erupted from the bottom up. By this time, Korea was as industrialized and urbanized as the countries in the West; the functional and vocational division of society was accelerating; the middle class expanded enormously; and farmers, workers, and other grassroots classes had matured. In such a social structure, authoritarianism cannot survive.

To say that Park's regime contributed to democratization through its failure is to say that when the regime abandoned democracy and adopted authoritarianism, a strong democratic force completely different from that of the 1950s emerged under that regime. Without the resistance of the anti-government *minjung*[19] force composed of citizens and workers, the collapse of the Yushin system would have been much delayed. The strong democratic force that finally ushered in democracy in the 1980s had its roots in the *minjung* movement of the earlier period.

In Korea, the breakaway path from authoritarian regime was paved by the democratization movement. According to Moore, modern democracy was led by the bourgeoisie who were the leaders of commerce. The bourgeoisie, or the *chaebŏl* in Korea, was created and nurtured by the authoritarian state and were the economic base of the state. A reform faction that could open a path to democracy would be unlikely to develop inside an overdeveloped state. An opposition party could exist only within the institutional boundaries allowed by the authoritarian state. The only possible source for a democratization movement was civil society. That path was set

19 *Minjung*: the people.

by the student movement, inspired by the tradition of the April 19 student revolution. The student movement later combined forces with the modern *minjung* movement, which was also reacting against the authoritarian development regime. Accordingly, while Moore argues that "there is no democracy without bourgeoisie," in the case of Korea, one would have to respond, "there is no democracy without a mass movement for democracy."[20]

The Legacy of Authoritarian Industrialization in Korean Democracy

The important issue from today's perspective is the impact of the Park Chung-hee-style industrialization on the democratization process in Korea. Of the many authoritarian legacies left behind, perhaps the gravest is the widespread and pervasive influence of *chaebŏl* in society. The Korean industrialization strategy was to create conglomerates and have them fulfill national goals. Today, however, the nation's economy and government performance depend on a small number of conglomerates owned by *chaebŏl*, and they now control the national economy. Democratization was synonymous with the withdrawal of the politicized military and heralding of market liberalization; when this happened, there was no power in Korea that could counter the influence of *chaebŏl*. Democratization made a transfer of power possible, where much of the power held in monopoly by the authoritarian regime could have been transferred to civil society and the people. However, much of that power was transferred to *chaebŏl*, not the people.

The *chaebŏl* began to develop as a state within the state, a mammoth independent organization impenetrable even by state authorities. As such, the ownership and decision-making structures of *chaebŏl* have come to exist outside of democratic control. In comparison to the monopoly power wielded by the private-interest-seeking *chaebŏl* in the liberalized market, the power of the state under democracy, which relies on the power of politics to create public goods, appears dwarfed. A *chaebŏl* might own a stake in production, distribution, service, leisure, education, culture, sports, mass media, and politics. In this way, *chaebŏl* wield enormous power and influence. In civil society, their hegemony is overwhelming. In the political world, as indicated by the phrase "politics and business in one flesh," the power of *chaebŏl* can debilitate the functional division between politics and business and control politics. In particular, it was difficult for *chaebŏl*, which were created and matured under Park's regime, to support democracy based on liberalism. Instead, as pious believers in the supremacy of economic and

---

20 Barrington Moore, Jr., *Social Origins of Dictatorship and Democracy: Lord and Peasant in the Making of the Modern World* (Boston: Beacon Press, 1966).

managerial efficiency, they formed a fortress of technocratic managerialism[21] and militarism. The conservative vested interests, the embodiment of this ideology, have become too firmly established in society; now they cannot change when time calls for them to change. In short, the *chaebŏl* structure and democracy cannot coexist. The legacy of the Park regime's authoritarianism is being handed down not by the military elite but by *chaebŏl*.

The second obstacle to democratization left behind by Park's military authoritarian regime is the deeply entrenched bureaucratic authoritarianism. The militarism strengthened bureaucratic authoritarianism and was in turn materialized by bureaucratic authoritarianism. The phenomenon that, today, power is concentrated at the center and at the apex, and that such power is manifested through a pyramid-like hierarchy of bureaucracy, cannot be entirely blamed on the legacy of the Park Chung-hee regime. Nevertheless, the strength of bureaucratic organizations that we witness today has its origin in the bureaucracy that President Park developed to pursue his ambitious modernization plan. By the late 1980s, when the call for a transition to democracy was in full swing, the bureaucracy had transformed itself into a huge interest group; it had become a force of resistance against democratic reform.

The third obstacle is the practice of authoritarian labor control, which was one of the most important macro-economic management principles under Park's regime. It was the other side of the coin of a *chaebŏl*-biased and growth-first policy. The government's labor policy in Korea has made it easy for industrialists and conservative political elites to dismiss and do away with the very concept of labor-management partnership. This authoritarian labor control brings serious negative effects to labor-management relations at the industrial level, and to participation at the political level.

---

21 Technocratic managerialism: This concept combines the goal-oriented rationality of bureaucracy in the theory of Max Weber and the managerial principle of maximizing profits in modern industrial organizations. Technocratic managerialism is a principle of organization and organizational management whose priority value is utilitarianism and efficiency, which is an apolitical or anti-political value. Technocratic managerialism, therefore, corresponds well to the organization of private enterprises and authoritarian political systems. It conflicts with the demands of democratic politics, which is based upon diverse conflicts of interests in society. The core principle of democratic politics is the coordination and integration of conflicts, rather than efficiency. Contrary to the principle of technocratic managerialism, by which decisions are made in the closed circuit of elites or professionals, the democratic political process and policy-making process require participation of many people, as well as openness and transparency under public control.

Perhaps it would be too much to insist that there should have been a labor-management policy of a liberal framework during the early period of Park's regime when industrial development was still in its formative stage. Today, the situation is different. Industrial development is stable; state intervention has diminished in all economic areas; and the relationship of one-way instruction between the state and business has changed to one where private-sector initiatives exceed those of the state. The problem is that authoritarian labor control still continues and has become a heavy burden. It impedes the transformation and development of labor-management relations that would better correspond to the advanced production structure of capitalism in Korea. Today, the Korean economy stands at a crossroads. It must wean itself from the Fordist mass production system, which depends on repressive labor-management relations, and transform itself into a modern production system of high wages, high technology, and flexible production to be competitive in the international market. The premodern and authoritarian labor-management relations can no longer serve any positive function. Moreover, such authoritarian labor-management relations cannot coexist with democracy. Democracy is by definition a system in which ordinary people realize their power through political participation, which in turn is realized through free and fair electoral competition among their associations. The working class cannot be considered simply as another social sector representing the diversity of social interests. It is one of the principal groups at the center of industrial productive and social relations. The suppression of political participation by the working class must be seen from this perspective.

Even if one conceded that a democracy cannot realistically allow political participation of all social groups, the system cannot be called a democracy when the political participation of such a core group is prohibited. To start with, the suppression of such a core group from participating in politics requires repressive state apparatuses of corresponding strength. The continued existence of authoritarian repressive apparatuses and the restriction of political participation by one of the core groups in society cannot but greatly distort the entire Korean political system, including the internal structure of individual political parties, the party system, and the activities of interest groups and voluntary associations, which are the building blocks of civil society. As long as this distortion remains, politics will continue to turn into a power game among elite groups, which in turn will lead to repetition of the "reforms from above" that continually alienate the masses.

The growth-first development strategy of Park Chung-hee was effective for implementing capitalist industrialization in Korea. If one were to say that democratization in Korea would have been difficult to achieve without the industrialization that took place after the 1960s in Korea, it follows then that the task of democratization had to be postponed until industrialization reached a certain level of development. In evaluating the Park Chung-hee regime, we cannot hold it responsible for all the possible negative aspects of a late-late-industrialized society. There are problems general to late-late-industrialized societies; such problems are not limited to Park's regime. It is also not right to take all the obstacles to democratic reform and the development of democracy, and attribute their structural origins to Park's regime. The governments of Kim Young-sam (Kim Yŏng-sam, Kim Yeong-sam) and Kim Dae-jung could not have been in a better position to pursue democratic reforms at the beginnings of their respective governments. They had enormous resources at their disposal to overcome the various problems left behind by Park's regime. If they had been more committed to doing so, the *chaebŏl* structure would have been reorganized so that it would now be more rational and liberal. Also, the government bureaucracy would have been more democratically reformed, and industrial relations would have been made more democratic. But the two governments after democratization did not properly utilize the social dynamics of the time and wasted their opportunities. Thus, if there are authoritarian elements with structural origins in the Park Chung-hee regime still remaining in Korea today, part of the responsibility must lie with the governments of Kim Young-sam and Kim Dae-jung for having failed to implement democracy to the fullest extent that they could.

Collusion between Political Power and the Press

Another negative legacy left behind by the Park Chung-hee and Chun Doo-hwan regimes is the collusion between power and the press. Tocqueville had observed as early as the mid-nineteenth century that the press in America was the secret to democracy in America.[22] The press, or the countless newspapers that were published in every city and rural county, narrated the interests common to both the individual and the group. They were the primary communication medium that held together what would have been a fragmented society if not for the newspapers' netlike connection of the diverse interests in society. The burgeoning of the press that spread to the edges of society empowered civil society in political action; it was the foundation of democracy in America.

22 Alexis de Tocqueville, *Democracy in America,* ed. J. P. Mayer (Garden City, NY: Anchor Books, 1969).

Of course, the press scene in Korea is far removed from this picture. The press has gone through technological advancements and is now run by giant corporations. Small newspapers have disappeared. Under these circumstances of modern capitalism, the status and role of the press today cannot be compared to those of the liberal press of the nineteenth century. Today, giant news companies reign above society and wield powerful influence. This is a general phenomenon found in modern capitalism, and it is thus not a unique situation in Korea. The particular pattern of the press overgrowth in Korea, however, has some unique historical characteristics. In the 1950s and 1960s, the press in Korea played an important role in narrating and socializing the most important issues of the time, namely democratization and modernization. The press also enjoyed a relatively high degree of autonomy from state power in 1950s. The press criticized without reservation and with rigor the growing authoritarianism of state power under Syngman Rhee and thus spoke on behalf of the democratic demands of society. A researcher had called the April 19 student revolution a "coalition of university students and the press,"[23] and in fact the revolution was possible because the coalition was possible. The role of the press as one of the central forces of the democratization struggle can be inferred from the 1959 closure of *Kyŏnghyang (Gyeonghang) Daily Newspaper*.[24] In the early 1960s, even after the May 16 coup, the press was still critical of the behavior and policies of the military junta. Moreover, the press also played a leading role in raising the issues of eliminating poverty and pushing modernization. This tradition of the press speaking on behalf of society and its demands continued until the Yushin Constitution was announced.

With the arrival of the Yushin system, the role of the press, which was relatively autonomous from state power, underwent a fundamental transformation. The Yushin system strengthened authoritarian repression and social exclusions, but fundamentally it was a very vulnerable system in that it could not create social order through ordinary legal procedures and police power. In short, the Yushin system was maintained through presidential

23 Hahn Been Lee, *Korea: Time, Change, Administration* (Honolulu: East-West Center Press, 1968).

24 Closure of the *Kyŏnghyang Daily Newspaper*: The biggest scandal involving freedom of speech during the Liberal Party regime. On April 30, 1959, the Syngman Rhee regime ordered the *Kyŏnghyang (Gyeonghang) Daily Newspaper*, an opposition newspaper owned by the Catholic Foundation, to be closed for violating the 88th Ordinance of the military regime. *Kyŏnghyang Daily* revived publication on April 27, 1960, right after the April 19 revolution.

emergency decrees[25] and the subsequent mobilization of military forces. It was an emergency system, and as such it was weak; allowing the smallest opposition would threaten its very existence. In this regard, the system was much like a human body with an immune deficiency: a minor attack from any pathogen threatens life. This explains why in mid-1979, a labor strike by about 200 women workers at a small unknown company called YH Trading Company[26] ultimately led to the collapse of the regime through a series of political and social chain reactions. It was because of this situation that press criticism of the regime was absolutely prohibited. Thus, the critical role of the press was completely sealed off during the period of the Yushin system. The basic structure and character of the news media in Korea today were formed in the 1980s. In the 1980s, the collusion between state power and the press deepened, and the press began to be actively mobilized to justify the authoritarian state. The result of the deepening collusion between the press and the state was grave. Some of the news companies now became giant corporations, the result of receiving special benefits in exchange for press repression.

During the period of the Yushin system and the Chun Doo-hwan regime, the military authoritarian system needed to justify itself, more than during the earlier periods. This was done through the news media. The press was reduced to a public relations agency for the government when the Yushin system was introduced. The period from then until the 1987 democratic liberalization can be divided into two, in terms of how the press carried out its role. Initially, the press was passive, having been forced to play the role of a government proxy. In the latter part, the press willingly played the role of government spokesperson to achieve its own objectives and benefits. When the Yushin system was first established, the press was given the role of a quasi-government agency, and most newspapers carried out the role under coercion. By the time Chun Doo-hwan arrived, they were playing the role

25 Presidential emergency decree: A special decree with constitutional force that was stipulated in the Constitution of the Fourth Republic (Yushin Constitution).

26 YH incident: In August 1979, about 200 female workers from the YH Corporation, a sewing factory, occupied the headquarters of the New Democratic Party and staged a sit-in. In the course of government intervention, one of the demonstrating workers, Kim Kyŏng-suk, was killed, and the president of the New Democratic Party, Kim Young-sam, was expelled from membership of the National Assembly. The YH incident started over an economic issue, resisting a lockout, but eventually it provided a political rallying point for all anti-regime groups, which brought about the Pusan-Masan Uprising and the fall of the Yushin regime in the end.

voluntarily. In return for accepting the role, news companies grew to be giant corporations with government favor, while at the same time journalists quickly emerged as a special group of intellectuals with a high salary range, a variety of fringe benefits, and access to power and resources. Along with the military elite, *chaebŏl*, and the technocrats of the state organizations, the press became a part of the core power bloc that sustained military authoritarianism in Korea. The press became the most vested among vested interests under the old system. After democratization the press became the fortress of Cold War anti-communism, and it played a central role in sustaining the hegemony of vested interests. We can see that the origin of the conservative press today goes back to this period that began with the introduction of the Yushin system.

4 The Conservative Outcome of the Democratic Transition and Regionalized Party System

1. Characteristics of the Democratic Transition in Korea

The Wonder of Democratization in Korea

The June 29 Declaration of 1987 was a historic moment when authoritarian rule ended and transition to democracy began in Korea. If we take this moment as the starting point for democratization in Korea, we can see that democracy in Korea progressed rapidly in comparison to Western democracies. When we look back at the historical and structural conditions in which the transition to democracy originated, certainly they were more favorable

TABLE 4.1

Chronology of Major Events, 1987–2001

1987	January 18	Student activist Pak Chong-ch'ŏl is tortured to death
	June 9	Student activist Yi Han-yŏl is hit by a splinter from a tear gas canister and dies
	June 29	June 29 Declaration is announced
	July–August	The Great Labor Struggle
	December 16	The 13th presidential election (Roh Tae-woo is elected)
1989	April–December	*Kongan chŏngguk* (a political state of "public security")
1990	January 22	*Chŏnno hyŏp* (National Council of Labor Unions) is launched
		Merger of three political parties
1991	May	*Punsin chŏngguk* (a political atmosphere of self-immolations) A series of students die in self-immolation in protest against the government
1992	December 18	The 14th presidential election (Kim Young-sam is elected)
1995	November	Korean Confederation of Trade Unions (KCTU) is launched
1997	November 21	Application for the IMF bailout loan
	December 18	The 15th presidential election (Kim Dae-jung is elected)
2001	June 15	The June 15 North-South summit meeting

Source: Author.

toward sustaining and strengthening authoritarianism than toward giving birth to a democracy. As we have seen earlier, the hegemony of Cold War anti-communist ideology and the effects of the north-south division were indeed powerful. In addition, the combination of an elite industrial group and an authoritarian government gave rise to authoritarian industrialization, known worldwide as the Park Chung-hee model of development, a legendary success. In present reality, this legacy is potentially more favorable toward further development of authoritarian rule. In this sense, the democracy movement of June 1987 and the subsequent democratization process is surely a wonder. It is all the more so when we consider that in many Latin American countries, the military, big or small, intervened even after a democratization process was in progress in situations similar to that of Korea. In Korea, there was no such "military guardianship"[1] after the June 29 Declaration. The withdrawal of the military from politics was definite and clear. How, then, was democratization possible in Korea? This is a major subject of interest to all who are interested in politics.

In this regard, another way of raising the question is, "Who or what social force led the democratization?" I have said on many occasions that democracy in Korea is a "democracy by mass movement." The mass movement was a combination of student movement and *minjung* movement with the labor movement at its center. Despite the north-south division and the hegemony of Cold War anti-communism, the military authoritarian rule could not last forever, and democratization by a popular movement was possible. It is interesting even from a comparative perspective that the student movement played a central role in this democratization movement. Since the 1970s, in the Latin American and southern European cases of democratization, people's movements such as workers' movements and democracy movements led by Catholics played leading roles. However, it is difficult to find a case where students, as in Korea, led the movement. Here, since we are not examining the history of the democracy movement, there is no need to describe its progress in detail. But it is important to see its overall pattern.

---

1 Military guardianship: A phenomenon of the military exerting influence in the decision-making of a civilian government with the justification that the military protects society from social unrest, corruption, excessive democracy, and economic uncertainty. In this case, the military and its organizational interests continue to exert influence and are reflected in the decision-making of the government, even after the authoritarian military regime has transferred its power to civilian political elites. In other words, the military's role as a government ends, but institutionally, its organizational interests and influence continue. Brian Loveman, "Protected Democracies and Military Guardianship," *Journal of Inter-American Studies and World Affairs* 36 (1994).

The Leading Role of the Student Movement in Democratization

Park Chung-hee established his regime through a coup on May 16, 1961. Since then, a number of landmark events occurred that chronicle the history of the student movement in Korea. The key events are as follows: the movement against normalization of Korea-Japan relations (1964);[2] the movement against constitutional amendment to allow a three-term presidency (1968-69);[3] the anti-Yushin movement (1973-74);[4] and the Kwangju Uprising followed by the "spring of Seoul" in 1980. These watershed events took place during certain periods of power vacuum during the Park Chung-hee regime and after its collapse. Even under the Chun Doo-hwan regime in the 1980s, the student movement remained strong from 1983 up to the June 1987 Uprising. In particular, except for the movement against the normalization of relations with Japan in 1964, all the other movements were democratization movements spearheaded by students. Why were students at the forefront of the democracy movement? More than anything else, it was the direct result of the fact that no strong opposition political party existed. Whether it was the New Democratic Party[5] during the Park Chung-hee

2 Student movement against normalization of Korea-Japan relations: The movement began with a demonstration that broke out in March 1964 and spread nationwide. The slogan was "Oppose the humiliating talks between Korea and Japan." More than 10,000 students and citizens participated in street demonstrations on June 3rd. At 8 pm that day, the Park Chung-hee regime declared emergency martial law in the Seoul area, and deployed four army divisions to Seoul to put an end to demonstrations that had been going on for three months (the June 3 Incident).

3 Movement against constitutional amendment to allow a three-term presidency: In 1969, the Park Chung-hee regime pushed for a sixth constitutional amendment, mainly to allow Park to run for the presidency for a third consecutive term. After months of political and legal maneuvering, the ruling party passed the amendment bill on September 14, 1969. The movement against the amendment began on June 12, 1969, when 500 law students from Seoul National University held a "Rally to Protect the Constitution." The movement continued until December 1969.

4 Movement against the Yushin system: This movement began due to the news reports by domestic and foreign media on the abduction of Kim Dae-jung in August 1973. After school began in September, students' demonstrations became an anti-dictatorship and anti-government movement. The movement spread nationwide and even to high schools. Several leaders of the opposition party, intellectuals, and religious leaders denounced the government for human rights violations, and led popular petition campaigns for constitutional amendments that would restore the democratic constitutional government.

5 New Democratic Party: The largest opposition party during the Third and Fourth Republics. It was established on February 7, 1967, when the conservative opposition forces, such as the People's Party and the New Korea Party, came together to form a single party, in anticipation of the 6th presidential election and the 7th general election in the same year.

regime, or the Democratic Korean Party[6] and the New Korean Democratic Party[7] during the Chun Doo-hwan regime, the established opposition parties did not properly carry out the role of an opposition in the parliament. For example, the issue of diplomatic normalization with Japan was the most significant foreign affairs issue faced by the South Korean government at a time when it had entered a stable period as a separate government in the aftermath of the Korean War. However, it was not the opposition party within the parliament but the students who raised issues about what was wrong with the government policy on Korea-Japan relations. It was impossible for the "loyal opposition party" within the established system to directly challenge the authoritarian regime. Subsequently, the first demonstration against the Yushin system was led by students, and it was again the students who first challenged the Chun Doo-hwan regime. Needless to say, the "Seoul Spring," the subsequent Kwangju Uprising, and the June 1987 uprising, were led by students. Under the strict authoritarian rules of the Yushin system and the Chun Doo-hwan regime, no one expected the opposition parties to carry out what the students did. Under these circumstances, school campuses were in the true sense the ground floor of the opposition, and the student movement was much like the ground troops at the frontline of a battlefield. They suffered the most sacrifices, leading the democracy movement at the forefront.

Many scholars who study social movement believe that the "political opportunity structure" elaborated by Doug McAdam, Sidney Tarrow, and Charles Tilly is the most important factor that generates a social movement.[8] In this scenario, a political opportunity opens up for a movement group; as the cause of the group gains sympathy from other significant but

6 Democratic Korean Party: Established on January 1, 1981, with a promise to be a critical and policy-oriented party. However, it soon abandoned its stated goals to become a political party in name only. It adapted itself faithfully to the pseudo-structure of party politics, conferring legitimacy to the ruling power.

7 New Korean Democratic Party: Organized on January 18, 1985, by leading members of the ex-New Democratic Party and the Council for Promoting Democratization. The majority were members of the Council for Promoting Democratization, composed of the Sangdo-dong group and the Tonggyo-dong (Donggyo-dong) group who supported Kim Young-sam and Kim Dae-jung, respectively. The New Korean Democratic Party emerged as the largest opposition party by winning 67 seats in the General Election on February 12, 1985. It became weakened, however, as its mainstream members left the party on May 1, 1987, and ceased to exist.

8 Doug McAdam, Sidney Tarrow, and Charles Tilly, "Toward an Integrated Perspective on Social Movements and Revolution," in *Comparative Politics: Rationality, Culture, and Structure*, ed. Mark Irving Lichbach and Alan S. Zukerman (New York: Cambridge University Press, 1997), 145.

scattered activist groups, solidarity of the movement is formed; the movement cycle then accelerates as the movement creates a series of events that cause insecurity among the ruling elite. But in the case of the student movement in Korea, the students did not wait for opportunities to come their way; instead, they created them. They then pulled other groups to enter into the movement. The Yushin system, particularly in the beginning, did not provide any form of political opportunity. Yet, when students demonstrated, a year after the declaration of the Yushin Constitution, a petition campaign to amend the constitution was launched by opposition-party politicians, religious leaders, academics, writers, and artists; a so-called "*chaeya (jaeya)* movement," or an opposition movement at large, was born to oppose the Yushin system. This development in the movement prompted the Park Chung-hee regime to invoke, in January 1974, the first of its many "emergency decrees," in an attempt to stop any public discussion of constitutional amendment. But the rule of the country by emergency decrees made the Yushin system weaker than any other system before it, and it triggered the regime's collapse that came years later. The subsequent emergence of labor movement in Korea, including that of the trade union movement in newspaper companies, became possible because of the political opportunities thus opened. In the same manner, the student movement under the Chun Doo-hwan regime did not emerge as a result of an opening in the opportunity structure brought by "liberalization." Again, students first created a political opportunity, which then became a driving force for spreading movements in other sectors of society.

The Growth of the 'Minjung' Movement

In comparison to similar movements in the 1950s and '60s, the democracy movement of the 1970s and 1980s, under the Yushin system and the Chun Doo-hwan regime, was very different in quality. In the latter period, under military authoritarianism, the democracy movement was stronger. One could say that the stronger the authoritarian regime, the stronger the democracy movement became, and certainly modernization played a role in this. With the spread of public education, the understanding of democratic values and ideas deepened and spread; the population of the educated urban middle class grew rapidly; as a result, a certain epistemological imbalance grew, one in which the value orientation that guided the political and social perspectives of the middle class did not conform to the experience of authoritarianism in reality. But to say that modernization was the cause of the democracy movement would be to understand the democracy movement only partially. To better understand why the democracy movement was stronger under military authoritarianism, one must pay attention to a more important factor than modernization. Rapid economic growth under the authoritarian industrialization policy in Korea shifted the Korean social structure profoundly toward modernization. In this process the regime created a broad sector of the *minjung* class, consisting of workers, farmers, lower-middle class, and urban poor, all of whom were alienated from the effects of modernization or otherwise not benefiting from it proportionately. This is not to say that the conditions of the *minjung* sector had deteriorated, or that the class structure had changed for the worse under military authoritarianism. However what is clear is that the rate of improvement in the economic and material status of the *minjung* sector was small in comparison with the upper and middle classes. This meant a development of a class entrenchment structure in society that aroused a sense of relative deprivation.

Clearly, the demand for material compensation for labor, the desire to live better, and the growth of the sense of rightful entitlement were important factors that brought together the democracy movement with the *minjung* movement. Thus, the spread of the labor movement and *minjung* movement was not the result of a deteriorating economic condition but of economic growth. Accordingly, there is a major qualitative difference between the democracy movements of the periods before and after industrialization in Korea. After industrialization, a strong *minjung* movement was developed, and when the student-led democracy movement joined forces with it, an explosive synergy was created.

After the mid-1970s, the labor movement began to spread in factories of the major industrial sectors. In fact, when Emergency Decree No. 9 was announced in 1975,[9] its primary target was this spreading labor movement. In order to control the growing labor movement, the regime had to increase the forceful use of public power, which in turn led the regime to become generally more authoritarian. Earlier, I had explained the establishment of the Yushin system with the concept of the overdeveloped state in contrast to the theory of bureaucratic authoritarianism. I had explained that the president of the Republic of Korea was in a position to control a vast array of state powers, and the maintenance of his power through the extension of presidential terms was the most important motive for the emergence

---

9 Emergency Decree No. 9: It was declared on May 13, 1975, and continued to exist for five years until the collapse of the Yushin system. The Emergency Decree No. 9 encompassed all the previous decrees, the first of which was declared on January 8, 1974.

of the Yushin system. The point of my critique was that the scholars of bureaucratic authoritarianism did not take into consideration as a major variable the tremendous strength of state power in Korea. Furthermore, I pointed out that the stage of economic development and the balance of power on the side of the *minjung* sector, including the labor movement, were very different in Korea compared to the situation in Latin America. In short, the theory of bureaucratic authoritarianism is too economics-oriented. However, in terms of the Yushin system's policy in dealing with the labor movement, the regime in Korea had much in common with Latin American bureaucratic authoritarian regimes. Under the Yushin system, the primary target group of the authoritarian repression was the *minjung* sector. Under the Chun Doo-hwan regime, it became all the more apparent that the authoritarian rule was an anti-*minjung* system. With the accelerated growth and the deepening industrial structure, the labor movement became the greatest opposition force faced by the authoritarian regime. The Yushin system, which seemed indomitable at one point, began to collapse when 200 young female factory workers at YH Trading went on strike, and the process accelerated when the same workers staged a protest sit-in at the office of the opposition New Democratic Party. The "Seoul Spring" in 1980 posed a great threat to the ruling power because the student movement and the labor movement actively emerged above the surface. The declaration of martial law on May 17, 1980, was made amidst the rapid spread of labor-management disputes, such as the Sabuk Mining Town incident[10] and the strike at Dongguk Steel Co.[11] In fact, during the rest of his regime, until the regime faced the culmination of the 1987 democracy movement, Chun Doo-hwan had to face a strong labor movement. The theory of bureaucratic authoritarianism contends that the need for a new industrial policy leads to the repression of the labor movement that then brings the rise of a military authoritarian state. If one were to apply this theory in Korea, it might be more convincing to do so to the Chun Doo-hwan regime than to the Yushin system.

10 Sabuk incident: On April 21–24, 1980, more than 6,000 miners and their families of the Sabuk Branch of Dong Won (Tongwŏn) Mining Company, the largest private mining company in Korea, went on a strike in protest against company-patronized labor union and the small wage increase they received. Their strike developed into bloody confrontations with the police on a massive scale.

11 Workers' Strike at Dongguk (Tongguk) Steel: The steel industry in general provided low wages and poor working conditions, but the workers of Dongguk Steel were working in even worse than usual conditions. They went on a strike during the period of April 28–30, 1980, for a wage increase and improvement in working conditions.

The Pattern of the Korean Democracy Movement

The first democratic political transition led by a popular democracy movement was not the 1979 Pusan (Busan)-Masan uprising that threatened the Yushin system, nor the June 1987 democracy movement that ended the Chun Doo-hwan regime. It was the April 19 Student Uprising that brought down the Syngman Rhee regime. To understand the essential characteristics of a democratic transition led by a popular movement, it is helpful to examine the April 19 Student Uprising. One sees the following patterns in the movement:

1. The central force of the movement was the students, and the educated urban middle class, in particular the intelligentsia—comprised of university professors, journalists, and writers—who formed the supporting force behind the students. Thus, the first popular democracy movement in Korea was not led by the newly emerging bourgeoisie or workers as in the West.

2. The issue was not the freedom of the individual or rights-oriented liberal demands; nor was it a class issue dealing with, for example, labor. The issue was first and foremost the overthrow of the dictatorship. In other words, it was a struggle against an authoritarian government that denied the principles and values of democracy, and as such the issue was the practice of democracy.

3. The regime was brought down by large-scale non-violent student demonstrations. The state was strong, but its support base was very weak. The stability of the regime's support base depended on how well the regime implemented and respected the norms and values of democracy. What this means is that by 1960 the norms of procedural democracy had taken root as an important value in Korea.

4. In terms of the movement's progress, the issues were presented in three stages. First, democracy issues were raised by students. As the movement spread and accelerated, and as political opportunities widened, labor issues led by the teachers' union followed. Then, at the last stage, there appeared attempts to address the issues of north-south division and national unification.

5. Because the central figures of the movement were students and workers, they could not play the role of central actors once the political upheaval and chaos had died down and institutional politics returned. The movement and institutional politics were separate; moreover, the threshold for entry into institutional politics was too high for the movement forces. This

phenomenon contrasts with the experience in the West where movement forces formed and participated widely in institutional politics.

6. The reform issues raised by the movement were not translated into policy, unless taken up by the political elite. For example, the third constitutional amendment of June 1960 took place as a result of the April 19 Uprising. The amended constitution introduced a parliamentary system, replacing the presidential system, and changing the existing power structure; it newly established the constitutional court to strengthen the judiciary branch; it introduced local-government elections for institutional reform; and it abolished restrictive clauses on various freedom rights and guaranteed freedom of the press, publication, assembly, and association. These reform issues had been delineated by the students during the April Uprising, but the reform demands were institutionalized top-down by the established political elite. I call this phenomenon "conservative modernization" or "passive revolution." A reform takes place, but the forces that raised the issues are not brought in as a part of the established political process or to play the role of decision-makers. Instead, reform issues are adopted on a selective basis and decided at the top by conservative politicians within the establishment.

7. As long as the movement is focused on issues of political democracy, it receives widespread popular support from society. But when the issues move on to socio-economic issues, such as those dealing with labor, North-South Korean relations, and reunification, i.e., when the issues become radical, social support for the movement breaks away, and military agitation and intervention follow. The policy and the attitude of the United States is the same in this regard. The United States is accommodating to the movement's goal of achieving procedural democracy; however, when socio-economic reform issues raise the possibility of compromising the secure base of the Cold War anti-communist system, and when the North-South Korean issues further threaten the Cold War system, the United States takes a very keen interest in the movement and the possibility of U.S. intervention increases sharply.

The Movement Splitting into Two

The April Student Uprising in 1960 and the democracy movement in June 1987 both brought about democratic government transitions. The Second Republic, brought on by the student uprising in April 1960, collapsed soon after it was established. It was ended by the May 16 coup in

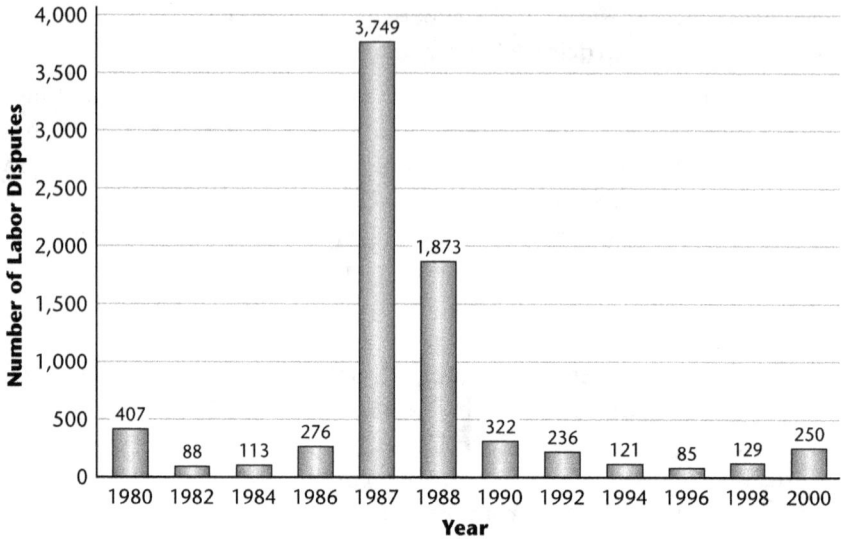

FIGURE 4.1 Labor Dispute Incidence after 1980
Source: Ministry of Labor.

1961. Thus, the consolidation of democracy[12] in Korea became possible only after the June 1987 uprising. But despite the long time lapse between the democracy movements of 1960 and 1987, there are many similarities between the two movements. To begin with, the democratic transition in 1987, as in 1960, was brought on by a popular democratization movement. Moreover, while the 1987 movement reflected the social changes since 1960 in that the number of participants and the scope of the social classes supporting the movement had grown incomparably larger, the overall pattern of the movement remained similar: 1) the central force of the movement was made up of students; 2) the educated urban middle class strongly supported democracy; 3) the primary issue was political democratization—as can be seen from the students' slogans, "Down With the Military Dictatorship! Democratic

12 Consolidation of democracy: According to Przeworski's definition, this means that democratic institutions become "the only game in town." In other words, it is a situation in which no one can act outside the democratic institutions, or in which the losers cannot but wish to compete again within the very system in which they have lost. The definition of the consolidation of democracy differs from scholar to scholar, but in general it refers to a changed situation in which a democratic political system maintains stability and continuity after its initial transition into democracy. Adam Przeworski, *Democracy and the Market: Political and Economic Reforms in Eastern Europe and Latin America* (Cambridge: Cambridge University Press, 1991).

Constitution Now!"—and this demand for procedural democracy received widespread civil support; 4) the movement issues progressively moved from political democracy to socio-economic reform; and 5) once again the movement was divorced from election-oriented institutional politics, and in this process the key forces of the movement could not participate in the process of institutionalizing democracy. On these points the patterns of the two movements are identical.

The students in 1960 cried "Down with the Dictatorship of Syngman Rhee!" In the course of the revolution, the students were joined by the labor movement, led by the teachers' union, as well as a radical faction of the student movement. The radical faction raised the issue of national division and demanded a north-south student meeting. When this happened, on the one hand, the issues deepened and the class scope of the movement widened, while on the other, the extensive support from the general public diminished. The status quo conservatives, both inside and outside of the Syngman Rhee regime, took such radicalization of the student movement as a real threat. But the radical faction of the student movement at the time was led by a very small group of students, such as those who made up Minjok t'ongil yŏnnmaeng (National Unification Alliance).[13] Also, considering the fact that the labor movement was led not by workers in the manufacturing sector but by teachers, the radicalization of the movement was not so much a real threat to the system as an ideological interpretation that exaggerated the facts. The 1987 democratization movement was quite different in this regard. The democracy movement that brought about the June 29th Declaration was led by students, and the "necktie troops"—the new urban middle class—joined the struggle in massive numbers. Afterwards, political opportunities opened up on a large scale, and the Great Labor Struggle followed immediately in July and August. Millions of workers staged labor strikes in large cities and industrial complexes nationwide for two months; in a tremendous explosion, the workers demanded rights that had been suppressed, and the ubiquity of the nationwide strikes had the effect of a general strike. This time, the widespread labor struggle posed a real threat to the conservative ruling structure whereas before it had not posed an ideological threat to anyone. It is interesting that a great democracy movement and a great labor movement did not take place simultaneously. If that had happened, the democracy movement in

13 Minjok t'ongil chŏn'guk haksaeng yŏnmang chunbi wiwŏnhoe (Federation of Korean Students for Preparation of National Reunification): A nationwide student organization for reunification movement that began when the National Reunification Alliance was launched at Seoul National University on November 18, 1960.

Korea would have taken a very different course. Why, then, did the two great movements occur separately? What was the power that separated the two? These questions contain answers that point to the direction of the democracy movement and the separation of the civil movement from the *minjung* movement after the democratic transition. Adam Przeworski, a leading political theorist, distinguishes hard-liners and soft-liners within a ruling block; he also distinguishes moderate and maximalist fundamentalists or moralists within a movement. He then argues that, in terms of strategic choices faced by both sides, the games led by the moderates are desirable for democratic transition.[14] At least from such a perspective, perhaps it was desirable, for the sake of a stable democratic transition, that the two movements in Korea took place separately. The situation, however, was not so simple.

2. Democratization Based on a "Pact" and the Formation of a Regionalized Party System

The Origin and Characteristics of Korean Political Parties

It would be wrong to say that the transition to democracy in Korea was accomplished solely by the democracy movement, because what Korea had was a combination of a democracy achieved by a popular movement and a democracy brought about by a "pact."[15] It was the democracy movement, and it alone, that brought down the old system. But the institutionalization of democracy was carried out according to a pact among political elites. The two processes were clearly separate. Thus one of the most notable characteristics of Korean democracy is the estrangement between the forces that dismantled the old system, on the one hand, and those that institutionalized democracy, on the other. To understand this situation, we need to take a look at the opposition party.

Earlier in this book we examined what I call the origin of the party system in Korea, how the ruling and opposition parties were formed during the

14 Adam Przeworski, *Democracy and the Market: Political and Economic Reforms in Eastern Europe and Latin America* (Cambridge: Cambridge University Press, 1991).

15 Pact: Pact is an important concept in the transitology of Guillermo O'Donnell and Philippe Schmitter. It refers to an explicit or implicit agreement by which the rules of exercising power are regulated in a way to guarantee the vital interests of parties participating in the new democratic system. The contents of such a pact differ from country to country and may include: constitutional institutionalization of the power structure; definition of the standard patterns for activities of the state apparatus, political parties and interest groups; and definition of overall economic relations. Guillermo A. O'Donnell and Philippe C. Schmitter, *Transitions from Authoritarian Rule: Tentative Conclusions about Uncertain Democracies* (Baltimore: Johns Hopkins University Press, 1986).

1950s. I have shown that the system was a product of Cold War anti-communism; that thus the competition between political parties took place within an extremely narrow ideological spectrum; and that the political representation system, including both the ruling and opposition party, did not represent a wide spectrum of social interests and demands but only the conservative layer with the most vested interests in society. One interesting phenomenon brought on by this party system was that often the authoritarian ruling party was more reform-minded than the opposition party. The case in point is the Syngman Rhee regime after national liberation. Neither the ruling nor the opposition parties had a wide support base. They had the common characteristic of being elite parties, parties of notables in society; both parties were far removed from the character of a mass party. Despite this commonality, the ruling party, as the government in power, needed political stability and a certain amount of public support, and thus it had an incentive to comply with the people's demands to a certain degree. This was the motive for the "reform from above"[16] by the ruling elite. On the other hand, due to their ideological limitations and the traditional characteristics of their organizations, the opposition parties had no will, no ability, and no incentive to be receptive to socio-economic demands of the time and to mobilize new support bases. The founders of the divided nation had locked up the framework of political competition in a narrow ideological space and reduced to a minimum the scope of political language and discourse for expressing conflicts and cleavages. When the extreme ideological conflict between the left and right quieted down, words such as *inmin* (people), *kyegŭp* (gyegeup, class), or *nodongja* (worker) had disappeared, because they were perceived as a part of "a communist language." As a result, the very act of expressing and representing social conflicts by a political party became difficult. Ultimately, the opposition party fulfilled its role and responsibility exclusively by criticizing the ruling party's monopoly of power, by selectively emphasizing certain democratic values and principles, and claiming that it is the democratic force in Korea.

To illustrate the reversed roles of the ruling and opposition parties, there is no better example than the implementation of land reform, which took

16 Reform from above: It refers to the phenomenon in which political elites carry out reforms in response to certain social demands of the time, but with the exclusion of the masses while political society and civil society are separated. Reform from above is the same concept as "passive revolution," "revolution from above," and "conservative revolution" used by Gramsci and Moore. Antonio Gramsci, *Selections from the Prison Notebooks* (New York: International Publishers, 1971); Barrington Moore, Jr., *Social Origins of Dictatorship and Democracy: Lord and Peasant in the Making of the Modern World* (Boston: Beacon Press, 1966).

place in April 1950 during the Syngman Rhee regime. The KDP and the Democratic Nationalist Party, the opposition parties, primarily represented the interests of the landed class, and they had strongly resisted land reform when it was first attempted under the U.S. military occupation, and they did so again in 1950. Their attempt to block reform succeeded under the U.S. military occupation but failed under the Syngman Rhee regime. It is commonly assumed that under an authoritarian regime the ruling party is conservative and the opposition party, which endlessly champions democracy, is progressive. In reality, it was the opposite in Korea. In this regard, what happened in the 1950s was repeated later under the Park Chung-hee regime. The ruling Democratic Republican Party (DRP) was a centralized bureaucratic organization. It was modern in its organizational structure, and it was pursuing modernization and reform as a matter of party policy. In the meantime, the organization of the opposition party, the New Democratic Party (NDP), was still based on a few factional groups each headed by its own group leader; it was still a party of notables. In other words, the most conservative political elite in institutionalized politics in Korea presented themselves as the spokespersons for democracy. Whenever a popular movement has produced a decisive moment for democratization in Korea, a paradoxical alliance has been formed between the strong reform forces outside of institutional politics and the most conservative group inside the established party system.

Changes in the Social Foundations of Political Parties

The political parties of 1950s and 1960s were not capable of generating broad social support. What brought a major change to this situation was the issue of regionalism that came from the Yushin system of the 1970s and erupted in the 1980 Kwangju Uprising. I have said in the past, the problem of regionalism was not an issue of a rivalry between two regions, i.e. between Chŏlla (Jeolla) and Kyŏngsang (Gyeongsang) provinces, but it must be defined essentially as a Honam question. My point was that to understand the problem of regionalism as a confrontation of feelings between the two regions is to succumb to false consciousness, i.e., an ideology. The Honam issue, the essence of the problem of regionalism in Korea, has three component elements. First, under the Yushin system, Honam figures were excluded from the make-up of the state and civil elite. Second, a strong emotional bond existed between the masses in Honam and Kim Dae-jung, the leader representing the hope of eliminating this regional alienation. Third, a collective experience of repression was formed in the Kwangju Uprising. The highly regionalized election results in Korea today first came about as a result of social mobilization by the authoritarian forces in the first election after the

1987 democratic transition. The ruling forces were interested in preventing the formation of a united front between the opposition parties and the democracy movement forces and in keeping them divided.

Regionalism emerged as the dominant element in party politics after the democratic liberalization and as a result of the political representation system molded largely by Cold War anti-communism. In other words, political competition based on the expression and mobilization of professional, class, or any other conflicts, interests, or passions, was difficult. Under the circumstances, regional support was the political asset that could most easily be mobilized by political elites and parties to win elections. Schattschneider emphasizes that the dividing lines of political conflicts can be formed selectively around many alternatives, and that an existing party system is the result of such a selection process where a particular axis of conflict has been selected over others that have been repressed.[17] Therefore, a particular party system in a sense brings together that which has been selected and repressed. From this perspective, the regionalism of the Korean party system is the result of the following set of selections that were made when mass mobilization became necessary in the wake of democratization and subsequent liberalization: 1) unlike in many similar countries, the masses were not mobilized along the lines of class, vocational, and functional interests and cleavages, which maximize the realm of political conflicts nationwide; 2) instead, within the old framework of the existing party system, the regions were vertically divided, and the masses were mobilized along regional axes. This is how the party system in Korea came to acquire its unique character of regionalism. This party system has institutionalized what Schattschneider calls the "mobilization of bias,"[18] which is greatly more advantageous to the interests of the elite than of the masses.

It must be emphasized, political parties after 1987 nevertheless were transformed. Unlike in the earlier periods, they were mass-based parties. In other words, during the democratization process, for the first time, the who's-who-oriented elitist parties came in widespread, direct contact with the general public. But these large-scale contacts were made based

17 E. E. Schattschneider, *The Semisovereign People: A Realist's View of Democracy in America* (Hinsdale, Ill.: The Dryden Press, [1960] 1975).

18 Mobilization of bias: According to Schattschneider, all forms of political organization have a preference for certain kinds of conflict, while they tend to repress other kinds. He called it the "mobilization of bias." For example, in U.S. history, racial conflicts have been used to offset class conflicts, or sectional conflicts have been used to control the influence of radical peasants' movements. E. E. Schattschneider, *The Semisovereign People: A Realist's View of Democracy in America* (Hinsdale, IL: The Dryden Press, [1960] 1975).

on parochialism,[19] personal connections, and hierarchical and regionally-divisive relations; these contacts did not develop into the kind of general political cleavages that one would find in the West. A political structure based on regionalism and personal connections is a structure fundamentally advantageous to the ruling group and the elite. Regardless of their regional affiliation, they are still part of the "concentric elite structure." Regardless of whoever wins an election, they do not contribute to decentralization of power, they do not share power, and they certainly do not represent or augment the interests of particular groups of masses nationwide or expand the scope of democratic participation. They do, however, expand their elite network and augment their status and vested interests. Therefore, when elections became completely open after democratization and a new party system emerged, what Korea found is a continuation of the "1958 system" that began with the founding election of 1958, the fourth presidential election in which the monopolistic party system was revealed. In other words, the regionalized party system in Korea is not distinct from the system based on Cold War anti-communism but is a political mechanism that guarantees its continuation.

Two Aspects of Regionalized Party System in Korea

There are two aspects to the regionalized party system that emerged after democratization. First, in terms of party system, none of the parties in electoral competition represented anything other than a conservative ideology. The parties had different regional affiliations, but their ideological orientations were largely conservative. The other aspect is the structural characteristics of the party organizations. A change can be seen in this regard. Due to democratization, political parties could not but make popular appeals. Thus a change in the recruiting structure of the party elite, and a subsequent change in ideological orientation, took place. For example, in the 1988 election for the 13th National Assembly, newly elected members occupied 50.4 percent of the total assembly seats. The fact that the conservative party system continued despite this fact indicates that perhaps it was like pouring new wine into old wineskins, or putting new changes in the framework of the old party system.

19 Parochialism: According to the theory of political culture proposed by Gabriel Almond and Sidney Verba, parochialism is a type of political culture that appears in pre-modern and traditional societies. It is an attitude of narrow local self-sufficiency that neither clearly recognizes the existence of a political system as such nor has any particular expectation or interest in political objectives. Gabriel Almond and Sidney Verba, *The Civic Culture* (Princeton: Princeton University Press, 1963).

Here, perhaps we can use the concept of a "hybrid party structure," which highlights the union or mixture of different elements in the makeup of a party. There are three elements in this mixture. The first is ideological conservatism. This is an element of the party structure that all political parties in Korea have shared since the 1950s. The second is regionalism. It became the central basis of popular support for parties. This is a popular characteristic that political parties acquired after 1987 as democratization restored the element of competition in elections. The third is the movement element, which corresponds to a certain degree to a social element. In the cases of Kim Dae-jung's Party for Peace and Democracy (PPD) and Kim Young-sam's Reunification Democratic Party (RDP), they were connected to the democracy movement at large to a certain degree, and their parties had relatively strong elements of the democracy movement during the 1980s. On the other hand, in the case of the conservative party of the old regime, the Democratic Justice Party (DJP) became the Democratic Liberal Party (DLP), which became the New Korea Party (NKP), which then became the Grand National Party (GNP). (DJP→DLP→NKP→GNP.) In the process, it tried to change the character of the party through a transfusion of new, mostly professional experts, such as journalists and legal professionals. Thus in this case, the term "social element" would be more appropriate.

In general, people regard the PPD→Democratic Party (DP)→National Congress for New Politics (NCNP)→New Millennium Democratic Party (NMDP) line as reformist, and the DJP→DLP→NKP→GNP line as conservative. The RDP–Kim Young-sam line and Kim's democratic associates are thought of as occupying a position somewhere between the two. On an ideological spectrum, however, there is no standard by which we can divide these parties into conservative and progressive categories. Within the narrow ideological representation system, all parties are conspicuously conservative and any ideological differences among them are insignificant. Any differences would come from disparity in past experiences and the support base of the party elite in the most general terms, and which members of the democracy movement are participating in which party activities and to what extent; thus, in terms of ideology, the differences are hypothetical and speculative. In the meantime, the three elements of the hybrid party structure put each political party in a constant state of identity crisis and instability. The three elements are linked together very intimately but often in a conflicting manner. For example, if we were to look at the Honam issue, the conservative and elitist elements in Kim Dae-jung's political party often clashed with the reformist characteristics of the Honam issue. Also, Honam parochialism, or the insistence on Honam particularism, clashed with the nationwide universalism of the movement, and the democracy movement element clashed with the elitist conservatism of old politics within the party. At the level of the party system, political elites compete with conservatism as a common denominator and under the influence of conservative hegemony. Their competition meshes with moral corruption, and changes in political alignment by means of *trasformismo*[20] become a routine political practice. Such a political environment brought fierce political fights that one would likely have seen in the post-liberation period of extreme ideological confrontations. On the other hand, frequent changes in political alignment made any demarcation lines between political parties questionable, and this resulted in political chaos.

Transition to Democracy and Its Institutionalization

Democratic theorists emphasize the importance of a pact between the reformist faction of the ruling power and the moderate faction of the democracy movement for successful democratization. This is because, should the radical element of the democracy movement control the leadership and take the situation in a revolutionary direction, chances are the ruling power's military hard-liners would gain voice and intervene with all their authoritarian powers in the rapidly progressing democratization. Such a path of democratization has certain relevance to the political circumstances of Korea. Although not completely identical to the circumstances assumed by this transitology scenario, the events that took place between the April student revolution in 1960 and the May military coup d'état in 1961 can be a case in point. During this period, a radical wing of the student movement raised certain radical issues. For example, they insisted on having a North-South Korean student meeting at Panmunjŏm[21] for reunification. Their demand was beyond the political boundaries and social scope allowed under the Cold War system. When this happened, the environmental "pull factor" for a military coup in fact increased. Also, as mentioned earlier,

20 *Trasformismo*: The concept originated from the behaviors of the Italian political elites since the late nineteenth century. It refers to political maneuvering of the ruling elites to win members of the opposition party over to their side, in order to break through their vulnerable status in the parliament and to build a stable majority. It also refers to the resulting unofficial patron-client relationship. *Trasformismo* is a system of political bargaining that occurs in the absence of competition among well-organized and developed political parties that have built strong social bases of support through distinct ideologies and programs; it occurs when politics is centered around a few "bosses" and their human networks.

21 Panmunjŏm: The Joint Security Area within the Demilitarized Zone between North and South Korea.

if during the 1987 democratization movement the radical elements of the student and labor movements united, and if thus a situation akin to that of the May 3rd Inch'ŏn (Incheon) incident of 1986 became prolonged and large-scale, the pull factor for a military intervention would have increased greatly. Nevertheless, the differentiation of the ruling power into soft-liner and hard-liner factions, the presupposition of transitology, was not borne out in Korea. Moreover, what happened in Korea was not a compromise that automatically guaranteed the path of conservative democracy, nor was it a case where alternative paths for further reform were completely sealed off. In this regard, the transitology requires closer inspection.

In institutionalizing democratic transition, major political actors enter into a pact through political compromises, decide on the type of power structure and a framework of political competition through constitutional amendments, and carry out a "founding election" according to the new rules for political competition. The most important question here is, who participates in the pact and how many of the democracy movement voices are represented. This is particularly important in cases such as Korea where the popular movement was the dynamic force that made democratic transition possible. Also, the entire democracy movement cannot be called radical, while the elite of the opposition parties cannot be said to represent the whole of the moderate faction of institutionalized politics. But in the process of transition to democracy in Korea, only the Cold War conservative political elites were represented in the transitional negotiation process to the complete exclusion of any major movement voices. A radical break was made. Here we find the most important cause for the eventual conservative outcome of the democratic consolidation process in Korea. Democracy theorists, such as Przeworski, deny that the mode of transition becomes the causal variable that determines the mode of consolidation.[22] This is an opinion that contrasts with that of O'Donnell and Schmitter who emphasize "path-dependency," or that the transition path and type has an impact on the subsequent development of democracy after the transition.[23] Przeworski sees the breakup of authoritarianism and democracy after transition as two separate processes. He believes that democracy after regime change is consolidated and transformed by itself through the effects of the democratic rule of game. However, the Korean experience shows that the type of transition almost

22 Adam Przeworski, *Democracy and the Market: Political and Economic Reforms in Eastern Europe and Latin America* (Cambridge: Cambridge University Press, 1991).

23 Guillermo A. O'Donnell and Philippe C. Schmitter, *Transitions from Authoritarian Rule: Tentative Conclusions about Uncertain Democracies* (Baltimore: Johns Hopkins University Press, 1986).

always defines the path of the subsequent development of democracy. Let us now take a look at how the transition was actually institutionalized in Korea.

The Conservative Character of Democratization Based on the Pact

The period from June 29, 1987, until the constitutional amendments were adopted in the National Assembly in October of the same year can be called the period of pact-making between the ruling and the democratic forces in Korea. The bilateral negotiations took the form of a political meeting between representatives of the ruling and opposition parties, participating on behalf of major political forces of the time. But these roundtable meetings for negotiating democratic institutions were a political game among the elites of institutional politics, and did not involve movement forces. The political meeting, composed of eight representatives[24] from the ruling and opposition parties, was a roundtable meeting among the old regime elites that to the maximum extent restricted the scope of participation, including that of Kungmin undong ponbu (Gukmin undong bonbu, The National Campaign Headquarters for Democratic Constitutional Amendment),[25] the organization that represented the voices of the democracy movement. There were no representatives from society and the democracy movement; a small number of politicians negotiated in closed meetings, and the negotiations were concluded quickly, giving a distinctly hurried impression of the process. These are the identical patterns Koreans witnessed in July 1948 when the constitution was enacted by the constitutional assembly, and when the amended constitution was negotiated after the April student uprising in 1960. The roundtable negotiations of the eight representatives selected to revise the constitution shows the constitution-making and democratization process in Korea. The format of constitution-making is very important, because it reveals that while party elites enjoyed the monopoly of representation, the movement activists as the main forces of democratization were not represented at all, thereby repeating the pattern of alienating the movement

24 The political meeting of eight representatives: After the June 1987 uprising, eight representatives of the Democratic Justice Party and the Reunification Democratic Party constituted a Special Committee for Constitutional Amendments. They proceeded to engage in political negotiations for constitutional amendments, while thoroughly excluding all other political forces.

25 National Campaign Headquarters for Democratic Constitution: The largest united front against dictatorship since the birth of the Republic of Korea. Its participants included the Reunification Democratic Party, social movement groups, religious groups, and student movement organizations. Established on May 27, 1987, it played the role of a political center coalescing various democratization forces during the June 1987 uprising.

voices from participating significantly in the democratic institutionalization. This is to say that the political representation system in Korea today still maintains the same essential characteristics it acquired under Cold War anti-communism, namely its disconnect from society. The constitutional amendment in 1987 was nothing but a product of negotiations between political elites. These negotiations took place without extensive civic participation in setting the agenda and without widespread discussion about alternative democratic institutions.

The characteristics of the negotiating bodies and the scope of participation directly determine the scope of agenda items. In the political meetings between the ruling and opposition parties, the central agenda items were issues dealing with the immediate exercise of political power by the two competing political parties. Agenda items included the term and qualifications for presidency, negotiations for institutional procedures that would impact the presidential election, and the strengthening of the National Assembly's authority regardless of the party in power. Thus, while the discussion of central agenda items focused on how to secure their own long-term interests and how to hedge risks in the case of defeat in the presidential competition, important social issues such as the amendment of labor laws and national recognition of the Kwangju Uprising were either excluded from the discussion or were handled vaguely. As explained by theorists who follow the minimalist conception of democracy in regard to such a political agreement, perhaps one could find meaning from the perspective that "the constitutional amendment for direct presidential election was a turning point for the institutionalization of uncertainty." However, it was not an "institutionalization of uncertainty" that took place in an expanded venue of electoral competition, a venue that would embrace new social conflicts and in the process make possible a change in the axis of conflicts. Rather, it was a repetition of the familiar game. This is because the institutionalization of newly agreed competition in the pact did not bring what is considered central in a democracy, namely the expansion of participation—or numerical and qualitative expansion of competing agents, expansion of the linkage between political parties and social bases beyond the scope of a game between elites, or expansion of the ideological spectrum in competition among political parties. The result is that, despite the giant change called democratization, no fundamental changes took place. The "1958 system" was intact. In the end, just as under the authoritarian regime, every administration elected since the 1987 democratic transition could not but struggle constantly to exclude socio-economic issues such as labor issues from politics.

The institutionalization of narrowly conservative competition is, as was mentioned earlier, a factor that made all political parties uniformly conservative in their ideology and organizational structure, even after democratization. Many democratic theorists seem to have overestimated the effects of democratic institutions and the pressure of competition to win a majority vote. They seem to assume that, under the pressure of competition to win a majority vote, each competing political party would mobilize workers, farmers, and the middle class and thus expand their social bases—and as a result, expand and deepen the connection between political parties and society. But the current axis of conflict in the party system has the effect of suppressing other potential axes of conflict that could expand and change the scope of conflict, because here, the interests of the competitors already participating in the existing axis of conflict are intermingled.

Furthermore, the maintenance of the narrow political representation system is deeply connected to the forces of strongly vested interests that have the giant conservative press as their spokespersons. The press controls political discourses and issues, and it exercises an overwhelmingly dominant influence in public forums. In this way, the press is not composed of commentators from outside of politics, but rather the internal instigators of ultra-conservative politics defending Cold War anti-communism. Ultimately, what happened in Korea after democratization was not an institutionalization of uncertainty where everything was open. Instead, new rules of competition were instituted, but the political horizon, or parameters, remained identical to what had been there in the past. For example, there is no question that the 13th presidential election of December 1987 was the "founding election" that created the framework of democratic competition. What emerged from this founding election were voting behaviors and a party system that are characterized by regionalism. However, despite the clearly new voter alignment, there exists no difference between the 1987 founding election for democracy and the 1958 founding election that stabilized the election framework in South Korea under division. In both elections, the participating parties each campaigned in an extremely narrow ideological space; the parties were not connected to social bases.

Earlier, I mentioned that the internal structure of the parties responsible for creating this political system has three components, namely conservatism, regionalism, and either a connection to a democracy movement or a corresponding "social element." If these three elements converged, and if in the process the movement element for democratic reform overpowered the other two elements through the effects of over-determination, perhaps the emergence of the regionalized party system could have been deterred. But such a scenario would have required a movement element strong enough to overpower the other two elements. It would have meant a movement strong enough to address nationwide conflicts and reform issues that are of national and universal significance. However, Honam issues did not turn up on a wider reformist agenda; instead they were localized as regional problems, segmenting political conflicts. When this happened, Honam issues became symbols of retrogressive parochialism, especially when the political party merged with the conservatives. Consequently, the regionalized party system is maintained to this day in spite of democratization, and the three elements still loosely coexist. Under these circumstances, the conservative element, representing the vital interests of Cold War anti-communism and the elites, and the popular movement element, pursuing universal democratic reform, essentially cannot coexist in a single political party. Eventually, any link between the two cannot but be broken and separated. For example, in the case of the PPD→DP→NCNP→NMDP party transformation, the three elements coexisted until the middle of the Kim Dae-jung administration. Then, the movement element was excluded, and the support base for the Kim Dae-jung administration weakened, and the administration's reform character was minimized.

3. Why Democratization Culminated in Conservative Democracy

There are three reasons why democratization in Korea took a conservative path. The first is the strength of the state that embodies Cold War anti-communism and economic growth ideology. The second is the method of transition that I call "two-step democratization," and the third is the fact that the institutional opposition party and the grassroots movement, the two moving forces for democratization, were divided from each other and weak.

The Strength of the State

Institutionalization of hegemonic authority is a very important aspect of a state. The state is not only the central embodiment of the institution of public authority within a territory, but in international relations it is also the central component responsible for carrying and practicing governing norms. In society, the patterns of expressing and organizing social conflicts and cleavages through political parties, in other words the horizon of party politics in society, are not freely created in a social sphere without any restrictions. They are largely defined by the characteristics of the state with restrictions in the social realm. If the state is strong in society, it also means that the state, more than society, has the wider bases of infrastructure to realize ideological hegemony. In this regard, current theories on political parties and party systems are excessive in their socially oriented approaches. An important exception would be Shefter who emphasizes a state-oriented approach.[26] In Daalder's analysis of political parties, too, the relationship between a bureaucratic system and a party system is suggested as an important variable, but the state is not considered a major variable.[27] Shefter takes the role of the state, in particular the development and role of the state bureaucracy, as an independent variable and compares the party systems and their developments in the United States and Europe. In the case of Korea, however, the role of the state is stronger than in these early democracies. There exists little empirical and detailed analysis of how much the role of the state influences the operation and transformations of the political system in such a case. In particular, not many theories use the strength or weakness of the state as a variable to analyze the transition and consolidation of democracy, or substantive changes that take place after democratization. The role and the degree of state hegemony determine the nature of the reform agenda. They put restrictions on the degree of reform and determine the horizon of negotiations among political players. Also, state hegemony is the power that maintains the existing conservative order. In other words, it is the power of the status quo.

Two-Step Democratization

To say that the transition to democracy in Korea is characterized by a two-step process is to say that there were two stages to democratization in Korea, the 1980 Kwangju Uprising and the June 1987 uprising. This implies that although the June 1987 uprising clearly marks the starting point of democratization, the character and path of democratization would have been significantly different without the 1980 Kwangju Uprising seven years earlier. In other words, this assumption raises the following question. If the "Seoul Spring" in 1980 and the subsequent Kwangju Uprising led directly to democratization, would Korea have witnessed the same kind of regionalism it witnessed in the post-1987 democratization? If the regionalized party system had not emerged, then the mobilization of social cleavages and conflicts would have taken a different form, and the axes of conflict and the political system too would look very different. Perhaps then, the party system, born

26 Martin Shefter, *Political Parties and the State: The American Historical Experience* (Princeton: Princeton University Press, 1994).

27 Hans Daalder, "Parties, Elites, and Political Developments in Western Europe," in *Political Parties and Political Development*, ed. Joseph Lapalombara and Myron Weiner (Princeton: Princeton University Press, 1966).

out of, and nurtured by, Cold War anti-communism and staunchly conservative, may have more easily and extensively changed itself with democratization better reflecting social conflicts.

The 1980 "Seoul Spring" and the Kwangu Uprising were, if we look at only the results, failed democratization struggles that could not stop the establishment of the Chun Doo-hwan military dictatorship. It was the democratization struggles throughout the 1980s and the June 1987 uprising that ultimately brought about democratization through a succession and extension of the struggles that began in 1980. The Kwangju Uprising symbolized and galvanized support for universal values of democracy and for the democratization movement throughout civil society. The Kwangju Uprising was thus a historic event that established a nationwide axis for the democracy vs. anti-democracy confrontation. It was also a decisive event in which civil society was revived as a movement in opposition to the authoritarian state. The Kwangju Uprising was the true antithesis not only to the Yushin system but also to the Fifth Republic (the Chun Doo-hwan regime) and all other forms of authoritarianism.

If the 1980 Kwangju uprising was the first opportunity for democratization, the June 1987 uprising was the second opportunity. The meaning of the Kwangju Uprising was renewed in the June 1987 uprising. If the authoritarian regime had chosen to suppress the June 1987 uprising with military force, it would have faced civilian resistance and sacrifices tens of times higher than in Kwangju. This played the decisive role in bringing a bloodless democratization in the June 1987 uprising. But the Kwangju Uprising did not result directly in democratization. As a failed movement, the uprising culminated in the establishment of the Fifth Republic. The Chun Doo-hwan regime had to legitimize its power and its rule. To do so, it mobilized various forms of political education and propaganda. They minimized and distorted the significance of the Kwangju uprising, saying it was not a democracy movement but a radical leftist insurgency, stoking anti-Honam regional sentiment. It was these ideological campaigns during the Chun Doo-hwan regime, more than anything else, that were directly responsible for the spread of anti-Honam sentiment in the 1987 presidential election. The 1987 election was the pivotal moment when the axes of political competition and conflict could have been realigned in the context of the newly introduced democracy. Here, the Chun Doo-hwan regime was the decisive variable that transformed the framework of the democracy vs. anti-democracy confrontation into a retrogressive frame of the Honam vs. anti-Honam regional confrontation. We can discover from various sources from this period that the June 29 Declaration by the Chun Doo-hwan regime already presupposes the ruling elite's strategy for division between Honam and Yŏngnam, i.e., the classic *divide et impera*[28] for division between the two Kims.

The Weakness of the Movement

More than the two factors cited above, democratization in Korea took a conservative path after the regime change in 1987 because the weakness of the popular movement and the weakness of the opposition political party overlapped. The weakness of the movement was the paradoxical result of the democratic transition in Korea. Such a popular movement maximizes the political instability of the regime and exposes the weakness of a regime that lacks legitimacy. At the same time, to maximize opposition, the street is used as the primary site of struggle where it confronts head-on the regime's authoritarian powers. However, a democratic liberalization means opening of electoral space that had been closed off or restricted. Political parties, on the other hand, are election specialists. The elite career politicians with a certain celebrity status from the era of the old regimes were members of these expert election organizations.

As the center of political gravity moved suddenly from the street to electoral politics, the center of power also moved in an instant from the movement to the existing political parties. Once the great cause of democratization was initially achieved, the movement groups, who had brought this about rapidly began fragmenting as they faced the new question of what kind of democracy there should be. In the December 1987 presidential election, which would become the founding election following democratization, the movement groups were split on the issue of which opposition candidate to support. There is no other phenomenon that illustrates better than this the "reversal of relationship" between the movement and party politics. In this election, the movement became subjugated to the opposition party. The movement was split under the following three banners: "single candidacy," "critical support," and "independent candidate." The fragmentation of the movement was in fact the reflection of its weakness.

Let us leave aside discussion of the independent candidate group here. The independent candidate had little chance of winning the election. But more importantly, it could not represent the movement and become the focus for channeling power of the movement into a national electoral politics. The

---

28 *Divide et impera*: "Divide and rule" is a technique of domination by the ruling class, a classical strategy of domination frequently used by ancient Romans. The ruler utilizes conflicts among the ruled, such as national sentiment, religion, social status, and economic interest, in order to cause conflict among them. This policy hinders the formation of a united opposition, and thus facilitates domination.

division between the advocates of "single candidacy (for Kim Young-sam)" and "critical support (for Kim Dae-jung)," however, meant two things. One was that the movement groups did not have a political party of their own through which they could represent and organize themselves as a political force. Someone else had to be the vessel to carry their position. The other is that the movement groups did not have strong enough influence to overcome the Honam vs. anti-Honam confrontational framework of the political elites. On the contrary, they themselves fell into it. It meant that the movement groups could not operate as an independent center in the electoral competition but became a dependent variable of the old politics of the elites.

It must be emphasized, however, that the weakness of the movement was not solely the result of Korean democracy's structural restrictions. It was also related to the subjective capacity of the movement. More than anything else, in the democratization process, the movement failed to develop and share any alternative ideology and vision. The predominant ideologies of grassroots groups during the democracy movement were formulaic, romantic, dogmatic, non-empirical, and abstract, following ideologies such as revolutionary socialism and radical nationalism. In struggling with strong military dictatorships, the movement groups tried to find strong weapons of struggle in the most radical and doctrinaire theories. The ideological radicalism of the movement meant that there was a negative perception of the election itself, a tendency toward abstentionism,[29] and a passive attitude toward electoral politics. It strengthened factionalism within the movement, marginalized itself from society, and prevented movement participants from empirically seeing reality. More than anything else, it was an element that impeded the channeling of its political power, preventing it from developing alternative ideologies and visions different from those of the existing conservative political parties. In other words, the ideological radicalism of the movement was not a reflection of its strength, but its weakness. As a result, with the presidential election, the movement lost its independent position and was dissolved around the issue of which opposition candidate it should support.

The Weakness of the Opposition Party

The weakness of the movement had a less direct impact than the weakness of the opposition party on making democratization conservative. The opposition party could not but be an alternative government against

---

29 Abstentionism: Refers to the negative attitude of radical leftists toward electoral politics and the arguments and actions associated with the attitude. The proponents of abstentionism interpret electoral politics as a bourgeois democratic system or as a formal means of legitimizing the ruling class.

authoritarianism, and democratization soon brought the opposition party into power. When the opposition party came to power, they had a responsibility to implement, to the greatest extent possible, policies reflecting the demands that had exploded during the democratization movement. When the question is no longer whether there will be democracy, the next question is, what reform policies will the democratic government carry out, and with what degree of efficiency? The question was the same in the Second Republic (1960-61), when the April student uprising brought in the new democratic government. Democracy had been achieved through fierce struggle and great sacrifice, and expectations were high for the leadership and performance of the democratic government. However, when the new democratic government did not respond to those expectations, disappointment followed. In fact, the larger the gap between expectations and performance, the greater the disenchantment. Democracy theorists have conceptualized this phenomenon as *desencanto*.[30] This is a general phenomenon that accompanies democratization. In the cases of the democratic governments of Kim Young-sam and Kim Dae-jung, they both received overwhelming popular support at the beginning of their terms. But toward the ends of their terms, their authority was lost, and they revealed incompetence so devastating that the government could hardly function, and public support fell precipitously.

Disenchantments with the democratic governments and the decline of their authority gave rise to nostalgia for authoritarian governments, and there is a risk that such nostalgia could strengthen negative perceptions about democracy itself. The extreme fluctuation between explosive support for a political party and its precipitous fall is a reflection that there exists a great gap between the party's ability to win an election and its ability to govern the country and to reform it. The two governments of the post-democratization period are both examples that dramatically illustrate this contradiction. The fact that not one but both governments followed this path suggests that there are certain structural causes. I think of this as "the democratization cost." During the long period of authoritarianism, opposition parties could not develop any roots in society. Thus their development was suspended, and they atrophied time and again. They were maintained

---

30 *Desencanto*: One of the core concepts of the theory of democratic transition. Refers to a certain feeling of discontent, or an awakening from excessive expectations, that many people experience after democratization, when reality proves to be short of what was expected of democratization. This disenchantment phase is inevitable in the transitional process, and democracy can take firm root only when democratic institutions properly operate at a certain threshold level in the aftermath of such a phase. Guillermo A. O'Donnell and Philippe C. Schmitter, *Transitions from Authoritarian Rule: Tentative Conclusions about Uncertain Democracies* (Baltimore: Johns Hopkins University Press, 1986).

as cult organizations with a few leaders and their followers at the center. In short, at the level of organizational quality, the opposition parties were the most backward organizations in Korea.

Towards the end of the military authoritarian regime, as the democratization movement began to gather momentum, the opposition parties expanded their contacts with particular regions and strengthened their regional bases of popular support. In this process they were joined with the movement elements. After democratization, when the two opposition parties each took a turn in taking power through election, they had no experience of formally running a large-scale organization. They became the ruling power, and suddenly they were in charge of running the largest modern organization in the country. Earlier, in discussing the character and structure of the Korean political parties, which would become important political resources for the ruling power under democracy, I pointed out conservatism as one of the main components. After the opposition parties each took turns to become the government as well as the ruling party, the problems of this conservatism were fully exposed.

When the opposition parties came to power, they typically went through the following transformation process during their term in office. As the core source of power, the regionalism element of the party joins the movement element to a certain degree. The movement element makes the reform character of the government strong, with its commitment to represent and implement demands for reform from below. In this process, the movement element inside the government unites with the movement element in the ruling party, and they thus contribute to the expansion of support from civil society outside the boundaries of the government and the party. However, the ruling elites and the conservative element of the ruling party restrict the strengthening of the movement element in the government. This restriction is accompanied by two phenomena. The first is that, in terms of the structure of the ruling elite, the regional element is strengthened and the structure becomes more closed. The other phenomenon is that because they are incapable of running the state organizations by themselves, especially with their closed structure, the union between the ruling elite and the state technocracy inevitably expands, resulting in the government's high dependency on bureaucrats. Such a phenomenon is one that can be compared to the deteriorating relationship between the Syngman Rhee group and the KDP, the two pillars of the divided nation during the First Republic. The closed-circuit nature of the new democratic governments was the result of the ruling elite's monopoly of power and personnel in the new government, and a complete exclusion of the movement element.

In modern Korean political history, the ruling power always had a closed-door policy of crony politics, rather than making itself more representative. There was no exception after democratization. In democratic governments, the retreat of the movement element was immediately followed by the retreat and disappearance of the reform agenda. This in turn caused reform-minded supporters outside of the government to end their support, at which point the conservative element of the party became stronger. Thus the vicious cycle continued. The elite cartel structure, which under Chun Doo-hwan and Roh Tae-woo (No T'ae-u, No Tae-u) was represented by the Taegu (Daegu)/Kyŏngbuk (Gyeongbuk) (TK) faction, was simply replaced with the Pusan/Kyŏngnam (Gyeongnam) (PK) faction under Kim Young-sam, and the Honam faction under Kim Dae-jung. The names have changed, but the closed-circuit power structure has not changed and is continuing. The decision-making style in the Kim Young-sam and Kim Dae-jung governments can be characterized as a combination of the closed-circuit method and technocratic methods. In the case of the former, the highest authority in the country and a small number of his closest cronies would make decisions. In this regard, one could say democracy has been regressing under democratic governments.

The failures of democratic governments are due in part to the hegemony of the conservative ideology, strength of vested interests, control of the National Assembly by the opposition party, and narrow social base for political support, i.e., the result of a party system based on regional competition and intense political rivalry that did not allow either party to build a nationwide constituency beyond their regional boundaries and affiliations. However, the weakness of the democratic leadership and the government's weak capability to govern, are the reasons that come before all others. Accordingly, the way to overcome the failures of democratic government is not so much to strengthen technocratic managerialism, but to expand democratic participation and thereby expand government capability to democratically run the state. In other words, constant democratizing of its own organization and leadership is the only way that a ruling democratic government can achieve competent performance. As emphasized by Anthony Giddens, what is important is to continuously democratize democracy.[31]

31 Anthony Giddens, *Runaway World: How Globalization Is Reshaping Our Lives* (New York: Routledge, 2000).

Part III

Korean Society after Democratization

5 The State after Democratization

1. The Problem of the State after Democratization

Democracy and the State

How did democratization change the state? This is one of the most important topics in examining the effects of democratization in Korea. Before democratization, the state in Korea was often described as an overdeveloped state, a developmental state, or a strong state. These are all concepts that describe the strength of the state. Strength became an essential characteristic of the authoritarian state in the process of nation-building and industrialization. Essentially, the state played a normative role in building the divided nation of Cold War anti-communism, and the state was the propeller and engine of modernization.

Max Weber said that the state is an institutionalized authority that has a monopoly on the legitimate use of force, while Tocqueville saw the state as a national bureaucratic agency that embodies the centralization of power. In the meantime, Peter Nettl emphasized the cultural aspects, such as the sense of legitimacy and value that people have about the institutionalization of power, and saw "stateness" as its essential factor.[1] These major theories on the state are consistent with the history of the strong authoritarian state in Korea. In Weberian terms, rule of the state is supported by ideological mechanisms of legitimization, such as Cold War anti-communism or developmentalism. In this way, since the time of national liberation until recently, a strong state developed in Korea in parallel, or in a mutually complementary relationship, with authoritarian regimes. With the democratic

---

1 J. P. Nettl, "The State as a Conceptual Variable," *The State: Critical Concepts*, ed. John A. Hall , vol. I (London: Routledge, 1994).

liberalization of 1987, the state in Korea was faced with an environment that it had not faced before. In other words, a new question had emerged, namely the question of the relationship between democracy and the state, or the question of the state in a democracy.

Authoritarianism in Korean society gave rise to, and developed, a very homogenous ruling elite. First, well-organized power groups, such as civilian political groups and then the military elite, obtained state power. They created a body of bureaucratic elites who controlled state apparatuses from the top, and under their control, bureaucratic administrative groups grew. Furthermore, they created political parties from the top down, and organized and supported the political elite in party politics and in the National Assembly. They created the corporate elite through state-led industrialization, with the most powerful *chaebŏl* at the apex of the group. Earlier, I have referred to this elite structure as a concentric structure in which various powers are centralized around the state. The ruling elite, composed of the political elite who have secured state power, the bureaucratic elite, and the corporate elite, are marked by great homogeneity in terms of ideology or value orientation. Moreover, authoritarianism is a political system in which the state and its elite arbitrarily allocate special privileges and benefits to specific groups and suppresses the rights and interests of other groups or individuals. With democratization, the nature and structure of the state changed rapidly.

Democracy is defined, more than anything else, by an elected government with a majority of popular votes. Thus, elections after democratization in Korea brought to power governments that would change the character and ideology of the authoritarian state, in contrast to the elections held under authoritarian regimes. What immediately followed was the separation of the political elite and the bureaucratic elite, which had been fused together under the authoritarian regime. Democratization demanded establishment of new relations between the elected political elite and the non-elected administrative bureaucratic elite, both of which run the state. Accordingly, two levels of the state emerged, centered on each of the two elite groups.

Democratization and the Two Levels of the State

To understand the changes in the state system brought on by democratization, first we must examine the state at two different levels. The first is the state at its infrastructural level. The state is commonly referred to as "a system of permanently institutionalized roles." By that, we mean the state as a giant bureaucracy that embodies the centralization of power, and the personnel involved in managing the bureaucracy. As Weber said, it is a large-scale public organization that has non-personal and non-individual personnel recruitment, public purpose, roles, and a performance evaluation system, and as such it is an institutionalized bureaucratic-administrative system. In general, when we refer to the strong state in Korea, this is what we mean.

The other level is the state as the government, not the infrastructure referred to above. We can understand a government as a political force that operates state apparatuses and exercises power in accordance with a certain set of rules, regardless of how it came to power; the government could have obtained power through an extra-constitutional use of force or through a democratic election. In other words, in obtaining and exercising power, the people at this level of the state want to organize and mobilize social support, and they have a particular ideological or policy orientation to do so.

Under the authoritarian regimes in the past, these two levels were merged together and therefore were difficult to separate. With democratization, however, the two levels of the state became separated, and this necessitated the establishment of a new relationship between the elected ruling political elite and the bureaucratic elite. Here, a question arises: who has the advantage of power and who is the subordinated between the two groups? Under authoritarian regimes, the ruling political elite had a natural advantage of power over the bureaucratic elite. The military elite had been the very creator of the modern bureaucratic elite in Korea. It provided the latter with clear national goals and instilled in its members pride and collective consciousness. The military also subjugated even the *chaebŏl* under the state bureaucracy, thus establishing a complete state autonomy, which meant establishing a bureaucracy completely autonomous from overall social pressures, including that from *chaebŏl*. Under democracy, such a relationship between the two groups was no longer possible. Roh Tae-woo was elected through a democratic election but the old regime continued in terms of the make-up of the ruling elite, and the changes in the state system caused by democratization were not easily noticeable. Thus, in the following section, we will examine the two levels of the state, using empirical indices from the democratic governments of Kim Young-sam and Kim Dae-jung, the two democratically elected civilian governments.

Earlier in this book, I made reference to the results of the opposition parties' power. In examining the relationship between the political elite and the bureaucratic elite in the state, it is very important to compare the early and late periods of these two governments. The two governments both came out of the democracy movement; and they came to power with the people's ardent wish for reform, which had become a national agenda in the process of the presidential election. Thus, at the beginnings of their terms, the two governments were both very popular. Entering the latter part of their terms, however, public support of the president's performance kept falling, and at the end it reached so low that the rule of government became difficult. Along the way, the relationship between the political elite and the bureaucratic elite also changed greatly. At the beginning of their terms, the political elite had an overwhelmingly dominant position over the bureaucrats. With the introduction of democratization, the protective membrane of special privileges provided to the bureaucratic elite was taken away, and their status was drastically lowered, and quickly. This was because the bureaucratic elite were considered of one flesh with authoritarianism, and they had very little moral authority over the new political elite. Now they were asked to serve the cause of democratic reform. However, as the initial period of the government passed, the political elite began to show signs of incompetence and a lack of judgment. Their own moral authority and the public faith in their capacity to rule diminished proportionately. On the other hand, the operation of government itself became difficult without the help of the bureaucratic elite, and the political elite's dependence on the bureaucrats increased rapidly.

At the beginning of their administrations, the political elite of these democratic governments exercised enormous power, because the electorate gave them the mandate[2] to reform. The more tasks there were for reform, and the stronger the longing for reform, the greater their reform mandate was from the electorate. And that was the source of their power. But the political elite of the democratic governments soon faced a great gap between the power they possessed and their ability to put into practice the reform agenda through concrete policies. When this happened, the bureaucrats came in to fill the gap. The power of the bureaucratic elite became even greater than during the authoritarian regimes. Toward the end of their terms, the democratic governments paradoxically became more co-opted by bureaucracy than the authoritarian regimes ever were. As a result, the decision-making process for government policies became no different from that under authoritarian regimes. Policy decisions were made within a very narrow scope of issues and in a closed-circuit and technocratic manner, without being widely linked to social demands and opinions.

2 Mandate: This refers to the view of candidates or political parties who have won an election and who claim that the voters have endowed them with an authority to realize their election pledges. The ruling party or the government generally uses it as a basis to claim legitimacy for their policies.

Normally, in our everyday language we do not make the distinction between the executive branch of government and the administrative bureaucracy. As a result, many people still believe in an authoritarian framework that career bureaucrats are in charge of the bureaucracy or the state executive branch. The two, however, are very different from each other. The executive branch refers to one of the three government branches that include the legislature and the judiciary. On the other hand, the state bureaucracy is a large-scale public organization that has a particular form of personnel recruitment and purpose and rules of duty that we refer to as "a system of career bureaucrats." If under a democracy, government bureaucrats still enjoyed vast state autonomy and exercised a great influence over the decision-making process and implementation of government policies, one could not say there was any real difference between democracy and authoritarianism. According to the definition of democracy delineated by Schmitter and Karl, democracy is "a system of governance in which rulers are held accountable for their actions in the public realm by citizens, acting indirectly through the competition and cooperation of their elected representatives."[3] In other words, democracy must have as its core elements representativeness and "accountability"[4] through elections. That is to say, assuming that accountability is the relationship that exists between policy performance results and sanctions against it, it raises the question of who is accountable for the consequences of the bureaucratic elite's enormous discretionary power in a democracy.

The Problem of Hegemony

In the case of Korea, the most salient characteristic displayed by the state after democratization is the incompetence of state as government. In the early 1990s, I had participated in an international workshop on the comparative study of democratization, with Eastern European and Latin American experiences as cases for comparison. The result of this joint research has been published in the book *Sustainable Democracy*.[5] The conclusion of that

3 Philippe C. Schmitter and Terry L. Karl, "What Democracy Is . . . and Is Not," in *The Global Resurgence of Democracy*, ed. Larry Diamond and Marc F. Plattner (Baltimore and London: Johns Hopkins University Press, 1993).

4 Accountability: Refers to the notion that when there is a demand from the sovereign people they represent, the representatives of the people should be held accountable for the causes and grounds of their actions and decisions in exercising the power delegated to them and in carrying out their duties.

5 Adam Przeworski et al., *Sustainable Democracy* (Cambridge: Cambridge University Press, 1995).

research was that in order to build a sustainable democracy that creates social growth, the centrality, or primary role, of the state must be emphasized. The common characteristic among the countries studied was that an incompetent government emerged in the transition process of political regimes. Accordingly, the question of how to turn an incompetent government into an energetic and competent one becomes a core issue in social development after democratization. About the time this study was concluded, the Roh Tae-woo government was ending and the Kim Young-sam government was still just beginning. Korea was still preoccupied with the problem of an excessively strong authoritarian government, not a government that would suddenly become impotent, incompetent, and weak. However, ten years later, Korea is faced with the problem of an incompetent state as government in a democracy.

There are many causes for the emergence of incompetent government. In comparing the Kim Young-sam and Kim Dae-jung governments in this regard, perhaps we can make a distinction between the two governments, based on which one did and did not gain hegemony. By hegemony, I mean the situation in which a government takes the dominant ideology of Korean society, Cold War anti-communism, as its core value orientation and receives support from the conservative vested interests, which have built themselves around this ideology. It also means the situation where a government embraces the value orientation of the conservative vested interests regardless of its regional, class, and ideological origin. In this sense, the Kim Young-sam government had hegemony, while the Kim Dae-jung and Roh Moo-hyun (No Mu-hyŏn, No Mu-hyeon) government did not. Even though it was considered a democratic government, the Kim Young-sam government secured the support of the old regime's conservative vested interests and inherited the regional and class support bases of the authoritarian regimes through the three-party merger.[6] On the other hand, no support came for the Kim Dae-jung government from the old regime's conservatives. Moreover, by announcing that it would pursue a policy of reconciliation and peaceful coexistence with North

---

6 The three-party merger: When the ruling party became the minority party after the 13th General Election in April 1988, the ruling Democratic Justice Party attempted to reorganize the political arena from above, against the people's wishes, for the purpose of creating a conservative alliance to fundamentally change power relations in the National Assembly. As a result, a gigantic conservative ruling party, the Democratic Liberal Party, was born by incorporating the three existing parties; the Democratic Justice Party led by president Roh Tae-woo (No T'ae-u, No Tae-u), the Reunification Democratic Party led by Kim Young-sam, and the New Democratic Republican Party led by Kim Jong-pil (Kim Chong-p'il, Kim Jong-pil).

Korea, the Kim Dae-jung administration severed itself from the old regime's Cold War anti-communist policy on North Korea. Despite these differences, and for different reasons, the two governments had the same problem of not being able to overcome the problem of the incompetent state. The power base of the Kim Young-sam government was the conservative vested interests. Accordingly, the very base and the character of its support put limitations on the power and the will required to carry out reform policies.

On the other hand, in the case of the Kim Dae-jung government, the lack of hegemony was a limiting factor that restricted the implementation of reform. The policy of reconciliation, cooperation, and peaceful coexistence with North Korea roused criticism, and Honam as a regional base was too weak to provide the necessary social support to the Kim Dae-jung government. Also, the ruling party was the minority in the National Assembly, which further restricted the government's ability to reform. Toward the end of its term, the Kim Dae-jung government faced a strong resistance akin to an all-out counteroffensive from the conservatives. There were major policy attempts from the Kim Dae-jung government that, if successfully implemented, could have changed the balance of social powers in Korea, such as the policies to reform *chaebŏl* and the press, and the Sunshine Policy. The resistance of the conservatives, with a few big mainstream newspapers at its center, was an important factor that reversed or weakened these reform attempts as well as the base of the government at the same time.

To say that the lack of hegemony, which focuses on the balance of power outside of political society, was the decisive factor in undermining the reform efforts and making the government incompetent would be to emphasize only one side of the problem. The very establishment of the Kim Dae-jung government meant that people supported those who struggled the most fiercely against the military authoritarian regimes. Therefore, the government had the mandate to carry out a full-scale democratic reform. In particular, because of the financial crisis that resulted in an IMF bailout loan, the Kim Dae-jung administration was given an absolute mandate to carry out reform. Concurrently, the status of the all-powerful *chaebŏl* reached an all-time low. Under the circumstances, support for the new government, and accordingly the power entrusted to the state, was enormous. We often hear that reform policies were sidetracked and the administration became weak because the ruling elite of the Kim Dae-jung government was besieged by vested interests. But it is merely an excuse for a lack of progress in reform and the subsequent weakening of the government. It was not the increased power of *chaebŏl* and the press that daunted reform efforts and completely weakened the political base of the Kim Dae-jung government.

The cause and effect are in fact reversed. To blame the hegemony of vested interests for the failure of reform is to overlook the fact that the early period of the Kim Dae-jung government was a historic opportunity to greatly and democratically change Korean society. It was as the result of the Kim Dae-jung government's failure at reform that the *chaebŏl* restrengthened their monopolistic positions in the market, expanded their social hegemony, and increased their political influence. Furthermore, toward the end of the Kim Dae-jung administration, a very small number of major newspaper companies not only strengthened their monopoly of the public opinion market but also took on political power. Such developments cannot but structurally damage democracy.

Perhaps one can find the cause of the reform failure internally, in the composition of the ruling elite. Or maybe it can be found in the more micromanagement details of the administration. For example, one could point out that there was not enough delegation of authority to lower-level officials in the government organization. One could also point out that there was lack of judgment in not organizing enough meetings where diverse and useful ideas could be collected, as such meetings are essential in operating large organizations such as government administrations. There could be many other such examples. But what was most seriously lacking were the principles of procedural universality and openness in operating public organizations such as government administrations. For example, open vs. closed organizations, visible vs. invisible powers are important distinctions for the discussion of democratic procedures. In regard to this point, there are no other organizations in Korea that have a more important function than those of the *pisŏn (biseon)* organizations;[7] the small, informal, and behind-the-scene networks of close personal confidants maintained by the president and other powerful political figures to work out special political tasks. This is a phenomenon that is not only endemic in Korea, where the division between the public and the private is not clear in political culture, but also frequently found in societies where the level of institutionalization of democracy is low. The *pisŏn* organizations represent the rule of a private power within a giant public organization, and at the highest level of the highly centralized state power structure.

The prevalence of *pisŏn* organizations meant that the ruling elite had a weak sense of responsibility toward its electoral supporters and that there was a lack of strong legal and institutional mechanisms to impose such a responsibility. This is the style of governing that has been shared by all the Korean presidents from Syngman Rhee to Kim Dae-jung, and the problem became more entrenched and noticeable under the democratic governments

---

7 *Pisŏn (Biseon)*: From *pisŏn chojik*, or "secret-line organization(s)."

of Kim Young-sam and Kim Dae-jung. The problem of *pisŏn* organizations lies in the fact that private power has decisive influence on personnel recruitment for state organizations and on major policy decisions. As can be seen in the extreme regional bias in personnel recruitment and the closed-circuit policy-making processes, this creates serious side effects that clash with the principles of democracy. Also, this private power becomes the apex of the network of special privileges that accompany the vast state power and it becomes the paramount hub of rent-seeking activities. It thus functions as a source and hotbed of corruption.

The Problem of an Opposition Party without a Social Base

The Korean experience shows that the question, "Why does an incompetent government emerge?" is directly connected to the question, "How does an opposition party come to power?" We can raise two further questions in regard. The first is, what plans for an alternative government did the opposition party develop in preparation to take over the state power during the period of the democratization struggles? The second is, suppose there were a plan for an alternative government; how did the party negotiate its terms and conditions with the existing hegemony, and what practical alternatives came out of such negotiation as the opposition came to power?

In regard to the first question, the opposition parties did not provide systematic alternatives to reform the government, *chaebŏl*, labor-management problems, or the market. Thus it is difficult to say that they had alternative visions and programs for replacing the existing state-led development model, and a new democratic development model that could translate such visions and programs into concrete policies and implement them on practical levels. Certainly, the election platforms and the policy directions announced at the beginning of the administration promised reform and democracy. But it is difficult to say that the promises were anything more than a vague orientation, or a rhetorical swing.

In regard to the second question, in order to avoid ideological attacks, the opposition parties attempted to put forth conservative alternatives during the election campaign process. As a result, any difference between the conservative ruling party and the opposition party became very small. To borrow Anthony Downs's spatial model,[8] this election strategy of the

8 Anthony Downs's spatial model: A theory to explain the voting behavior of the electorate and the strategic choices of political parties. The core explanatory variable is the position of the various political parties or candidates in competition on the ideological spectrum, or their distance on the coordinates of ideological orientation. Anthony Downs, *An Economic Theory of Democracy* (New York: Harper and Row, 1957).

opposition presupposes the median voter[9] to be conservatively disposed, and to support Cold War anti-communism and development ideology. This phenomenon was not limited to Kim Dae-jung. In every major election, the so-called reform candidates, without exception, tried to appeal to conservative voters. Accordingly, elections were won after the platforms became conservative enough for the conservative vested interests to embrace them.

In the previous chapter, as regards the weakness of the opposition party, I discussed the results of a weak opposition party suddenly coming to power after democratization. This problem also raises two questions. The first is, whom does a political party, in particular an opposition party, represent? The second is, are there enough intellectual resources to formulate alternative ideology and policy visions, and to translate them into concrete policy plans? In the past, opposition parties and their candidates were excessively conscious of the effects of Cold War anti-communism. Thus, rather than suggesting a clear ideological identity and policy positions in election campaigns, they consciously opted for "strategic ambiguity." Accordingly, elections in Korea came to have no meaning as a procedure where the voters delegate ideological and policy aspirations and hold the supporting parties accountable for them. As a result, the relationship between voter support and the responsibility of elected officials is very loose and ambiguous rather than concrete and direct. As was mentioned in the previous chapter, the three heterogeneous elements of conservatism, regionalism, and a democracy movement coexisted in opposition parties in Korea. After a party came to power, these elements within the party separated, and the support base of the party disintegrated in the process. The coexistence of the disparate elements, as well as their disintegration afterwards, was possible because of the loose relationship between voters and the ruling party. This looseness of representation, therefore, was translated into the ruling party's loss of identity.

Using the Latin American experience as a case example, Guillermo O'Donnell conceptualized a situation where there is no accountable relationship between elected leaders and voters as a "delegative democracy."[10] It is a

9 Median voter: The middle voter on the ideological and policy spectrum of a simple dimension that two competing political parties struggle to win over in order to gain majority. Anthony Downs, *An Economic Theory of Democracy* (New York: Harper and Row, 1957).

10 Delegative democracy: A type of government in which it is presumed that the president's role is to define and protect the national interest, and that the president elected by popular vote is bestowed with the authority to rule in a way that he or she views to be proper during his or her term. Delegative democracy refers to the typical characteristics of democracy in Latin America after democratization, and was conceptualized by O'Donnell as the opposite concept from representative democracy. The main difference

concept that attempts to explain a situation where the government, with an elected president as its highest leader, does not represent the forces that supported it in the election and is not restricted by its own social base. Rather, the government has power delegated to itself for a certain period of time and exercises power arbitrarily, unhinging itself from society. O'Donnell's study conceptualizes an extreme situation in Latin America where, because of a unilateral rather than a bilateral relationship between elected representatives and voters, accountability cannot be established. The situation is not completely irrelevant to Korea. It is the identity of a political party that is crucial in having power delegated to its elected officials. The party's very function of representation is also defined by its identity. Assuming that what is central in shaping this identity is the party's intellectual capacity to formulate alternatives, the capacity of the party becomes a central issue.

The issue of intellectual capacity is a problem that is not limited to political parties only, but also to the entire democratization movement. The task of framing alternative consensuses cannot be left to political advisory groups or think-tanks for political parties and a few of their political leaders. In order to formulate alternative consensuses in opposition to the hegemonic conservative consensus, it is necessary to have a comprehensive intellectual infrastructure formed over the long-term period, as well as the public sphere for policy discussions where various plans for alternatives can compete with one another. In the current Korean reality, asking a politician or a political party to deliver such a vision would be like looking for fish in a tree. The political elite of the opposition party came of age, as had the politicians under the old regime. When they finally came to power, they became preoccupied with factional competition over patronage and the pursuit of their own career interests.

---

between delegative democracy and representative democracy is the principle of accountability. In representative democracy, the ruling government is limited by horizontal accountability, as it is constantly checked by other apparatuses or institutions, such as the legislature and the judiciary. In delegative democracy, however, the president is above any other political party or organized interest. The parliament, political parties, or courts of law are perceived to be institutional obstacles hindering the president's political will. The president frequently bypasses these obstacles to make or change policies. Accordingly, policies are easily made and changed under the direction of the president. Initially, after the president takes the power, people welcome the president's policies as a means to realize social harmony. Soon, unexpected costs occur in the course of carrying out those policies, and opposition and resistance arise. Due to the low level of institutionalization, the president is personally held responsible for the failure of the policies. Consequently, the president enjoys high popularity at the beginning of his reign, but such a president often becomes the object of criticisms that are akin to a curse in the end. Guillermo A. O'Donnell, "Delegative Democracy," *Journal of Democracy* 5, no. 1 (1994).

2. The Problem of the Bureaucracy

The State Seized by the Bureaucratic Elite

The problems of the state after democratization begin at a point when the newly arrived ruling elite meet the existing administrative bureaucracy or the bureaucratic elite, one of the central forces of the status quo hegemony. Let us leave out of this discussion the Roh Tae-woo government, since its elite were an extension of the old authoritarian regime. Examining only the governments of Kim Young-sam, Kim Dae-jung, and Roh moo-hyun, it is difficult to say that the ruling elite in these governments had any concrete ideas about the role of the state in a democracy. The ruling elite of these democratic governments came to rule the country overwhelmingly influenced by the ideology and values of technocratic managerialism. In this regard, it is difficult to say that there was a significant difference between the civilian and the earlier authoritarian governments. A certain degree of difference appeared with the inauguration of the Kim Dae-jung administration, but it was not because the new ruling elite had a different principle of state operation. It was because the Asian currency crisis and the subsequent bailout by the IMF created a lasting shock. Under the influence of neoliberalism, the Kim Dae-jung administration emphasized small and efficient government. Except for the slight downward realignment of bureaucracy, mainly through mergers or abolishment of government agencies and personnel retrenchment, there was no earnest attempt to scale down the government to ease centralization and to functionally and spatially decentralize power.

Assuming that there is a need to create a new paradigm for a democratic state administration, it would require establishing a national development ideology and goals appropriate for the norms of democracy, and reforming the government bureaucracy that grew out of the past authoritarian development model. Unfortunately, the new ruling elite did not earnestly pursue any of these activities. For example, at the beginning of his term, when president Kim Dae-jung announced that there would be "parallel development of democracy and a market economy," it was expected that this entailed a vision for a new development model.

The parallel development of democracy and a market economy, however, was avowed but not concretized as a general path for reform policy. Thus, everything became ambiguous. The scope and principle of a democratic government's intervention in the market was not defined. Thus, the only way to overcome the "IMF crisis" was to passively implement the reform package outlined by the IMF. In regard to the question of how the market must be organized in a new environment of globalization, a model was not provided where the issues of *chaebŏl* restructuring, privatization, labor, employment, social welfare, etc. could be discussed within a single comprehensive framework. In the meantime, following the authoritarian development ideology, market efficiency and market fundamentalism began to gain power as a new hegemony. Through a new dogma, a vulgar theory of the dichotomy between the state and market became dominant; the new dogma argued for the maximum reduction of the state role and the expansion of the market. Did the state then become a "minimal state" from a "maximal state" through neo-liberal globalization?

The state remained the same on the infrastructural level, and centralization was preserved and strengthened. It is difficult to say that under democracy the strong state has changed, but the state has become incompetent. Shifting without direction between the inertia of the maximal state and the aspiration for a minimal state, the democratic government went through one confused period after another. The model of the Park Chung-hee style development was abandoned, but its spirit remained in the state sector. The new ruling elite failed to provide a democratic development model. In the face-off between the new ruling elite of the democratic government and the old-line bureaucratic elite, the state failed to establish a dominant position over the government bureaucracy. Thus the former allowed a counterattack by the latter, which by now had become one of the vested interests in society. At the beginning of the administration, their relationship was characterized by mutual cooperation and coexistence. As the political elite could not provide a new development model, and became increasingly dependent on the bureaucrats, the relationship soon changed to one where the former was dominated by the latter. In short, the elected elite of the government could not provide a development model for a democratic nation, and they came to consider the government a venue for allocating public offices. When this happened, the task of setting up and making decisions on policy agenda items fell in the hands of the bureaucrats. In the meantime, the technocrats, who are protected by presidential power, have been singing the same old tune about growth, efficiency, order, and stability. The myth of representation is thus completed by the separation of the representative and the represented.

Democratization and the Problem of Incompetent Bureaucracy

When we say that Korea has a strong state, it is a reference to one of its core characteristics, i.e., the state's well-developed bureaucracy, which is the heart of a strong state at the infrastructural level. During the authoritarian regimes, and in particular under Park Chung-hee, Korea had the reputation of having not only a strong state but also a competent and high-performing state. How did bureaucracy change in Korea with democratization? Under democracy, does it perform as well as it did during the development period? These are interesting questions. But if anyone said that bureaucracy after democratization, i.e., under the Kim Young-sam, Kim Dae-jung, and Roh moo-hyun governments, was reliable, competent, and responsible, it would be far from the truth. Under democracy, the government bureaucracy as a whole was timid and passive, irresponsible, lacking professionalism, incompetent, corrupt, complacent, sycophantic, and confused about the chain of command. From the standpoint of performance, the change was negative in almost every category. The change from a competent state bureaucracy to an utterly incompetent one after democratization is dramatic. What are the factors that led to this change? The following are some answers we can consider.

1) Unlike in the Park Chung-hee era, there are no national goals, such as growth achievement targets, that come from the top. In a democracy and in a market-led economic system, such goal-setting by the state is no longer possible. 2) Unlike in the past, there are no authoritarian state agencies such as the Korean Central Intelligence Agency (KCIA) and the National Security Agency. Under the authoritarian regimes in the past, the national intelligence agencies controlled, regulated, evaluated, and disciplined the enormous government bureaucracy. By doing so, the agencies helped the president, the highest authority in the government, to mobilize the government bureaucracy to achieve the state-established goals. Under a democracy, however, government intelligence agencies cannot continue to play such a role. Instead, what is needed is "horizontal accountability,"[11] the kind referred to by O'Donnell. After democratization, such accountability was neither established nor practiced within the bureaucracy of the democratic governments in Korea, as there was no reform of the bureaucracy. 3) After democratization, the presidency was limited by the democratically amended

11 Horizontal accountability: A contrasting concept to the vertical accountability that is achieved through an electoral mechanism. It refers to the accountability of public officials secured through a system of mutual checks and balances among state apparatuses. To achieve this, the authority and activities of independent apparatuses must be institutionalized, and such apparatuses should be able to make sanctions against the abuse of power, dishonest acts, or neglect of duty by public officials. The government board of audit and inspection, independent statistical institutions, anti-corruption committees, and ombudsman systems are examples of such organizations and institutions. Horizontal accountability was conceptualized by O'Donnell, on the theoretical basis of republicanism. Guillermo A. O'Donnell, "Horizontal Accountability," in *The Self-Restraining State: Power and Accountability in New Democracies*, ed. Andreas Schedler, Larry Diamond and Marc F. Plattner (Boulder, CO: Lynne Rienner, 1999).

constitution to a five-year single term. There was to be a change of government after each term. This weakened the long-term career stability of individual bureaucrats. When the state bureaucracy in a democracy shows that it cannot function properly due to the democratic changes of its government, it is a telling sign that the system lacks the rule-binding autonomy that public organizations under the democratic control must have. 4) Personal connections that allowed the maintenance and stability of bureaucratic career positions shifted after the democratic change of the government, and confusion arose in the bureaucratic chain of command. Consequently, the government bureaucracy became even more characterized by sycophancy, timidity and passivity, lack of professionalism, incompetence, and irresponsibility.

Ultimately, one can say that these underlying causes of the bureaucratic incompetence after democratization in Korea are the consequences of the democratic governments' failure to develop a paradigm for democratically operating the state bureaucracy.

There are criticisms that corruption in the government bureaucracy has become more serious under democracy than under authoritarian regimes. I wonder if such a notion is not actually an image manufactured by the big newspapers in Korea. After democratization, the mass media have undertaken the role of a surrogate court. Competition among political parties was focused not on practical policy issues but almost exclusively on individual politician's personal flaws and scandals, fundraising irregularities, and corruption. In this process, the major newspapers function as a quasi-judicial entity, exposing the scandals and passing judgment on the cases. Of course, this is not to say that public officials under democracy are not corrupt. Rather, the difference between the type and scope of the corruption must be mentioned. Under the old regimes, corruption was structural and large scale. Under democracy, with the increasing transparency and democratic control, large-scale corruption becomes difficult. The fact that rent-seeking activities in the public sector become hotbeds of corruption is the same today as it was in the past. In short, under democracy, incompetence and irresponsibility increase in comparison to the earlier authoritarian periods, but not corruption. The scope and content of corruption can vary greatly depending on how it is defined. The corruption in the government sector, the waste of government funds, the waste in large national projects, private appropriations, and waste in the management of public funds are serious problems under democracy, as they are under authoritarian regimes. What must be emphasized here is that there are more serious problems of corruption, namely the corruption in the big organizations in the private sector, more so than in the state sector. They have become power institutions for private individuals. The evasion of the law and other forms of corruption among the most privileged in our society have been revealed in part in the process of the government's tax investigations into the largest newspaper companies, and in the process of parliamentary confirmation hearings for high-level government officials.

There is another important question of how autonomous the bureaucrat was within the ruling coalition of the authoritarian regimes. Even if one grants that the state bureaucracy was the most modern and efficient organization in Korea under Park Chung-hee, the same cannot be said of it after the 1980s. Private businesses grew rapidly. In fact, the Fifth Republic's ability to control *chaebŏl* had disappeared soon after Chun Doo-hwan came to power. After democratization, under weak civilian governments, the problems of the huge bureaucracy became further entrenched.

3. Democratization and the Problem of the Presidential System

Incompetent Government and a Strong President

In this section, I will discuss the new phenomenon of how the following two seemingly contradictory elements coexist under democracy: 1) an incompetent government, the characteristic feature of the state in the post-democratization period in Korea, and 2) the presidential system, which implies an institutionally strong state. Earlier we have observed how the government in Korea has become weak since democratization. This phenomenon may appear contradictory to the statement that the presidential system is an instrument that institutionally embodies a strong government. Let us first consider, what is the nature of the presidential power in Korea that made the state in Korea strong? We will then examine how this presidency has changed after democratization.

In a period of less than 40 years, from the year the nation was founded until 1987, the constitution in Korea was amended nine times. There is nothing else that better symbolizes the perilous journey traveled by the constitution of Korea. It also speaks of the instability of the political system and the low level of democratic institutionalization. Except for the fourth amendment that took place in the wake of the April student revolution, all the others were without exception about the power structure of the government and election regulations, the term and authority of the highest leader of the government. In other words, the history of the instability of the government in Korea is mostly related to the presidency.

What is interesting is that although the questions regarding such issues as choosing a type of government and defining presidential authority and term limits were of paramount importance, there were no public discussions or debates. Nor were there any thoughtful designs that would have followed such a process in society. Perhaps one could make excuses for the founding constitution, allowing that the circumstances were exceptionally chaotic then. After the April student revolution, however, why was the presidential system changed to a parliamentary system? The change in the form of the government took place without any public discussion or debate. By then, the presidential system was perceived as representing dictatorship, and when the Syngman Rhee regime collapsed, the new government almost automatically chose the parliamentary system.

After the June 1987 uprising, the situation was the same. Because the idea of the "minimalist conception of democracy" had become widespread, the transition from military authoritarianism to democracy meant more than anything else a transition from indirect to direct presidential election. Direct election was adopted because it was the antithesis of the authoritarian regime. Any public discussion of the merits or demerits, or the social effects, of the presidential system itself was overlooked. Consequently, it did not become customary in Korea to reflect on the universal standards beyond the scope of factional interests, on such matters as how a particular system, or a particular set of rules of competition, might or might not represent the interests and demands of society and the people, or how it might or might not contribute to the advancement of democracy.

Is the Presidential System Pre-disposed to Authoritarianism?

The political system in Korea changed after democratization in that the highest authority of the state administration is now elected by popular vote, whereas during the military authoritarian era the president was elected indirectly. Despite this change, to the extent that the government still runs on a presidential system, there is little difference between the old and the current system. Under democracy, the president is a catalyst for a political party. As such, through an election, and as the representative of the people, the president embodies democratic leadership among people. More than anything else, democratic leadership has the responsibility to answer to the demands of the people in accordance with the powers and responsibilities defined by law, and by performing public duties that are defined more widely and flexibly than by law. At the same time, the people must monitor and supervise elected representatives to insure that they carry out public duties properly, and the people must have at their disposal various practical and institutional methods to exercise restrictions. This bilateral relationship is at the core of democracy, and it is in this way that the relationship of public responsibility is established.

In speaking of the democratic system in late-eighteenth-century England and the election of lower house members, Rousseau made the following criticism: "The English people believes itself to be free, it is gravely mistaken; it is only free when it elects its members of parliament; as soon as the members are elected, the people is enslaved; it is nothing." Two hundred years have passed since that remark was made. In modern representative democracies, it seems that establishing a relationship of high responsibility between the electorate and elected representatives is still not an easily realized goal.

When there are strong elements of authoritarianism and patriarchy in the political culture or tradition, there is a high risk of the presidential system turning into an authoritarian government in a democracy. The risk is even greater when this political culture has a powerfully centralized state government combined with a low development of pluralism. Considering that, historically and in contemporary culture, Korea has a strong authoritarian legacy, the risk increases all the more. Before we examine abstract reasons for explaining presidential authoritarianism in Korea, it would be useful to look for clues in the physical environment of the president's everyday work and life.

From the moment he takes office, the president is overwhelmed by his rapidly changed status and the change in his physical environment. The president of the democratic government, elected by the people, is physically separated from the public, for security purposes, the moment he wins the election. First, the heads of national security and intelligence agencies will make reports systematically on various national secrets. Other important public officials will follow them. This is merely the beginning of the process of changing the thought structure of the president to fit his office. The presidential residence and office buildings are isolated from the living- and workspaces of ordinary citizens, and the interiors of these buildings have a palatial atmosphere. The size of the Korean presidential security service is probably the world's largest, relative to the size of the country. The structure of the office of the president's chief of staff is such that it could be called a cabinet on top of the actual cabinet, and its office forms a bureaucracy of its own. Such an environment may fit right in with authoritarianism, but it cannot coexist with democracy. Even if a president is elected democratically, unless he is a philosopher-king referred to by Plato, it is impossible for him to be a democratic president in such an environment. This is to say that the physical environment that surrounds the president is highly susceptible to authoritarianism. Unless such an environment is completely reformed and democratically reorganized, democratization of the presidency, or democratization of the state, would be very difficult even if everything else were to be democratized. Under these conditions the debate on "the imperial president" emerged as an important political issue.

The Problem with "Imperial Presidency"

The discourse on "imperial presidency"[12] has both realistic and fictional aspects. On the one hand, under democracy, an authoritarian president, characterized as an "elected monarch," can be even more strongly maintained than before. There are legitimate grounds for this discourse that could attract a broad social consensus. Issues that give this discourse its basis in reality are: the "winner-take-all" system, the excessive concentration of power in the presidency, the enormous power granted to the president, the lack of mechanisms to check the presidential power, the ambiguity of the legal and institutional boundaries that make arbitrary use of power possible, private appropriation of enormous public power, and the corruption resulting from it. On the other hand, there is a large part of the discourse that distorts the truth, and the distortion is caused by the excessively conservative partisan politics contained in the criticism of the system.

Those in Korea who make the criticism that the president has too much power call the president "imperial." Their reasons are as follows: The president is not simply authoritarian, he is much like the monarchs of the Chosŏn dynasty who enjoyed absolute power without checks; the president privatizes government power and therefore corrupts; the president frees himself from the responsibilities "delegated" to him by voters, and rather than working with the parliament through proper procedures, rules by emergency decrees; through populist political propaganda that mobilizes the masses from the top down the president relies on personal charisma to govern by ochlocracy, or mob rule; and the president, who must represent the public interest as the leader of the nation, subjugates national interests to partisan interest by maintaining the highest leadership position in a political party. Thus, they argue, in order to escape from this "worst form of rule" it is not enough to simply divide and limit the presidential power. What is needed, they argue, is a transition to a new paradigm of a "CEO president." There

12 Imperial presidency: This notion came from the name of a book written by Arthur Schlesinger, Jr. in the early 1970s. Schlesinger criticized president Richard Nixon for his abuse of power; Nixon waged war against Cambodia without the approval of Congress, used the emergency power given to the president for the purpose of suppressing domestic political opponents, and wiretapped the offices of his political opponents. The concept of imperial presidency, along with "Caesarian presidency," has been used in a partisan way to criticize presidential power in the United States. Arthur Schlesinger, Jr., *The Imperial Presidency* (Boston: Houghton Mifflin, 1973).

are two problems connected to this argument. The first is that, in the post-democratization period, are presidents in Korea really as "imperial" as they are described above? The other is, can the "CEO president" be an alternative? Let us examine the second, simpler, question first.

There is a fundamental problem with the argument for a CEO president proposed as an alternative to the imperial president. The CEO president is at odds with the fundamental tenets of democracy. Democracy is not possible unless the presumption of the separation of politics from economics is made. Fundamentally, the market principle and the democratic principle are at odds with each other. The former is based on pursuing private interests, while the latter is based on the one-person, one-vote principle of equality, or the right of universal suffrage. Furthermore, as a private organization pursuing profit, a company values efficiency, and its organization is characterized by a hierarchical structure that can best realize efficiencies. In its organizational essence, the corporate structure cannot but be basically authoritarian. A government is also a giant organization, so it could embrace the same principle of efficiency as its principle of operation. But the government is a public organization that represents and pursues the interests of the whole society, whose aim is to unify the whole society, maintain an orderly market, and realize public welfare through principles of citizenship and distributive justice. The operational principles of private corporations and the leadership of a CEO who is in charge of such an organization are fundamentally different from the leadership of a president who is the head of a government, the representative body of a sovereign people.

Clearly, the debate on the CEO president is a product of the neo-liberal or neo-conservative ideology that is dominant in the world today. It tries to eliminate the difference between economics and politics. It would like economics to be more dominant, and to have everyone believe that politics should be subordinated to the economic power. The proponents would argue that conceptually they are still separate but that normatively politics should be subordinated to economy. The most salient characteristic of this ideology is that it is market-oriented, international-capital-oriented, negative toward politics, and anti-political in attitude. This attitude is in line with the neo-liberal argument that politics is corrupt; politics is irrational; and the government is not a solution but a bundle of problems. Furthermore, such an argument opposes any and all efforts by a country or a government to implement an active labor market policy, to increase social welfare or strengthen social policies on the one hand, and to control market inequality effects and the influence of capital on the other. To justify such an opposition, they would like to eradicate the very basis for the existence of government, and this would pose a threat to democracy itself, inevitably.

Next, before we answer whether or not the president in Korea after democratization could be called imperial, it would be interesting to examine the U.S. context in which the term "imperial presidency" was first coined. The origin of this term, which was first used to criticize authoritarian behaviors by the president, goes back to the founding of the nation. More recently, the former advisor to president Kennedy, Arthur Schlesinger, Jr., and the American political scientist Bruce Ackerman have used the term to criticize the Republican foreign policy of the Nixon and Bush administrations, respectively. It is clear what they mean by the term. Both criticize the supra-legal exercise of presidential authority and power, the making of decisions on matters of war and peace without the approval of Congress. There are several elements of an imperial president: the growth of direct presidential bureaucracy, the Cold War and War on Terror pressures that isolate the president and diminish a sense of accountability, secrecy in the name of national security, the president's arbitrary decisions on the matters of war and peace, the weakening of the traditional party structure, and the phenomenon of the president becoming the focus of political decisions. Thus the criticisms have usually been made under conservative Republican governments, targeting Nixon or Bush, by Democrats or liberals in the country. In other words, the debate on the imperial president in the United States has been a debate on the president's foreign, not domestic, policies, because the United States, as a superpower in the world, can exercise enormous power through its foreign policies. The concept is not an academic one but one that is generally used to express the partisan liberal criticism of the presidents' conservative and expansionist foreign policies.

Let us now examine who uses the term in Korea, and why, when, and under what circumstances the discourse is propagated. The term first appeared in 1996, when the Kim Young-sam administration arrested Chun Doo-hwan and Roh Tae-woo, the two former presidents. The term was also used by the past authoritarian regime forces as a part of the criticism against the Kim Young-sam administration's attempt to "correct history." A full version of this discourse began to appear in the leading conservative press only at the end of 2001, under the Kim Dae-jung administration. The discourse appeared among several factors: pressure on the president to resign from the party chairmanship, the administration's retreat from major reform attempts including a tax investigation of newspaper companies, falling popular support for the president, and a conspicuous weakening of presidential leadership. It was a period in which critical attacks from the opposition and press against President Kim Dae-jung and his administration began to surge.

Any discourse on "the imperial president" in Korea had direct bearing on democratic reform attempts made under the Kim Young-sam and Kim Dae-jung

administrations. It was also directly related to the already weakened leadership of each of these presidents and the weak support base in the assembly for them and their governments. In particular, during the Kim Dae-jung
administration, the fact that the discourse on the imperial presidency had
such a powerful effect as criticism, has to do with these two elements. In
other words, the opposition had the majority in the parliament, and at the
same time the popular ideological support base of the administration was
narrow. These are the factors that compose the situation I referred to as a
government without hegemony. Under such circumstances, we see what we
might call a "discourse alliance" building around the debate on the imperial
presidency. This alliance is between the big newspapers and conservative opposition party. Unlike the case in the United States, this critical discourse on
the presidency came out not when the president was actually imperial but
when the presidency was feeble, and the discourse was used to further ema-
ciate the already weak government. Furthermore, it was not a weapon used
by liberals to attack the conservatives, but the other way around.

Because of the strong power of the president and the executive branch
of which he is the head, the state in Korea has been characterized as strong.
However, this situation changed greatly when democratization came,
and the heart of this change is the changed relationship between the executive and legislative branch. The greatest task faced by any government
elected after democratization was how to secure a majority of the National
Assembly seats. I have said that the Roh Tae-woo and Kim Young-sam governments had hegemony while the Kim Dae-jung administration did not.
The relationship between the administration and the parliament constitutes
the key element of this hegemony or its absence. With a minority of seats
in the National Assembly, the Kim Dae-jung administration proved not
only its weakness in leadership but also the institutional vulnerability of the
presidency.

At the end of the Kim Dae-jung government, in terms of the relative
power relations between the executive and the legislative branches, what
became more powerful was not the president but the majority opposition
party. The president was made feeble and incompetent by the power of the
majority opposition party in the National Assembly, by the influence of
giant voluntary organizations in society such as the press and *chaebŏl,* by
public opinion, and by his own weak leadership and corruption. Thus, one
could say the president in Korea has not been very representative, but neither has he been the head of the "delegative democracy" that O'Donnell
refers to, in which he would be completely free of responsibility to the voters. Against a strong oppositional parliament, the president in Korea did not

rule by emergency decrees as might have been the case in delegative democracies. He could not even exercise the power of veto guaranteed to him by the constitution on decisions made by the legislature. In the meantime, the opposition party had powerfully established hegemony and held a majority in the National Assembly. At the slightest perception of any disadvantage to itself, it rendered the executive powerless and, in a similar fashion to what the authoritarian regimes did in the past, exercised undue influence by intervening in the investigative activities of the courts and the press.

What I am arguing here is not that the power of the National Assembly in Korea must be checked by instituting a new mechanism but that the abuse of that power is a problem. I do not criticize the discourse on imperial presidency in Korea to argue that the authority and the strong power of a president must not be checked. Rather, I criticize the discursive form of the argument. The discourse holds a particular president and a particular government responsible for problems that are caused by the immaturity of democracy in Korea, and its main purpose is to attack the incumbent president. It thus avoids focusing social attention on the real causes and problems of the issues pertinent to society. It is important for the president to greatly decentralize and delegate his authority and exercise a new democratic leadership. However, this is an issue that must be approached from the perspective of improving and democratizing the presidential system, not from the narrow, partisan perspective that incapacitates the fulfillment of presidential duty itself.

Democratic Leadership of the President

How democratically did the state in Korea change after democratization? How democratically did the presidency change after democratization? Any discussion of institutional changes regarding the presidency must address these questions as basic issues. At the same time, discussions on these questions must be based on a wide perspective on developing a framework for a democratic relationship between the state and civil society, and between the state and the market. More specifically, to realize such a framework, the discussion must also include questions on what kind of party system is desirable under the presidential system. Otherwise, the discourse cannot be effective, nor can it contribute to the development of democracy. Despite the fact that the discourse on the imperial presidency points to the problems of the presidency in Korea after democratization, it fails to touch the heart of the problem, because it fails to properly identify the cause and effect of the problem. In other words, presidential authoritarianism is not the cause of all evils, but rather it is itself the product of various problems of the political system in Korea. The problems visible at microscopic levels are secondary problems. They include such problems as the authoritarian and patriarchal behaviors of the president; the confusion in state affairs caused by excessive dependence on "secret lines," i.e., close personal aides; corruption committed by close family members of the president; and personalism revealed in the privatization of power. Would solving these problems create a more democratic presidency?

What makes the presidency authoritarian is the fact that what the president says, what he does, and what he has promised in election campaign platforms do not bind him to the voters. The president is the highest authority in the country; he is the leader of the government and the political party, which is the intermediary between the government and civil society, a body that represents and is accountable to the voters. The authoritarian presidency stems basically from a weak political party. If the president can freely control the political party of which he is the head, as if the party were his own private property, then the problem is not that the president is authoritarian but that the party is so feeble. The base of the political party is not rooted in society, and the source of political power does not come from that base; these are the problems. At the center of the problems surrounding the presidency is the party. Therefore, the heart of the matter in addressing the problems thus engendered is the question of how to democratically develop political parties and a party system. What then is the most serious problem of the party system in Korea? Simply put, it is the gap between the political party and society. The gap must be narrowed. In other words, political parties must have their roots in real social conflicts.

What I have been emphasizing all along in this book is that Cold War anti-communism has imprisoned the party system in Korea within a very narrow framework. The system left very little room to represent conflicts. Moreover, since the 1950s the hegemony of Cold War anti-communism has made any expression of conflicts difficult, insisting on the virtues of unqualified social harmony, and making conflict-free discourse a dominant form of social discussion. This is not to say that the value of harmony and consensus is not important. However, through a political process, harmony and consensus have to be the result of the expression, organization, and negotiation of various social conflicts, not the beginning and the end of such a process. Politics assumes the existence of conflicts and society thus divided; it is a process where such conflicts are democratically expressed and settled through competition and compromises, with political parties as intermediaries. Social harmony is achieved as a result of such a process. Accordingly, harmony is not achieved simply by avoiding conflict in discourses. Harmony in such a case means nothing more than increased repression in the interest of serving vested interests and maintaining the status quo. Conversely, unresolved conflicts harm and disintegrate society at the bottom. To suppress the expression of this, repressive structures would be further strengthened in every sector and at every level of society.

Before the accumulation of such conflicts finally explodes, society would suffer enormous adverse effects and the cost would be high. A social situation where conflicts cannot be expressed and resolved politically feeds the cravings of the political elites to free themselves from their responsibilities to the voters and to arbitrarily expand their power. It thus contributes to the vicious cycle of political corruption. Seymour Lipset, who laid the theoretical foundation of modern democracy through his study of modernization, evaluates society by using two basic criteria, i.e. conflict and consensus. He emphasizes that both are essential for democracy. In the introduction to *Political Man: The Social Bases of Politics*, which has become a classic in political sociology today, Lipset states as follows:

> Surprising as it may sound, a stable democracy requires the manifestation of conflict or cleavage so that there will be struggle over ruling positions, challenges to parties in power, and shifts of parties in office; but without consensus—a political system allowing the peaceful "play" of power, the adherence by the "outs" to decisions made by the "ins," and the recognition by the "ins" of the rights of the "outs"—there can be no democracy. The study of the conditions encouraging democracy must therefore focus on the sources of both cleavage and consensus.[13]

Lipset further states: "Cleavage—where it is legitimate—contributes to the integration of societies and organizations."[14] In Lipset's dialectics between conflict and integration, and looking at elections as a "democratically institutionalized class struggle," an absence of conflict is the evidence that a particular group in society is being excluded from the public decision-making process. Living in a conflict-free society would mean that certain groups are being excluded from political competition. I emphasize the importance of the political party for developing democracy, because political parties belong to the realm of civil society, yet they are the intermediary between civil society and the government. In emerging democracies, political parties are feeble, which means that democracy is weak in these societies. This is because the political parties in these countries do not have deep social roots. Because they are not rooted in social cleavages, differences between parties in elections are not meaningful. Furthermore, because the link

13 Seymour M. Lipset, *Political Man: The Social Bases of Politics* (Garden City, NY: Doubleday, 1960), 1.
14 Ibid.

between political parties and social cleavages is weak, elected officials are not accountable to voters. The principle of accountability does not operate, and therefore what politicians say is not binding. Politicians make campaign pledges and use rhetoric, but they are not bound by society and voters to their utterances. This situation, in which political parties are based on elite interests and personal bossism, cannot but result in a situation that guarantees the hegemony of vested interests. Accordingly, it is most important now to dismantle the old party system embedded in Cold War anti-communism. This would mean transforming the base and structure of political parties, so that they would take root in the new conflict structure created by rapid and widespread social change.

4. Democratization and the Problem of the Concentration of Power

Hyper-concentration: Geographical Concentration and Concentric Overlapping of Elites

At the beginning of this book, I pointed out the causes and problems of centralization. My argument is that one of the most important factors that weakens democracy is centralization. To argue this, it is first necessary to define what is meant by centralization in Korea. Here it means a combination of geographical concentration and the concentric overlapping of elites. In other words, it means a spatial concentration in Seoul but also the overlapping of elites in major social sectors. It is possible that the geographically small size of the country or the traditionally centralized Confucian bureaucratic culture have contributed to this condition. However, the phenomenon is deeply related to the homogenized value structure created by the virulent Cold War anti-communism. It goes without saying that a rigidly uniform value structure, such as that found in Korea, cannot contribute to the strengthening of a pluralistic character of society. Can democracy develop in a society where pluralism is weak? If not, what are the ramifications in Korea?

The most recent historical development that gave impetus to centralization is authoritarian industrialization. After the 1960s, industrialization-era authoritarianism had two axes of concentration: political power and economic wealth. One might ask, with this structure intact in society, is real democratization possible? That is to say, concentration here means hegemony and the structure of vested interests. There are two ways to address the question. The first is to reverse the structure through decentralization of political power, localization of governments, dispersion of *chaebŏl*, decentralization of education, and pluralization of values to create a pluralistic society. The other is, because the decentralization and pluralization of society are enormous and revolutionary tasks, to soften this structure as much as possible and in the meantime replace vested interests, that have benefited from centralization, with new elites. The first direction is too unrealistic, and such a revolutionary direction would be hard to realize unless there were a national consensus. The second approach is feasible, but even if it were realized, it would create only a partial replacement of elites. A major structural change would be difficult to expect. Whatever the answer might be, the important point here is that no government since democratization has raised this issue as an important political agenda, and the same is true of civil society.

Centralization means basically an elitist structure catering to vested interests. The structure is concentrically overlapping and is concentrated at the top so that fundamentally it is not a structure in which the alienated strata in society and *minjung* can broadly participate and access limited resources. It is oriented toward catch-all politics and the economy of full-scale mobilization from above with the state's growth-first policy. In politics, it tends to strengthen a strong government, and in economics and the market, a *chaebŏl*-oriented structure. Catch-all politics is favorable to the state in establishing its political agenda and creating conditions that make it difficult for the various interests created by social cleavages to enter political competition. For example, suppose there is a plan to build a satellite city near Seoul with significant public funds going into the project. The development interests directly connected to this project would be strong enough to overpower any grassroots demands.

When the economic growth rate of a nation depends on the performance of a few *chaebŏl*, issues such as social welfare, distributive justice, and labor problems cannot but become secondary to pro-*chaebŏl* economic policies. Undoubtedly, centralization will make political competition escalate to new levels of ferocity. The winner-takes-all structure is not so much a problem of the presidential system. It is rather a problem of centralization where the president is in a position to allocate resources that are centralized. The regionalism in Korean party politics is the direct and inevitable result of the combination of elitist politics and centralization. When the political elite, active at the center with bases in particular regions, win an election at the center and monopolize the political resources of the center, the losing elite are put in the opposite situation. In other words, the structure of regionalized parties in Korea is not based on competition among plural political forces that have self-supporting regional bases. Instead, it is the product of centralization, i.e., competition between elite political groups at the center. Thus, the result of competition is either all or nothing. In such a structure, the masses are mobilized top-down in election campaigns, but they do not receive victory dividends. This happens in the arena of political competition, i.e., elections, and in other arenas competition is structured similarly.

For example, there is now fierce competition in education, and the reasons are not much different. All cultural, educational, and economic resources are concentrated in Seoul, and the university ranking system has the same centralized concentric structure. Under such circumstances, the intensity and the convergence of the college entrance competition cannot be alleviated. The focus of all schooling is concentrated only on college admission. Under these circumstances, changing the rules of competition, i.e., changing the college entrance system, serves only to further burden the students to adapt to a new system in addition to dealing with the competition. Educational reform will be effective only when it is linked to reforms that comprehensively alleviate the structure of centralization. In other words, education reform will remain an empty slogan unless there is reform on the demand side of education, i.e. the structure of social pull, not the supply side or what is released to society.

Hyper-concentration under Democracy in Korea

From such a perspective, one could pose the following questions. What efforts were made by political elites after democratization to relax centralization and to build a pluralistic structure? How much did the democratic governments contribute to easing centralization? Looking at the record of performance, the democratic governments did not contribute to reducing centralization but rather contributed to its further entrenchment. Table 5.1 shows the percentages of different sectors that are located in Seoul and the Seoul metropolitan area.

The statistics show that as of 1998 the population of Seoul is 22 percent of the national population, or in other words, the population concentration of Seoul is 22 percent. Concentration levels in every other category are between 20 percent and 50 percent. The sectoral categories include the industrial sector, which has figures on employment and local production, higher education, the medical care industry, and the financial and service sectors. Considering that Seoul occupies 0.6 percent of the total national land area, one can see how serious the concentration is. More than 20 percent of the entire population lives in this limited space. A comparison of the population concentrated in the capital cities of other countries also makes the point. According to statistics from 1995, Korea's population concentration in the capital was 23 percent. In comparison, Portugal and France, two countries with the highest concentration of population in their capital cities in Europe, had 19 percent

TABLE 5.1

Degree of Concentration by Sector (1998, %)

	Categories	Seoul	Seoul Metro Area
	Land Area	0.6	11.8
	Population	22.9	45.6
Industrial	Total employed	22.2	47.8
	Local production	23.9	45.9
University	Universities	25.0	42.3
	University student population	26.3	40.5
Medical	Hospitals/clinics	27.1	49.0
	Doctors	37.0	52.5
Financial	Total deposit	49.5	65.9
	Total credit (loans)	46.1	61.7
Public	Government-investment org.	14.3	85.7
	Government-contribution org.	67.7	83.8
Research Institutes	Government/university/industrial	31.3	61.2

Source: National Statistics Office.

and 16 percent, respectively. Excluding countries such as the United States and Australia, where the rate is the lowest, in England, Germany, and Japan the rate is 12 percent, 5 percent, and 9 percent, respectively.

The percentage of universities and university students in Seoul are 25 percent and 26 percent, respectively, of the national total. The number of hospitals and physicians are 27 percent and 37 percent, respectively. But in the case of bank deposits and loans, the concentration is close to 50 percent. The table only shows quantifiable values. When taking into account qualitative values, the concentration in Seoul would be much higher. Also the concentration of population and economic power, and the concentration of venture companies and emerging-industry companies in the Seoul metropolitan area became more entrenched after democratization. For example, the population concentration in the Seoul metropolitan area was 35 percent, 43 percent, 46 percent, and 48 percent in 1980, 1990, 1999, and 2004, respectively. The local production concentration was 35.7 percent, 43.9 percent, 44.6 percent, and 47.7 percent for the same years. As of 1998, the degree of concentration in venture and emerging industry-companies was even more serious. Statistics show that software companies (82 percent), venture companies (62 percent), KOSDAQ-registered venture companies (72 percent), Korea Stock Exchange–listed companies (78 percent), information and telecommunications companies (53 percent), various research institutes (62 percent), and venture investment companies (75 percent) are concentrated in the Seoul metropolitan area. Even in the emerging-industry sector, such as various venture businesses and knowledge and information industries, which began growing rapidly under the Kim Dae-jung administration, an overwhelming concentration in the Seoul area is also the case.

A New Approach to Easing Hyper-concentration

How can the concentration be eased? If we understand concentration as only a geographical issue in Seoul, the alternative would be to ease the geographical concentration, and that would mean spatial dispersion of resources to the provinces. Until now, in discussing the concentration issue, the alternatives were mostly understood as deterrence of development in Seoul and the metropolitan area and dispersion to the provinces. Accordingly, government policies were developed with the idea of decentralizing power and economic, cultural, and educational resources to the provinces. The concept of local self-government was introduced as a result, and policy alternatives for college education, such as the decision to develop local colleges, were also introduced.

Given the situation that elite concentration is still very high in all sectors of the society and that the personnel recruitment structure is still concentric, it is very doubtful how much the decentralization and dispersion efforts mentioned above can ease the hyper-concentration in Seoul and the surrounding area. In the context of the concentric elite structure, it is difficult for such decentralization and dispersion policies to have any practical effects. Even if decentralization and dispersion are gradually achieved in some quantitative ways, that achievement would not change the dependence of local governments on the center, or the existing relationship between the center and periphery. Moreover, such a situation would create a double elite structure where there would then be an elite structure in the center and elite structures in the peripheries.

To approach the problem of centralization differently, one has to define the problem differently. As mentioned earlier, I refer to the concentration phenomenon in Korea as hyper-concentration. This is because the two aspects of concentration in Korea, i.e. the geographical concentration and the functional concentration of the concentric circles of elites, produce synergy effects that increase the level of concentration. Accordingly, ways to ease concentration should start with the separation of the two. Geographical dispersion efforts should continue, but what is more important is the breakup of the concentric elite structure. Dismantling the concentric elite structure, in which the elite circles in politics, economics, culture, and education overlap, requires above all strengthening the independence of each sector. University reform in this regard is very important. There is probably no other country in the world except Korea where the graduates of a single university occupies close to a half of all elite positions in politics, economics, society, culture, and education of the nation. If we add a few more universities, one can safely say that almost all high-level elite positions in Korea are occupied by graduates of a few universities. Add to that a standardization of values and a lack of ideological diversity, and one can easily see why Korean society has such a uniform and homogeneous elite structure as well as overall social structure.

Strengthening the independence of major sectors of society means developing society's pluralism. This is why it is important to expand the ideological spectrum in the political sphere, and for political parties to compete in wider ideological spheres in order to ease the concentration phenomenon in Korea. Increasing competition between parties would mean that political parties would have stronger and more stable social bases, and that social groups, in particular the working class and other alienated groups not represented in politics so far, would participate as important agents. In other words, this would mean that politics would no longer remain the arena of activities solely reserved for the elites. Therefore, the current elite-centered party system and the conservative party structure, in which the differences between the parties do not mean much, must be pluralized by accepting new participants from society. A structure that can widely distribute political power would mean decentralization. Until now, the centralization of politics was the product of a political cartel where a few elites monopolized political resources and power. Political pluralism will be an important starting point for spreading pluralism in other spheres of society.

6 The Market after Democratization

1. Democratization and Market Reform

What Kind of Market Did Authoritarian Industrialization Create?

In this chapter I will examine the market and democracy. By market, I do not mean the market in the economics sense of the flow of goods or the microeconomic behaviors of corporations and consumers. What I wish to discuss here is the market structure in Korea as a particular political-economic system that has been institutionalized by an authoritarian state and that has imposed certain limitations on the development of democracy in Korea.

The fact that the market in Korea was developed on a path that was fundamentally different from those of the West is well known. The market did not begin and develop from the private sector. It was created by the state through major political acts. In other words, the market in Korea did not develop as previously existing market elements grew and transformed; rather it was created in the process of state-led authoritarian industrialization. Of course, this is not to say markets did not exist before, but the market only meant a place to buy goods. Only under the authoritarian state in Korea did the market become functional as an institution where the circulation of goods and services and individual economic activities are regulated in a particular manner. Accordingly, the structure and character of the market in Korea have special characteristics deriving from authoritarian industrialization.

The market shaped under the authoritarian industrialization process has three distinct characteristics. First, the state established the economic growth target, mobilized private corporations, and directly exercised influence on the allocation and distribution of resources; it was a market led by a strong state. Second, in this process a few giant corporations nurtured by the state acted as a surrogate government in pursuing the growth targets of the state's macro-economic policy; this is the *chaebŏl* economic system. Third is the exclusion of labor. This means that—whether in the government policy-making process, which influences the allocation and distribution of productive resources, or in the conservative monopolistic political system— the participation and representation of labor, the major producer group in society, was not allowed. The authoritarian regime was a market-fostering developmental state. It drafted and executed economic development plans, including plans for the nation's economic growth, export targets, and investment strategies. It also guided the allocation of resources to fit macro-economic policies. The state's basic weapon was the supervision and control of finances. In short, the authoritarian and monopolistic structure existed not only in politics but also in the economy. Monopoly and exclusion became the dominant principles of the economy, and transparency and fair competition, the essential characteristics of a market economy, were not actualized.

The strong interventionist role of the state in the market led to bureaucratic authoritarianism taking root in Korea. The state was successful in motivating a national ambition for the single goal of pursuing modernization, and it achieved certain macro-level outcomes. Under these circumstances, the role of an expansive bureaucratic body that established a national target and efficiently distributed and allocated available resources cannot be denied. In the market structure shaped by authoritarian industrialization, the *chaebŏl* grew rapidly. Today, the nation's economy and government performance depend on a small number of corporations, and the fact that they control the nation's economy does not require a separate explanation.

During the authoritarian era, the *chaebŏl* grew to be colossal independent organizations so it became difficult for the state to penetrate them. *Chaebŏl* ownership and governance structures existed outside of democratic control. At the same time, the *chaebŏl* became increasingly more influential in various spheres of society, and their hegemony in civil society became overwhelming. Also, the *chaebŏl* held the fort in advocating efficiency, technocratic managerialism, and militaristic ideology, the building blocs of the authoritarian value system. It is not difficult to understand then, that the authoritarian exclusion of labor is one side of the coin whose flip side is the *chaebŏl*-biased ideology of growth. Whether it is at the level of labor management or politics, exclusion of labor has a great negative impact on the development of democracy. Under conditions where labor participation is excluded from policy-making processes, politics cannot but permanently be a game among upper-class elites. Under such circumstances, even if resistance and demands for reform from the bottom are accepted, such an acceptance cannot but repeat the "reform from above" that alienates the masses from politics.

The Economic Significance of Democratization

In Korean society, what social and economic meaning does democratization have? In brief, it would mean reforming the existing authoritarian market structure.

More than anything else, *chaebŏl*-centered market economy is at odds with democratic politics. The coalition between *chaebŏl* and the authoritarian regimes made rapid growth possible in the past, and the growth was the core of the authoritarian state. Thus the fact that the same system continues means that there is a repetition of vested interests and special privileges for one social group as well as alienation and exclusion for the others in society; it means the maintenance of the social divisions and cleavages from the authoritarian regimes.

Furthermore, the collusion between politics and business, the other face of the *chaebŏl* system, had been a hotbed of corruption, irregularities, irrationality, evasion of the law, abnormality, and inefficiency. It guaranteed special monopoly and privileges to *chaebŏl* in the market and stunted the development and creativity of other economic actors. Accordingly, to continue a *chaebŏl*-centered economy even after democratization was to continue a colossal structure of corruption.

The market structure created by the state-*chaebŏl* coalition is one side of a coin whose flip side is unequal development between *chaebŏl* and small, medium-size businesses, between regions, sectors, and social classes. The development strategy based on this model was pursued in parallel to the phenomenon of political authoritarianism and the strengthening of the unequal economic structure. In short, the policy of growth first, accompanied by huge inequality, was pursued at the cost of serious alienation and social division that spurred authoritarianism in politics, the strengthening of vested class in society, and the exclusion of labor. Under the democratic system, the exclusion of labor has created a vicious cycle where it promotes conflicts, which in turn require an authoritarian state mechanism. Furthermore, it has lowered the enthusiasm and dedication for work and has made the cultivation of public spirit difficult; ultimately, it has the negative effect of obstructing social integration. Accordingly, without reforms that break up this structure and create a transparent relationship between politics and the economy, any democratic reform will become an empty mantra, and the realization of social justice and the rule of law would be difficult.

Two Opportunities for Reform: Democratization and Globalization

What real changes did democratization bring to the existing market structure? If the market in the past was structured to form a pair with authoritarianism, did Korea develop a new market structure corresponding to democracy after democratization? There were two historic occasions when the market structure of the authoritarian past was raised as an agenda item for reform. One was democratization and the other was globalization.

The massive democratic June 1987 uprising was the first time in Korea when the force of the democratization movement was strong enough to demand a structural change in the market. Thus, the June 1987 struggle marks a historical turning point in social movement. There was a consensus that the movement must focus its power on political democratization to solve the structural problems of society. As a result, for the evaluation of how democratic the established political forces were, their attitudes toward *chaebŏl* and on labor issues became the most important criteria.

Afterwards, the task of democratization in Korea included issues not only on the political but also on the socio-economic level. For example, even the Roh Tae-woo government, which was a continuation of the authoritarian regime of the Fifth Republic, proposed *chaebŏl* reform and harmony with labor as policy objectives. In practical terms, it restricted the *chaebŏl*'s use of non-business-purpose real estate and pursued a business specialization policy. The Kim Young-sam government, which came to power with vested interests as its power base through the three-party merger also, implemented the real-name financial transactions law[1] that contributed to the breakup of collusion between politics and business. But the fact that these governments came to adopt *chaebŏl* reform and labor-management harmony as policy goals under the influence of democratization is a separate matter from how much democratization actually contributed to reorganizing the old market structure.

Next, let us take a look at globalization. Chronologically, globalization was embraced before democratization as a government policy. It was in the early 1980s that globalization was initially embraced in Korea, and then it came on much like a storm with the 1997 IMF-imposed structural adjustment regime. From a discursive perspective, globalization means liberalization according to universal world standards. But in fact, it meant something more

---

1 Real-name financial transactions law: This law imposes a system in which one must use one's real name instead of a false or borrowed name in transactions with financial institutions. This law covers all financial transactions in South Korea and was introduced on August 12, 1993, by the "Emergency Order on Real-Name Financial Transactions and Confidentiality."

specific in Korea; it meant embracing the specific policies of neo-liberalism, or the "Washington consensus."[2] In general, the policy of globalization consists of market liberalization, privatization, deregulation, and tight fiscal policy. What must be emphasized here is that globalization and the subsequent demand for changes in policy came not as a result of changes in political-economic conditions in Korea but as a way of accepting changes in the global economic policy cycle led by the United States.

It is important to understand that although globalization has neo-liberal content, its political-economic effects and significance are not always the same. For example, before the 1997 IMF bailout crisis, globalization in Korea meant largely pro-*chaebŏl* and anti-labor policies. Globalization entailed policy support for Korean corporations to strengthen their competitiveness in the global market. Accordingly, labor demands were defined and suppressed as an element that eroded corporate competitiveness. In the early 1980s, the economic technocrats under Chun Doo-hwan pursued a neo-liberal policy, and its main features were the consolidation of redundant investments among *chaebŏl,* forced liquidation of insolvent companies, and the establishment of much stronger repression and control of labor. Consequently, under this policy the *chaebŏl*-centered economic system was strengthened; in particular, a rigid hierarchy of economic structure developed with the five largest *chaebŏl at* the top, and the macro-economic management of the country became difficult without the cooperation of *chaebŏl.* Afterwards, an internationalization policy under the Roh Tae-woo government, and a globalization policy under the Kim Young-sam government repeated the same policy with the same result.

On the other hand, the globalization that came after the IMF bailout crisis brought anti-labor and anti-*chaebŏl* effects at the same time. The fact that neo-liberal globalization brought anti-labor effects after the financial crisis is not difficult to understand. More than anything else, one of the core aspects of the structural adjustment was the elimination of labor-market protection policies, such as employment security. Massive corporate restructuring took place as a part of the IMF-imposed structural adjustment regime, and this was accompanied by large-scale lay-offs.

2 Washington consensus: Refers to strategies to expand the U.S.-style market economy system abroad, or policy prescriptions according to neo-liberal principles. The term originated from John Williamson's presentation in a forum in 1989, in which he called the reform prescriptions for Latin American and other developing countries given by economists from international economic organizations in Washington a "Washington consensus."

Globalization had anti-*chaebŏl* effects, because the implementation of the IMF conditionality significantly threatened privileges enjoyed until then by *chaebŏl*. For example, the institutionalization of publishing corporate financial records alone was a big burden for *chaebŏl*. Such transparency had the risk of lowering their asset valuation in the financial market; it would dampen the free reign that *chaebŏl* enjoyed until then on mismanaging funds through accounting fraud; ultimately, it would reduce the social influence of *chaebŏl*. Other anti-*chaebŏl* measures included the restriction on cross-lending among affiliate companies within a corporate group, the strengthening of the rights of small shareholders, and forcing an outside director system. All of these would eventually weaken the power and influence of the large shareholders of the largest conglomerates in Korea, or *chaebŏl*.

Accordingly, it was through the 1997 financial crisis that globalization served as an opportunity to reform the market structure that had been shaped under military authoritarianism in Korea. Did the demands and opportunities that came from both within and without due to democratization and globalization reform the market structure in Korea? Did the *chaebŏl*-centered economic structure change by the end of the Kim Daejung administration, which had the unique opportunity to do so as both the democratization and globalization forces overlapped in demanding *chaebŏl* reform in an unprecedented historical manner?

2. Did Democratization Change the Authoritarian Market Structure?

Democratization Was Too Weak for Chaebŏl Reform

It must be noted that after democratization *chaebŏl* economic concentration became stronger than during the authoritarian era. The governments that came to power after democratization promised, without exception, to carry out *chaebŏl* reform. But after the initial period of each administration, the promises became empty words. In the case of the Kim Young-sam government, after the initial reform commitment faded, *chaebŏl*-friendly policies became dominant in the administration's economic program. In

TABLE 6.1

Change in General Concentration of Chaebŏl, 1988–2006

	1988	1990	1992	1994	1996	1997	1999	2001	2002	2003	2004	2005	2006
Top 50 chaebŏl	30.3	30.0	32.0	32.2	34.4	37.1	38.0	36.8	35.7	36.6	38.5	38.9	39.2
Top 100 chaebŏl	38.1	37.7	39.2	39.2	41.2	44.2	45.1	43.7	42.5	43.2	45.0	45.5	45.7

Source: Fair Trade Commission.

fact, the *chaebŏl* restriction measures that had been put in place by previous governments, such as regulations on credit management, acquisition of non-business-purpose real estate, and business specialization[3] were eased. Furthermore, huge national projects, such as the privatization of public enterprises, building social overhead capital with private investments, and building a mobile telecommunications network became government largess for the *chaebŏl*. It was under the Kim Young-sam administration that the government abandoned the business specialization policy for *chaebŏl*, which had been introduced and proceeding from the time of Chun Doo-hwan era, and allowed Samsung to enter the automobile manufacturing industry.

In regard to the Kim Dae-jung government, the fact that the Daewoo group and Kia Motors went bankrupt is evaluated very enthusiastically by some people who believe that it is a positive sign of changing times that even *chaebŏl* can go bankrupt. To be more accurate, this phenomenon was the result of an external shock brought on by the 1997 financial crisis, not a result of government policy to reform the *chaebŏl*-centered economic structure in Korea. Moreover, the issue of reforming the *chaebŏl*-centered economic structure must not be equated with the success or failure of individual *chaebŏl*. The figures in Table 6.1 give a simple but powerful testimony of how the *chaebŏl*-centered economic structure has become more entrenched in the fifteen years since democratization.

Was the *chaebŏl* system weakened through democratization or strengthened in spite of it? We can say it has been strengthened. In particular, the concentration of economic power in the top five *chaebŏl* has deepened. *Chaebŏl* interests and perspectives represent the dominant discourse and ideology in Korean society today, and as such they hold the hegemonic position. It would not be an exaggeration to say that the press and universities that were in the past controlled by the authoritarian state are now under the overwhelming influence of *chaebŏl*.

Democracy without Labor

Before the June 1987 uprising, the labor movement was directly suppressed by the authoritarian regimes. However, the labor movement proved

3 Specialization of business activities: This was the goal of the government policy that induced *chaebŏl* to concentrate their resources on their most competitive businesses, rather than expanding "octopus-like" into a fleet of different businesses. For example, in the policy introduced in 1993, the government selected two or three core businesses and core companies per *chaebŏl* and allowed certain regulatory exemptions. The Fair Trade Act restrictions on investment, and bank loan restrictions according to the credit management laws, were eased for such companies.

itself to be the central social force that contributed to democratization in Korea through the July and August labor struggles that followed the June 1987 uprising,

After the April 26 general election of 1988, in which the ruling party lost their majority in the National Assembly, and because labor movement was growing rapidly after democratization, the Roh Tae-woo government faced pressure to reform the authoritarian market structure that excluded labor. However, the labor policy under the Roh Tae-woo government continued to be repressive and exclusive. The "atmosphere of public security" in 1989 reinstated the labor control of the authoritarian era. Just as the introduction of the Yushin system was not unrelated to the growth of the labor movement at the time, it is not an accident that the launching of Chŏnnohyŏp (Jeonnohyeop) in January 1990 coincided with the three-party merger. The merger signaled the counterattack of the conservatives against demands for labor and democratic reforms that had been building since democratization. There was, on the one hand, the continuation of the policy to exclude labor through the use of physical force. On the other hand, the labor movement had grown rapidly since democratization. Between these two phenomena, conflicts increased. Despite the government's authoritarian control, the balance of power between management and labor in labor-management relations changed greatly after democratization. The labor's standing became stronger. The labor market had never been more favorable to the labor movement in the nation's history. It was a time of high economic growth, improvement in the income distribution structure, low unemployment, and labor shortage.

During the Kim Young-sam administration, there were attempts to make labor policy more democratic. The newly installed civilian government could less easily afford the price of repressing labor. Accordingly, at the beginning of the administration, attempts were made in parts to reform labor policy. The "new economic policy"[4] and the "policy of sharing the burden" are some of the examples. At the same time, the labor movement during this period was still strong. Solidarity beyond company-level unions expanded, as can be seen in the formation of Chŏnnodae (Jeonnodae).[5] Legal

4 New economic policy: The economic policy suggested by the Kim Young-sam administration in its initial stage. Following the neo-liberal ideology that emphasizes the failure of the state and the efficiency of the market, the new economic policy presented anti-regulatory measures oriented to strengthening the function of the market.

5 Chŏnnohyŏp (Jeonnyhyeop): Chŏn'guk nodong chohap taep'yoja hoeŭi (Jeon'guk nodong johap daepyja hoeui, Korean Council of Trade Union Representatives). It was formed in June, 1993. Major democratic trade union groups active at the time, including Chŏnnohyŏp, Hyŏnch'ongnyŏn (Hyeon chongryeon), the Daewoo group trade union alli-

and institutional mechanisms that supported the repression and exclusion of labor became in large part ineffective or unenforceable due to the growth of the labor movement. In labor-management relations, however, the government's neutral position and the guarantee of the autonomy of labor unions reverted to past practices. After the Hyundai group strike led by Hyŏnch'ongnyŏn (Federation of All Hyundai Group Trade Unions), the direction of labor policy reforms was reversed. Under the government-led discourse on economic revitalization, it was deemed that labor demands were excessive and responsible for a decrease in corporate investments. On these grounds, the government took hard-line actions against strikes staged by labor unions at Hyundai Motor Co. and Apollo Industrial Co., a subcontractor of Hyundai Motor. Afterwards, hard-line government intervention in labor strikes followed, as in the subway and railway workers' strikes. For example, the strike at Korea Telecom in 1995 was defined by the government as "an attempt to overthrow the government." At the same time, major newspapers, broadcasting companies, and business organizations strengthened their counterattack. With the slogans "no work, no pay," and "protection of management rights," they stepped up their offensive. The character of the labor policy under the Kim Young-sam government is well captured in the administration's response to the general strike[6] (December 26, 1996–March 13, 1997) waged in protest against the December 1996 passage of the labor law amendment. The general strike, and the negative social atmosphere opposing the government and supporting the strike, put the Kim Young-sam administration in a crisis. At the same time, the situation clearly illustrated that the labor policy under Kim Young-sam supported corporate rationalization and excluded labor as before.

Globalization rapidly swept through Korea in the wake of the IMF crisis. One of the key demands of the IMF reform package was labor-market flexibility. The result was generalized employment instability. The major content of the IMF reform package is usually summarized as requiring *chaebŏl* restructuring, financial reform, public enterprises reform, and labor-market reform. However, it must be emphasized that the outcome of the four major

---

ance, and an alliance of industrial-level unions formed a single national body. In total 1,048 trade unions and 420,409 workers were represented by Chŏnnodae. Source: http://www.kctu .org/2003/html/sub_01.php (English) & http://www.nodong. org (Korean), June 12, 2005.

6 1996 general strike: On December 26, 1996, the ruling New Korea Party rushed eleven bills through the National Assembly by surprise, including the KCIA law and a labor-related law, by voting when the members of the opposition party and independent members were absent. Then, a general strike began in resistance to this, demanding that the resolution be overruled. It lasted for three months, and 3 million workers took part in it.

reforms were all closely linked to labor issues. These reform policies brought a shock to all sectors of society, i.e. *chaeböl*, the middle class, and labor. But the labor sector was the hardest hit, and the middle class also had to absorb much of the shock. For the old upper-class, income from financial investments soared during this period, while working- and middle-class life became much more unstable. Income gaps increased, and employment instability for wage earners became greatly more aggravated. Under such grave conditions of economic crisis, labor policies could no longer be conceived separately from wider social policies that include welfare programs. As a result, under the Kim Dae-jung administration, a new type of conflict emerged regarding labor issues. The conflict arose not so much around labor-management relations itself, but regarding labor policy, which would significantly influence the framework of labor-management relations. This was a signal that a change was taking place in traditional labor-management relations, which had been rife with conflicts that were focused mainly on the collective bargaining agreements at the shop-floor levels.

If the traditional labor-management relations were changing, did the labor policy and its results under the Kim Dae-jung administration also change from those of previous governments? Could government policy support the changing nature of the labor-management conflicts? It is difficult to answer these questions positively. Contrary to expectations, in reality, the government's policy tilted singularly toward the market economy priorities. Social policy, including welfare and labor policies, was considered a sub-category of economic policy. Whether it was a labor policy or a welfare policy, it had meaning only as a complement to economic restructuring. In the decision-making processes for economic policies, labor neither participated nor was represented. Many people believe that through the Korea Tripartite Commission,[7] labor participated in the decision-making process on relevant policies. They defined the establishment of the tripartite commission as an example of the corporatism[8] that functioned in the welfare states of the West. The tripartite

7 Korea Tripartite Commission: An advisory committee that reporting directly to the president. The Tripartite Commission was formed of representatives of labor, industry, and government as a way to overcome the IMF economic crisis in 1997. Major representatives of labor withdrew from it because of the problems of layoffs and the contract work system, and other agreements also had not been carried out correctly. It ceased to function in 1999.

8 Corporatism: A system of interest representation that is in contrast to pluralism. In the pluralistic system of interest representation, interest groups can be organized plurally according to the functional categories of interests, voluntarily and competitively. There is no permission, approval, or financial aid from the state, and the election of their repre-

commission, however, in its decision-making and policy-implementation process, was a far cry from the corporatism of the West, where the participation of labor is well institutionalized. If we must use the concept of corporatism here, one could stretch the concept and say that what happened was an experiment in "supply-side corporatism"[9] in that the commission was established as a consultation body for labor, business, and government with the goal of realizing labor-market flexibility. Even this experiment could not continue when the Korean Confederation of Trade Unions (KCTU), the key representative of labor, walked out of the process after a year.

On the whole, even under the Kim Dae-jung government, labor remained an excluded group. In the market, the workers' position is more vulnerable now than at any other time before. During the high-growth period of the past, the government was authoritarian but there existed a macro-economic framework that united workers with full employment and rising incomes.

---

sentatives or the expression of their interests is not controlled. On the contrary, in a corporatist system, interest groups are organized compulsorily, hierarchically, and without competition. They monopolize the representation of interests in particular functional or occupational categories, and in return, get supervised and controlled by the state. Philippe C. Schmitter defined corporatism as a system of interest mediation for the first time in the theory of corporatism, and developed his theory systematically. The theory of corporatism can be applied to any interest group, and is particularly useful when applied to the producer groups, such as employer groups or labor unions. Pluralism can be compared to free market competition, while corporatism can be compared to market competition under oligopoly. Philippe C. Schmitter, "Still the Century of Corporatism," *Review of Politics* 36 (1974).

9 Supply-side corporatism: Corporatism up to the 1980s was generally based upon Keynesian demand-side economics. It focused on coordinating macro-policies among the representatives of major labor and industry organizations and government. The core content was a mutual exchange of wage control and social welfare. Supply-side corporatism is the same as the existing corporatism to the extent that it is a mechanism of cooperation based on the tripartite negotiations. Yet, its issues and goals are completely different from those of the demand-side corporatism in that it is an institutional mechanism dealing with important issues that are newly emerging, such as the increasing demand for labor market flexibility and rising unemployment due to neo-liberal globalization. Furthermore, supply-side corporatism encourages wide policy discussions not only at the national level, but also at the levels of economic sector, industry, and shop floor. It mutually exchanges labor market flexibility with employment stability, and it tends to make cooperative relations between labor and capital. Unlike the demand-side corporatism that includes an aspect of policy input, supply-side corporatism seeks mainly for cooperation in the execution process of neo-liberal policies. Franz Traxler, "From Demand-side to Supply-side Corporatism? Austria's Labour Relations and Public Policy," in *Organized Industrial Relations in Europe: What Future?*, ed. Colin Crouch and Franz Traxler (Aldershot, UK: Avebury, 1995).

TABLE 6.2

Yearly Labor Disputes Under the Kim Dae-jung Government

Category	1998	1999	2000	2001
Strikes	—	129	250	235
Lockouts	—	15	35	24
Criminal complaints by employers	262	281	586	1,053
Interventions requested for unfair labor practices	837	1,042	1,031	1,454

Source: Ministry of Labor.

With the IMF reform package, that framework disappeared. The exclusion of labor from party politics did not change under the Kim Dae-jung government. The tripartite commission remains in name but not in function. Participation of labor at the enterprise level, at the level of political representation, and at the policy decision-making level has been closed off. Consequently, when it became clear that the labor policy under the Kim Dae-jung administration was meaningful only as an extension of neo-liberal economic policy, the mainstream labor movement, as represented by KCTU, confronted the government. The government responded to the situation only as a matter of maintaining law and order. In the process the administration's labor policy regressed to that of the authoritarian regimes of the past.

After democratization, the Roh Tae-woo, Kim Young-sam, Kim Dae-jung, and Roh Moo-hyun governments each responded to the labor situation with different labor policies under different circumstances. From a broad perspective, there is a clear distinction between before and after: the IMF crisis is the dividing line. Before the crisis, even if an economic crisis were in progress in the form of a bubble economy, at least on the surface, favorable conditions for the labor movement continued, such as high economic growth, low unemployment, and labor shortage. On the other hand, after the crisis, an unprecedented era of low growth and high unemployment arrived, and labor-market flexibility became an unavoidable condition. Nevertheless, labor exclusion continued in party politics, policy decision-making processes, and even in labor-management dialogues. Neither was there a political attempt to transform the framework of the Cold War anti-communist development ideology. As a result, old government patterns repeated. In other words, at the beginning of each of these administrations, the government emphasized reform for the sake of harmony with labor, but in the latter half of their terms, each administration regressed to authoritarian policies. In the end, even after democratization, a shift in labor policy that went beyond the level of general discourse, i.e., a substantial change in labor policy, did not materialize.

3. IMF-led Globalization and Economic Reform

Globalization as a New Social Cleavage

As was pointed out earlier, globalization as an implementation of policy began in Korea in the early 1980s. By then the free market, privatization, deregulation, and competitiveness had become an ideology, and each succeeding government since the early 1980s attempted to more fully embrace the demands of globalization, as if each were trying to outdo the other, mobilizing rhetoric such as "internationalization" and "new economy." Based on discursive output, it looks as if the Kim Young-sam government reached the summit in pursuing globalization. A government-wide globalization committee was formed, support for academic research on globalization increased rapidly, and there was a flood of special features on the topic in the mass media. It was an era when a proposal was made to change even the ruling party's leadership system so that the party would be "more predisposed to globalization."

Interestingly, until then, i.e. before the financial crisis, the shock of globalization could not produce a new level of cleavage in Korean society. On the whole, before the crisis, the government and vested interests mobilized the globalization discourse mostly to avoid the demands of democratization and reform. For example, in arguing that competitiveness must be enhanced to survive in the world market of limitless competition, labor demands were criticized as a cause for increasing costs excessively, and demands to reform *chaebŏl* were denied on the grounds that it would weaken their advantages in the world market from economies of scale. Furthermore, under the influence of globalization, making Korea a desirable place for doing business became the goal of the government. Thus, globalization had the effect of accelerating the subjugation of politics to economics, and this resulted in the deterrence of government intervention in economics and the stabilization of the *chaebŏl*-oriented economic system. But it did not create a new cleavage as the IMF bailout crisis did. In short, before the bailout crisis, the cleavages around government economic policy existed in a single axis with two poles; on one side was the argument for government-led economic intervention, and on the other side was the argument for free market system. Globalization was no more than an additional aspect of the existing axis of cleavage.

Globalization after the IMF intervention was different. We can express the cleavage structure brought on by the crisis in Table 6.3. Before the "IMF era," cleavages around economic policies involved only the horizontal axis, i.e. confrontation on the degree of expansion of the role of the market. However, after the IMF era, the vertical axis, i.e., conflict over how much the globalization norms should be embraced, was added. The policies of the government, which accepted the IMF conditions for bailout, belonged to quadrant (2), which meant transformation toward market economy in step with the norms of globalization. In the case of *chaebŏl,* who have argued for a free market and government deregulation, logically it seems that embracing the globalization norms should be consistent with their interest. To *chaebŏl,* globalization meant transparency and accountability in management and fair competition; it meant not only the elimination of the special privileges they have enjoyed in the Korean market but also a restructuring that would have a direct impact on the very survival of *chaebŏl.* Accordingly, even as they argued for greatly reducing government regulation and for allowing autonomy of the market that they controlled, they argued that hasty application of globalization norms would weaken the development of Korean industries. Thus their position belonged to quadrant (4). The labor sector was opposed to the globalization norms that demanded labor market flexibility. At the same time, it demanded government policies to protect labor market. Thus their interest lay in quadrant (3).

Had these changes functioned as axes of political conflicts, the existing party system and political cleavages might have been very different now. In reality, the lines of the cleavages were not made clear, and they were manifested in much more chaotic forms. In other words, although the IMF era had arrived and there were now two axes of conflict in the Korean economy, this did not lead to clear formulation of the axes of political competition but only contributed to making previous issues more confused. Government economic policy makers could probably say that by embracing the IMF reform package they were attempting to make the Korean economy transparent in

TABLE 6.3
The New Cleavage Structure in the IMF-led Globalization Period

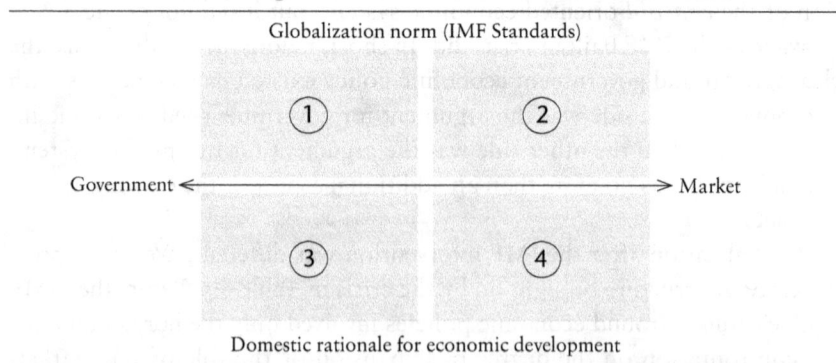

Globalization norm (IMF Standards)

Government ←————————————————————→ Market

① ② ③ ④

Domestic rationale for economic development

Source: Author.

line with the norms of globalization. More than anything else, such policies confront the interests of *chaebŏl*. What is interesting is that the market
reform policies were resisted by both *chaebŏl* and the labor movement, because corporate restructuring according to the standards of globalization is
accompanied by employment instability. Accordingly, the labor movement
opposed the government policy as "neo-liberal restructuring." In this case,
chaebŏl and organized labor, whose relationship with each other is usually
characterized by extreme confrontation, came to share a common interest
in opposing the government's efforts to implement globalization policies.
Furthermore, as we can see in the case of the LG Semiconductor Company,
which was one of the companies on the Kim Dae-jung administration's target list for the "Big Deal"[10] merger in early 1999, the trade union joined
hands with the conservative opposition party to resist government efforts.
We can call such a phenomenon a displacement of alliances, or substitution
of cleavages. Examples of such phenomena can be found in the relationship
between the labor and the civic movement. Although people on both sides
agree on the basic principle that *chaebŏl* must be reformed, they reveal nu-
anced differences and opposition on specific issues of how *chaebŏl* should
be restructured.

After the financial crisis, the globalization cleavages hit hard and greatly
transformed the structure of social conflicts in Korean society. Yet, why did
the axes of cleavages and forms of alliances become more divisive and confused? This was because social conflicts were not politically mobilized and
represented. As I have pointed out earlier, democracy is a decision-making
structure where private interests in social conflicts are not repressed but developed as public-interest alternatives through a political party, and where
alternatives thus developed compete with one another for public support.
In a democracy, the function of politics is to develop and integrate various
social conflicts into public policy alternatives that society as a whole can
embrace. To do that, there must be political parties that clearly delineate the
axes of conflicts and alliances, and such political parties then must develop
competitive alternatives based on the interests of different social groups.
Although the cleavage structure has changed and demands by various social groups have been voiced due to the arrival of IMF-led globalization, no
political party responded to the situation. No political party attempted to
integrate the elements of conflict and develop them into a realistic political

10 "Big Deal": Cross-exchange of core businesses among the top five *chaebŏl* groups
in Korea according to the general principle of industrial, or business, specialization. For
example, under this government-initiated policy, the LG Semiconductor company was
merged with Hyundai Electronics, now Hynix Semiconductor Inc.

alternative. Consequently, the opportunity was lost to develop the demands of various social forces and groups into practical policy alternatives, and Korean society became even more divided than before.

Why Was Korean Democracy Ineffective at Substantive Reform?

Democratization in Korea was effective in ending authoritarian rule. More than anything else, this is an achievement that the democracy movement in Korea can be proud of. However, fifteen years of experience show that democratization has been impotent in bringing about a substantive change, i.e., socio-economic reform. Despite democratization, the class structure became more entrenched and the *chaebŏl*-oriented economic structure has been strengthened; at the same time, the exclusion of labor continued and the intellectual foundation of our society has become further ravaged. Democratic governments showed strong reform commitment at the start of their terms, as if they were in a competition to do so. But they soon retreated and became conservative in the direction of stabilizing the establishment.

Why was democratization in Korea so impotent in bringing real reforms? How did it become conservative? Reform requires two conditions for success at a substantive level, such as at the level of reforming the *chaebŏl*-centered market structure. The first condition is the presence of the idea, vision, and program of the reformer. The other is the presence of reform capability to mobilize support and to impose the inevitable losses and disadvantages of a successful reform to *chaebŏl* and other constituents of the conservative class seeking to preserve the status quo. From the vantage points of these two standards, perhaps it would have been difficult to expect a reform beyond sending the military back to the barracks, i.e. a procedural reform, until the end of the Kim Young-sam administration. That is to say, perhaps it would have been difficult to expect a substantive reform that would change the system of existing vested interests during this period. After all, Kim Young-sam came to power through a coalition with the vested interests, and it was not easy for his administration to pursue a reform that would contradict its own support base. In fact, the Kim Young-sam government's motto of building "a New Korea" became an empty slogan. Beyond the slogan, no serious attempt was made to carry out any socio-economic restructuring or to develop an ideology, vision, or program that could support such an endeavor.

The fact that *chaebŏl* restructuring finally became an actual reform agenda item, not just rhetoric, during the Kim Dae-jung administration prompts two observations. First, the ruling clique of the Kim Dae-jung administration were the marginal elite who had been alienated from the homogenous elite structure that became hardened and fixed over the long period of the rule of the authoritarian regimes. In other words, it meant the arrival of a government whose supporting base was not rooted in vested interests, which was not the case for the Kim Young-sam administration. This also meant that there was at least some overlapping between the social forces that could be mobilized to support *chaebŏl* reform and the population that supported the Kim Dae-jung administration. Second, there was the shock from without, in the form of the IMF bailout crisis that was accompanied by a radical program of globalization in Korea. As can be seen in the IMF reform package, globalization worked as a force for restructuring the existing *chaebŏl*-centered economic system. But the only way to overcome the crisis also depended on the government's crisis management ability. In other words, as long as the Kim Dae-jung government was in charge of breathlessly negotiating with the IMF and rapidly restructuring, it could be said that vested interests had clearly turned over their hegemony to the government. At least in the beginning, the Kim Dae-jung government enjoyed a certain kind of autonomy over vested interests that no other government before it had enjoyed. Accordingly, had the Kim Dae-jung administration prepared itself with a reform theory and programs appropriate for Korean reality and developed political conditions to implement them, it would have been possible to greatly change the existing economic system.

When the Kim Dae-jung administration came to power, the word "reform" carried two meanings. Broadly speaking, one was the IMF-imposed "structural adjustment," a survival strategy to overcome the financial crisis at the time, a reform induced from without. In this sense, it meant a passive reform. The other was the "structural reform" internally demanded by the historical changes in society brought on by democratization. In other words, there was a need to reform, with or without the financial crisis, or IMF intervention. In this sense, it meant an active reform. This referred to a reform that would establish alternative models for economic development and social policies, as well as practical policies and concrete programs to implement within democratic frameworks. That is to say, with or without the IMF crisis, for the sake of democracy, Korean society could no longer afford to continue the *chaebŏl*-oriented economic structure, the exclusion of labor, and the growth-driven macro-economic policy.

Even under the IMF bailout regime, there was room to make some choices. One was to create a market economic system befitting democracy, one that was different from the authoritarian growth model used during the Park Chung-hee era. Another was to interpret the implementation of the IMF reform package as a transition to a market economy. Under this scheme, the negative effects created by a market economy would be mitigated by democratic reforms. Whichever approach the government took, it would have given the Kim Dae-jung government an opportunity to carry out a reform beyond "adjustment" by allowing it to distinguish democracy from market economy and to thus come up with alternatives appropriate for Korean reality. In this regard, the parallel development of democracy and a market economy, as announced at the beginning of the Kim Dae-jung administration, was important. But whether one calls it parallel development or "a democratic market economy," the policy vision and ideology of the Kim Dae-jung administration were never fully defined and realized in real policies. They ended as rhetorical discourse.

In fact, given the conditions Korea faced, it was inevitable that the government would embrace neo-liberal doctrine and implement the IMF reform package. As mentioned above, this meant structural adjustment of the existing macro-economic model, and this response had the characteristic of responding promptly and fully to the impact of the bailout crisis. This was the direction of government policy, and its goals were defined in terms of accomplishing the four major reforms: participating actively in globalization; restructuring the "chimney" industry-oriented manufacturing sector; realizing global standards; building a flexible, open, and freely competitive economy; and nurturing the growth of the knowledge and information industry. However, if the Kim Dae-jung administration stopped at these passive reforms, what was its particular raison d'étre? Kim Dae-jung came to power as a heroic defender of democracy after a long history of struggles. For this to have any meaning, his administration should have initiated long-term and autonomous structural reforms beyond "adjustments," in order to provide for further development of Korean society. It would have meant going in the direction of the parallel development of democracy and a market economy and taking the "democracy" aspect seriously. Wholly unconnected to the external restrictions imposed by the IMF, some major tasks waited to be carried out. For example, there had to be a new party system that would allow the labor sector to play a major role in it, and a dismantling of the regional party system. Also, work needed to be done to include labor in policy-making and implementation processes, and to expand collective-bargaining rights in the labor market. These were some of the more important tasks, again unrelated to externally imposed conditions, that could have been achieved if the government developed a strong enough popular political base. Such political changes should then have been combined, on the market side, with *chaebŏl* and financial sector reforms, free and fair market competition, and corporate transparency.

Had the Kim Dae-jung government pursued political reforms centered on a socio-economic structural reform that widely mobilized and represented the interests of the working and middle classes, its somewhat incomplete policy visions and programs could have been complemented by social ramifications. The Kim Dae-jung administration, however, made no serious attempt whatsoever to reform the regionalized party system and the conservative-monopolistic political structure. In regard to forming political alliances, the policy of the Kim Dae-jung government was to maintain the ruling coalition with the United Liberal Democrats (ULD), the conservatives. Even after the 2000 general election, after which the coalition had broken down, the administration was consistent in wishing to resume the coalition. While no reform-minded political forces could support the Kim Dae-jung government, the vacuum was filled by bureaucrats nurtured during the authoritarian era who now carried out government policy. These bureaucrats could not plan and pursue any alternative economic policy. In fact it was unrealistic to even expect that changes, such as *chaebŏl* reform and a transformation of labor policy, could be possible under such circumstances.

The Legacy of the Failure to Reform

Despite the internal and external shocks brought on by democratization and globalization, there were no major changes in the general framework of the market structure in Korea. After democratization, the unilateral advantage of the state disappeared in the power relations between the state and *chaebŏl,* and *chaebŏl* now had power and influence that could not easily be controlled by the state. The exclusion of labor from the economic system continued. Despite certain legal and institutional changes, no practical changes appeared, either at the level of consciousness or in terms of influence on policy or the agenda in which the labor could participate. That is to say, the market structure formed in the authoritarian industrialization process continued after democratization. In short, what had to be changed did not change under the Kim Dae-jung administration. What result did this bring to democracy in Korea?

More than anything else, it allowed a particular political perspective, one that we can call neo-liberalism, to widely permeate Korean society. This perspective manifested itself in the belief that state intervention and regulation are bad; in the anti-political belief that politics is irrational, incompetent, inefficient, corrupt, and morally depraved; and in the belief that the state must not interfere with the flow of the economy. In terms of its effect on reality, these beliefs led to the stabilization of the *chaebŏl* system dominating the economy. Clearly, such beliefs would eventually lead to the expansion of cynical and negative views on democracy. Already, we see nostalgia cropping up. It is nostalgia for authoritarian politics and its efficiency, for the Park

Chung-hee regime that successfully created a development model based on quantitative growth. We also see in many places that such nostalgic sentiments make a mockery of the reform discourses. In the face of the prevailing power of the discourse that disparages and derides politics, views the role of the government negatively, and furthermore subordinates the meaning of democracy to economic values, democracy today in Korea is completely impotent.

It must also be pointed out that a change is being delayed in the perception of democratic labor-management relations. The perception of the labor movement as spread by the conservative press is still authoritarian. The following headline quotations are representative of the general tone of the press: "the strike by militant union destroys national economy;" "the egoism of the labor union;" "the lukewarm implementation of the law against illegal strikes by trade unions;" "the future of the Korean economy is gloomy as long as labor unions are not controlled." In this situation, where anti-democratic views are so dominant, democratic foundations for peaceful institutionalization and arbitration of conflicts are constantly threatened. Thus, today we live in a reality where there is no awareness that, for economic development and growth and for political stability, a partnership with labor is unavoidable. There is no awareness that if labor is excluded from the political process, social stability, never mind democracy, cannot be maintained. Under the circumstances, it is difficult to expect the labor movement to grow as a leading political force in our society, equipped with a practical ideology and objectives.

The predominance of neo-liberalism since the 1990s has greatly weakened the cohesion of the labor movement. However, the leaders and activists of the labor movement are still prone to hold unrealistically idealist and radical ideas, which prevent them from taking full advantage of the remaining opportunities for action. The ideological radicalism that has been characteristic of many labor union leaders since the time of the democracy movement in the 1980s made these officials largely unable or unwilling to exert a restraining influence over the trade unions of large enterprises. Nor did they sufficiently represent the interests of those low-income social groups who were particularly severely affected by globalization. For these reasons, the South Korean labor movement needs to undergo certain much-needed changes. It is somewhat paradoxical that the raison d'être of the labor movement was questioned under democracy, rather than under the pre-1987 authoritarian regime.

After democratization, the South Korean administrations have not made any sustained attempt to reform such earlier practices of economic development as bureaucracy-centered policy-making and a growth-first policy. Instead, they regarded the *chaebŏl* groups as the main vehicle of implementing government policies. Despite the vague and optimistic expectations of many rank-and-file supporters of the democracy movement, the state hardly played a reformist role in managing the economy and regulating markets. The dominance of the *chaebŏl*, which was so characteristic of the authoritarian era, has remained unchanged under the democratic administrations. In fact, the new democratic administrations drastically imposed the model of neo-liberal reform not only on the economic production system but also on every other social sphere, including culture and education. This process has aggravated socio-economic inequalities, worsened the living conditions of the lower social strata, and ensured the *chaebŏl's* economic hegemony over social and cultural life. In the light of this evidence, the new democratic governments seem to have been far less capable of restraining the *chaebŏl's* power and socio-political influence as many supporters of the democracy movement expected and desired.

7 Civil Society after Democratization

1. The Development Context and Characteristics of Civil Society in Korea

What Kind of Civil Society?

In this chapter, we will deal with the structure of civil society and change after democratization in Korea. Given that democracy in Korea has not further developed in either content or quality, is there any value in discussing civil society? Would it help us better understand the issues that Korea faces?

Civil society is hard to define, and the subject is difficult to approach analytically. There are many differences of opinion among scholars in defining civil society. A student came to me once and asked, "What is civil society?" and I had to pause for a long time before I could say anything. However, I do not wish to belabor readers with an elaborate discussion of the theoretical and abstract issues necessary in defining civil society even before we have begun to discuss the topic for the chapter. Before we go any further with the subject, I would like to define civil society as "a sphere of activities by voluntary associations that exists between the state and the individual or family." This is one of the standard definitions. Assuming that civil society is a voluntary intermediary sphere between the state and the individual, it has three major components. The first are the interest groups, such as physicians' associations and pharmacists' associations, voluntary associations formed to maintain and expand the special interests of a particular, homogenous group. The second are non-governmental organizations and networks that cannot be grouped as interest groups. They deal with ideology, culture, education, and social consciousness. The press and religious, educational, and youth-related social organizations are major groups that belong to this category. The third is mass movements. Its level of institutionalization is low, its scope of organization unclear, and its continuity short; but it refers to collective actions and their organizational bodies that mobilize the masses to realize a particular value and objective, and in particular to pursue the public good.

Assuming that civil society is the social realm composed of voluntary associations between the state and the individual, civil society in Korea clearly exists. This definition, however, is too general. The more important question is, what kind of civil society is it? How was it formed, and how did it change? The best way to answer these questions and to understand civil society in Korea is to take a comparative approach.

Comparison with Civil Societies in the West

In the West, the concept of civil society, in terms of historical development, appeared in sixteenth- to eighteenth-century England and France with the emergence of the bourgeoisie. In terms of intellectual development, it appeared with the emergence of liberalism and Enlightenment philosophy. The contributors to the theorization of civil society, such as Hobbes, Locke, Montesquieu, Rousseau, and Adam Ferguson, were all liberal Enlightenment thinkers. In concept and in theory, civil society was meant to protect the private sphere or commercial interests from the state, which represented the public authority. Thus, civil society in the West has an intimate link with liberalism. The boundary between the state and civil society, between the public and private spheres, became very clearly demarcated. Conceptually, civil society's role was to legitimize resistance against the state authority intruding upon the private sphere. In short, we can understand the starting point of Western civil society as the liberalism that is strongly suspicious of the expansion of the state's public authority. In Korea, the concept of civil society appeared during the 1980s' democratization movement. During this period, the concept of civil society began to be widely circulated in academic and movement circles. What this means is that in Korea, the issues of civil society and the democratization movement have an intimate relationship. In Latin America and the socialist countries of Eastern Europe, the concept of civil society also saw a rebirth in the 1980s, the period when changes began to take place in spheres that were autonomous from the state.

When the concept of civil society began to take root in Korea, it was used to represent the relationship of tension and conflict between the highly centralized authoritarian state and democratic civil society. Civil society meant "civil society against the state." It was an attempt to define the democracy movement as a civil rights movement, and demands of those who opposed the authoritarian state, and civil society, accordingly, as the social base of the democratization struggles. In this way, civil society was defined as a popular movement space where the universal and public interests of the citizens are organized in opposition to the authoritarian state. Thus, the formation of civil society in Korea is very different from its original birth in Western Europe.

Earlier I defined civil society as "a sphere where voluntary associations are organized." What this means is that civil society is fundamentally representative of and is based on the sphere of private interests, and that any interest and participation of it in the public sphere also represents, and is based on advancing and promoting private interests. In contrast, civil society in Korea acquired meaning as a mass movement space where the universal rights of the citizenry in general, or the public interest, were pursued. In this movement space, the individual is understood as an "active citizen" pursuing the public interest. This created a very negative perception of the expression of private interests and any organized activities based on such interests in Korea. In short, the concept of civil society in the Korean context, unlike in its original context, acquired meaning as a public sphere created by "active citizens."

Liberalism and Civil Society

As seen in the writings of Hobbes or Locke, the state or political society in liberal political philosophy was the end point of a deductive logic that began with the principle of the private sphere, and it includes the principle that individual rights and freedom have priority over the state. The principle of the minimal state and the freedom of the individual from coercion constitute the nucleus of the liberal theory. To David Hume, Adam Smith, Adam Ferguson, John Miller, and other Scottish Enlightenment thinkers, civil society is even more clearly defined. They defined civil society to theoretically justify the social changes that can be best described as commercial activities, commercial society, or money-making society. In their theory, civil society has the first role, and that of the state follows as the maker and implementer of the rules that complement civil society and also as the maker of institutions. To these Enlightenment thinkers, the distinction between public and private spheres is clearly made. Locke defined civil society through the concept of the state of nature. To Locke, the state of nature was one in which each individual was born with freedom and equality but one where social conditions were somewhat unstable. Civil society is a condition where order is added to the state of nature, and the state has a meaning only as a surrogate civil society.

In contrast, in the case of Korea, the distinction between public and private spheres is very unclear because civil society in Korea was built on a different foundation and under different conditions from those of the West. In Korea, civil society was not created on the foundation of the priority of property rights or for the purpose of protecting private economic interests in the market. Rather, it was the struggle against centralized political power, the protection of democracy, and the democratic public sphere that were the primary purposes of the formation of civil society. Accordingly, civil society in Korea is weak in liberal tradition but very strong in its democratic orientation. In short, in Korea, the context and tradition of the democracy movement were very important in the formation of civil society and the public spirit, or the value of the public good, as expressed by the movement dominated its discourses. In this regard, it is difficult to understand civil society in Korea through the dichotomous prism of public vs. private spheres; nor can one understand it as that which represents the private sphere as opposed to the state or the political society that represents the public sphere. If an attempt were made to define civil society strictly in terms of public and private spheres as discussed above, one would find that no civil society exists in Korea where the ideas of the private sphere and the individual are weak.

Civil Society and the Development of Democracy

The question is then, does the development of civil society automatically result in the introduction of democracy and its flourishing? The experience of the West in the 1920s and 1930s illustrates that it does not. There is no better example of this than the emergence of the Nazi regime. Sheri Berman's study of the collapse of the Weimar Republic merits attention in this regard.[1] The strong development of voluntary associations in society constitutes the core building block of civil society, as discussed by Tocqueville. The Nazi example in Germany, however, shows the result of a reverse relationship between the strong development of free associations in civil society and the intransigence of national political institutions and structure. The immature political structure and party system in Germany did not respond to the demands of the increasingly mobilized masses. On the contrary, the political structure interfered with meaningful participation of the masses in public life. Consequently, the energy and the interests of citizens were channeled into the activities of private associations limited by narrow private interests. The activities of a dynamic civil society contributed, not to pushing political parties and politics to address public interests, but to holding them back. By doing so, they gradually and increasingly weakened the power and

---

1 Sheri Berman, "Civil Society and the Collapse of the Weimar Republic," *World Politics* 49 (1997).

importance of political parties and politics. Ultimately, when a critical situation presented itself, the Nazi party, with its unified vision, program, and proposals for bold solutions, took the opportunity. Thus, the Nazi party ruled legitimately, having come to power by election in a democracy. In a context different from that of Berman, E. E. Schattschneider emphasizes the difference between interest group politics that privatize and localize conflicts and the party politics that broaden conflicts nationwide;[2] in this way he emphasizes the fact that for democracy the latter is essential.

In Korea, too, before democratization, private interest groups were widely organized as in the West. It is too simple and formulaic to look at democratization or democratic development as a function of the existence of civil society or the quantitative growth of civil society. What is important is not the quantitative expansion of civil associations, but their political content. One could say that civil society is for and of citizens, when voluntary associations can reach a certain public consensus with democratic values at its center. In this context, civil society in Korea went through cycles of expansion and contraction. The expansion cycles took place with the following periods as their apexes: the post-liberation period of 1945 to 1948; the April 19th revolution period of 1960 to 1961; the "Seoul Spring" and Kwangju Uprising period of 1979 to 1980; and the June Uprising in the period of the late 1980s. These were the periods of heightened mass movement and they were marked by a condition in which the state had difficulty in imposing its demands on society.

2. On the Thesis of "Civil Society against the State"

The Democracy Movement and Civil Society

Earlier in this chapter we observed that the concept of civil society in Korea emerged in the process of the democratization struggle against the authoritarian state; that civil society in this context was understood as representing the public interest; and that this can be understood as exemplifying the thesis of "civil society against the state." I also pointed out that these aspects of civil society were most easily seen in the heightened periods of the democracy movement, during widespread mobilization of the masses in civil society against the state. Does this fully explain the special characteristics of civil society in Korea? What is the nature of civil society when the movement is not at its peak? Is the explanatory model of "civil society against the state" applicable in the post-democratization era? To answer

2 E. E. Schattschneider, *The Semisovereign People: A Realist's View of Democracy in America* (Hinsdale, IL.: The Dryden Press, 1975).

these questions, it is necessary to examine how the interest groups, other voluntary associations, and the democracy movement—i.e. the building blocks of civil society—existed and functioned under the authoritarian rule in Korea. Only then can one understand why the elements of civil society, with the exception of the movement, failed to have an impact on building civil society in Korea.

The core of voluntary associations in modern capitalist societies is composed of interest groups. Primarily, the growth and power these groups enjoy are functions of economic development. The interest groups in Korea also grew in the process of economic development and have increased their influence accordingly. In the case of Korea, economic development did not take place at the level of the private sector, independent of the political conditions defined by the authoritarian regime; rather it was the result of the authoritarian state policy. Accordingly, the existence and the activities of voluntary interest groups were vertically and hierarchically integrated by the state for the purpose of economic development and political stability. Large and powerful interest groups were controlled by the authoritarian state through state support of such organizations, and smaller interest groups were integrated as a part of these larger umbrella organizations. In other words, in return for accepting authoritarian state control, these interest groups received opportunities to maximize their special interests. Korea Employers Federation, Federation of Korean Industries, Federation of Korean Trade Unions, National Agricultural Cooperative Federation, and Korean Federation of Teachers' Associations are major examples of such large and powerful interest groups. During the authoritarian period, these groups formed the flourishing *kwanbyŏn tanch'e* (*gwanbyeon danche*) or "government-circle organizations," and maintained close ties with state organizations in which give-and-take exchanges took place. This is a typical relationship found in state corporatism[3] where the state provides interest

---

3 State corporatism: Corporatism has two sub-types; one is societal corporatism, and the other is state corporatism. In the former, the development and activities of interest groups are represented and mediated from below, freely and spontaneously, without any external restriction or intervention by the state. In the latter, however, the state imposes the system of corporatism for the purpose of controlling major interest groups from above. O'Donnell applied the concept of state corporatism to his theory of bureaucratic authoritarian state. He defined state corporatism as a system in which the state imposes a repressive system by force in order to incorporate, or exclude, the popular sector, especially the working class, from political system. O'Donnell identified state corporatism as the core element of a bureaucratic authoritarian state. Philippe C. Schmitter, "Still the Century of Corporatism," *Review of Politics* 36 (1974); Guillermo A. O'Donnell, *Modernization and Bureaucratic Authoritarianism* (Berkeley: University of California Press, 1973).

groups with protection and special privileges for the monopoly of representation in their functional interest areas in exchange for the groups' support and loyalty to the state.

However, it is too narrow to define civil society merely as a lineup of non-governmental or private organizations and institutions. Civil society also deals with the ethics and morals of society by producing and defining knowledge, ideology, culture, and norms. What is essential in civil society at this level is the absence of ideological and institutional dictatorship. No doctrine or ideology must be worshipped as sacred; and any social order or consensus must be the result of free and rational communication. From this perspective, the important question to ask is not whether civil society exists, but how it exists. Ultimately, what is important is the level of structural and ideological pluralism. In this regard, civil society in the authoritarian period in Korea was extremely limited. The state, the non-governmental institutions, and ideology in general were strongly hierarchical, homogeneous, and monopolistic. The repressive structure created by the strong authoritarian state, the non-governmental institutions and organizations that were hierarchically bonded to the state, and the Cold War anti-communist ideology, fundamentally restricted the plurality and autonomy of civil society in Korea. Under the circumstances, it was only the grassroots movement, not the private interest groups or institutions that could create the space and public sphere, that were autonomous from the political power and the state.

The Characteristics of Authoritarian Industrialization and Civil Society

Unlike in the West, the Korean private interest groups and the liberal ideology that has roots in such groups, did not function to promote civic order and public consensus. More than anything else, the divisions between political system and the economy, and between state authority and private interests, were ambiguous and the vulnerability of civil society was unavoidable. In Korea, it was not the bourgeoisie but students and intellectuals (the "active" group among the educated urban middle class) who created the public sphere to realize the great cause of democracy and to realize civic values and norms. They led the movement. Given that private interest groups were bonded to the authoritarian state and monopolized the representation of national interest, civil society, or the voluntary public sphere, could only be created by the collective struggle of the supporters of democratic values, i.e., those whose participation was excluded from policy decision-making, the weak in society, marginal groups, and socially critical forces.

As has been pointed out earlier, in its origin, civil society has a close connection with capitalist industrialization. While a strong authoritarian developmental state led the industrialization of the country, the *chaebŏl* in Korea were the greatest beneficiaries and locomotives of economic development. Their power and influence were indirect in the political arena, but in the economy and social spheres they were direct and overwhelming. Basically, civil society was subjugated to the economy. Liberal ideology was weak, and conditions were very limited for the ideology and values of democracy to develop through normal institutions. It is difficult for state authoritarianism at a political level, authoritarianism in the private sector including non-governmental organizations and corporations, and intolerant Cold War anti-communism to coexist with democratic or liberal values. The democracy movement and *minjung* movement emerged from within and without the private organizations that were controlled by state corporatism. However, the mass movements did not have institutional characteristics, for a grass-roots movement was by nature organizationally unstable, intermittent, and short-lived.

Political Society Separated from Civil Society

In Western political thought, viewed in particular from a modern liberal perspective, the state is not a natural institution but merely a human convention. Even in the medieval period, where the liberal ideology of the state and civil society has its origin, political authority was viewed as one of many institutions in society. In Western liberalism, the dualism of civil society and political society presupposes that a basic homogeneity exists between the state and society. In Lockean terms, in essence, the development of civil society from the state of nature starts with the creation of the parliament, the legislative body. Therefore, to Locke, civil society and political society were one and the same. It needs to be pointed out that Locke contrasted civil society with the state of nature, not with the state as we do today. Here the concept of representation connects civil society to the state, and the state then has meaning as the representative body of civil society.

The logic of liberalism expands along the following line of argument. First, the fundamental base of society is the individual who has inalienable natural rights. Next, civil society is composed of these independent individuals, and it has a tendency to be self-sufficient. Finally, the state is elected by individuals in civil society and is composed of representatives that those individuals have agreed upon. In the West, classical liberalism and the long struggle for modern constitutionalism against absolute monarchy from the seventeenth to the nineteenth century have created a mistrust of the state, along with the concept of "negative" liberty.[4] Accordingly, the principle of the priority of civil society over the state was developed, from philosophical perspectives, with a focus on individualism, the individual rights and freedom of private interests, the private sphere, etc. Consequently, as Locke said, the state was merely a "fiduciary" of civil society.

The situation in Korea was fundamentally different from the West. In the Korean intellectual tradition, the state existed before individuals, and the notion of society did not exist. The supremacy of the state in Korea has its historical roots in the long centralized bureaucracy that never had a feudal system with plural centers of power. Philosophically, the notion has been maintained through Confucian tradition. Moreover, the experience of Japanese colonial rule, the U.S. military occupation that ended with the partition of the Korean Peninsula into two states, and the Cold War further preserved and strengthened the priority of the state. In the process, the foundation for arguing the legitimacy of the private interest over the public interest was very weak. The public and private spheres, the state and civil society may have been separated, but the boundaries were ambiguous, and civil society was subjugated to the state to the extent that one could say that the former was absorbed by the latter. Accordingly, the formation of civil society as a separate sphere from the state began with the opposition movement against the authoritarian state.

The party system, the mediator between the state and civil society, became a top-down system, an auxiliary body to the state. Accordingly, political society was characterized by its separation and alienation from civil society. After the Korean War broke out in 1950, political society in Korea became institutionalized, centered around political parties on the right of the ideological spectrum, and around interest groups controlled by the state. Afterwards, civil society in Korea was divided between organizations that collaborated with the state through the network of state corporatism, on the one hand, and the marginal forces that were alienated and excluded from it, on the other. The former was integrated into the structure of Cold War anti-communist hegemony, and it could be characterized as the depoliticized sector of civil society. The latter, marginal elements, were not integrated. The

4 Negative liberty, positive liberty: Two concepts of Isaiah Berlin's. Negative liberty is the liberty from certain external authority, such as the state, or from others' coercive intentions. On the other hand, positive liberty is the liberty to do what one wants to do, or to achieve one's goals. In political science, negative liberty often means the right not to be violated or intervened in by the state, while positive liberty means the right to participate in the management of a community or the state. Isaiah Berlin, "Two Concepts of Liberty," *Four Essays on Liberty* (Oxford: Oxford University Press, 1969).

fact that the institutionalization of political society took place under Cold War anti-communist hegemony where entry into politics was allowed only to the right wing meant that there was a large gap between political society and the rest of civil society. When a civil society that is founded on a liberal social order cannot be widely represented with an open ideological spectrum, it is inevitable that the party system does not properly represent it.

3. A New Thesis: "Civil Society vs. Civil Society"

The Change in Civil Society after Democratization

The thesis of "civil society against the state" has limited application after democratization. In other words, civil society in Korea no longer has the integrity that it demonstrated during the democratization struggles. Civil society after democratization is in a condition where it can no longer play the role of the guardian of democracy, to protect it and to advance its causes. Thus, civil society after democratization in Korea must be understood with a new thesis, i.e. the thesis of "civil society vs. civil society." The fact that civil society after democratization must be understood differently from before is intimately related to the theme of this book. What changes have there been in civil society after democratization?

One can understand civil society by its placement within the structure of a particular relationship between the state and civil society. Under the authoritarian regimes, the state and civil society had the following relationship. First, the state managers—i.e., the president and the non-elected authoritarian ruling elite in the administration and the parliamentary elite who make up the majority of the elected representative body—constituted the membership of the conservative elite cartel of society. They shared a very homogeneous ideological and personnel profile. Under the authoritarian state and the hegemony of Cold War anti-communist ideology, civil society was co-opted and controlled through the apparatus of state corporatism. The autonomy and pluralism of civil society against the state were severely restricted. Accordingly, the state was concentric in structure, and Cold War anti-communism was the dominant ideological influence. Under this condition, civil society against the state was a realm that was not fully integrated into the authoritarian state rule. Instead, the non-integrated realm emerged and was expanded as an activated and politicized social space, on the margins of the strongly integrated civil society within the authoritarian state rule, or the conservative hegemony, to bring together forces against the state. Indeed, they became the social and political base for the democracy and *minjung*, or popular, movements in Korea. In other words, under the authoritarian regimes, civil society was divided into two camps. One was the conservative civil society integrated within the state-centered hegemonic structure, and the other was the non-hegemonic civil society that functioned as the base of the democracy movement.

On the other hand, after democratization, the relationship between the state and civil society changed. First, the state managers, i.e., the elected ruling elite with the president at the center, and the government bureaucrats who came of age in the authoritarian regime, had great differences between them in terms of their interests, ideology, and political orientation. Many of the parliamentary elite elected after democratization had the experience of participating in an opposition party or democratization movement. Unlike in the past, these National Assembly members were not the conservative elite cartel members. Thus, the state structure became eccentric, with the state bureaucrats and elected officials no longer forming a homogenous group. With such profound changes in the overall personnel makeup of the state system, the role of the civil society that was formerly integrated as a part of the state system under the authoritarian regimes also changed. Under the democratic governments, this civil society was no longer vertically integrated. Increasingly, its members were vociferous detractors of the heterogeneous elements that had newly entered the state sphere, such as those who were involved in the opposition party or the democratization movement in the past.

The Substitution of the Authoritarian State by the Press

A new phenomenon that emerged after democratization is that the dominant conservative newspapers came to play a greater role than ever in the public sphere where public opinions are formed. Currently, the press in Korea functions as the guardian and spokesperson for the old order and the Cold War anti-communist hegemony. At a time when the overall makeup of the state power structure is becoming increasingly more heterogeneous, or eccentric, and when the Cold War anti-communist hegemony is becoming weaker in comparison to the past, the press took on the role of strengthening the hegemony of the status quo within the state system, and of coalescing and maintaining the conservative hegemony in civil society. Why has the press come to play such a role? In the military authoritarianism of the past, it was not necessary for the press to take this role. The state maintained the concentric character of its ruling elite structure and secured its hegemony. Democratization, however, was the very force that changed the concentric structure of the state, and it changed the personnel makeup of the ruling elite. In other words, a certain dislocation has taken place in the relationship between the ruling elite of the state and the formerly hegemonic sector of civil society. It was the conservative sector of civil society that attacked the ruling elite under such a condition, and the press spoke on behalf of the detractors. After democratization the press came to represent the voice of the most upper-class segment of the supporters of the status quo and to coalesce its demands.

Under these circumstances, the ideological issues surrounding the Cold War anti-communist hegemony intensified the conflict, and the forum for public debate in civil society, i.e., the press, became the central axis of the conflict. The focus of conflict also shifted from that between the state and civil society, to that within civil society. In other words, conflicts were focused now on those between the conservative hegemonic sector of civil society and the movement sector, the post-Cold War generation critical of the old order. Today in civil society, at least in appearance, the conservative sector has the ideological hegemony. As a result, democratization and ideological pluralism that must further be developed as sub-system levels of society are being delayed. In the political system in general, further development of democratic processes are being hindered.

The structural changes in the state and civil society began with the launching of the Kim Young-sam administration (1993–1997), but the outlines of the changes became clearer during the Kim Dae-jung administration (1998-2002). In terms of birth origins and life experiences, the ruling elite in the Kim Dae-jung administration were much different from the members of the conservative elite cartel. Also, the shift in the North Korea policy during the Kim Dae-jung administration, in which the government pursued the "Sunshine Policy" of seeking "harmony and coexistence" with North Korea, began to clash ideologically with the status quo Cold War anti-communism; the clashes resulted in large structural changes in the state and civil society.

After democratization, hegemony was the most important standard that distinguished the Kim Young-sam administration from the Kim Dae-jung administration, the two democratic governments. By embracing the conservative sector of civil society and Cold War anti-communism, the Kim Young-sam government secured a hegemonic base, while one could say that the Kim Dae-jung government was a government without hegemony. What happened to this government without hegemony? First, there appeared a phenomenon in which the nucleus of state power with the president at its center began to link and cooperate with the movement sector of civil society. The Kim Dae-jung administration had an inclination toward democratic reform, but only an intention; it did not fully have a support base within the state structure in terms of ideology, program, and leadership. Accordingly, it needed to secure support and backing from civil society, from outside the sphere of the state. To state the conclusion first, solidarity between the ruling elite and the movement sector of civil society did not allow the Kim Dae-jung government to secure hegemony in favor of reform. By not taking a firm stand against the conservative hegemony of vested interests, the Kim Dae-jung government failed to secure active support from the movement sector of civil society. Ultimately, the government's non-hegemonic position did not change, the conflict with the conservative sector of civil society escalated, and both the government and the civic movement became weakened simultaneously.

Should the Thesis of "Civil Society against the State" Be Discarded?

Should the thesis of "civil society against the state" then be discarded? Has the axis of the conflict between an authoritarian state and democratic civil society disappeared? The answer is "no." This answer is not based on the theory of substantive democracy or the perspective of the maximalist conception of democracy of the revolutionary socialist tradition, which argues for the abolition of the state; rather it is rooted in a Tocquevillian notion. When Tocqueville analyzed the results of the French Revolution, he pointed out the paradox; the old system was changed by democracy, but the *ancienne société* is preserved because of the weakness of civil society, and in step with this the centralization of state power continues. This is the phenomenon that Tocqueville took as the central theme in his study of the French Revolution.[5] In Korea also, the centralized bureaucratic administrative bodies have continued to develop even after democratization, and their dominant position over society has continued. In fact, as far as centralization is concerned, nothing has changed after democratization. Accordingly, the thesis of civil society against the state can still provide a theoretical support for emphasizing and practicing freedom of association, decentralization of urban centers, and decentralization of the concentric power structure of the elite. With democratization as the starting point, the axis of the greatest social conflict shifted from that between civil society and the state to within civil society. Despite this fact, at another level, the strong state-centered character of Korean society must still be monitored closely.

Now there remains the question of how civil society in Korea has fulfilled its role under democratic governments, and how it has contributed to enhancing the quality of democracy. I mentioned above that the conservative

5 Alexis de Tocqueville, *The Old Regime and the French Revolution* (Oxford: Blackwell, [1856] 1947).

hegemony in civil society has strengthened after democratization. What this means is that in the case of *chaebŏl*, for the large-interest groups from the private sector, and entrenched ideological bodies and institutions—in other words the sub-systems and organizations in society that have their material base in the economy and which were the prop and stay of the authoritarian state—their autonomy from the state has been fortified. Did the increase in their autonomy mean that they contributed to the strengthening of the liberal foundation in Korea and thereby contributed to democratization? The answer is obviously no, because, more than anything else, these sub-systems and organizations function as classrooms for authoritarianism dominated by the culture of Cold War anti-communist ideology, patriarchal authoritarianism, and paternalism. The amount of resources they could mobilize is large enough to overwhelm society, and their hegemonic influence in the venues of public discourse is secured through the big newspapers. As long as they constitute the core of Korean conservatism and resist democratic reform, it would be difficult to expect substantial development of democracy in Korea.

4. The Weakening of Civil Society and Democracy in Korea Today

Civil Society without Pluralism

During the Kim Dae-jung and Roh Moo-hyun administrations, civil society in Korea expanded. However, it was a passive result brought on by the incompetence and weak leadership of the ruling power. In other words, it was not the result of an expansion of the sector of civil society that aspires to active democratic reform; rather, it was the result of a growth of conservative civil society. This is a phenomenon where the expansion and contraction cycle of civil society under authoritarianism has been reversed.

Many Koreans understood democratization as freedom for the market and the private sector—freedom from authoritarian state intervention or restrictions. Indeed, after democratization, it can fairly well be said that business liberalization and the eruption of individual self-interests have become the most prominent features of Korean democracy. This trend became more firmly entrenched in Korean society after the IMF bailout crisis, when the government pursued a neo-liberal economic reform, and when the neo-liberal values, such as market efficiency and competition, and meritocracy, became pervasive throughout society. In tandem with this, the two central axes of civil society in Korea, one pursuing the organization of private interests and the other pursuing public interests, have greatly expanded and become active. I am not aware of any data that show that bolstering market autonomy and actively feeding individual self-interests resulted in expanding the number of free associations in civil society. Nevertheless, without doubt, a quantitative expansion of volunteer associations can be expected, and the scope of civic movement has expanded greatly to include such areas as the anti-nuclear peace movement; voter participation campaign and election-monitoring activities; evaluation of political party candidates; the anti-corruption movement; consumer information and protection; environmental protection; and the women's movement. At the same time, as for the hegemonic forces from the old regime, instead of becoming weaker as a result of the spreading democratic values, they have become stronger through conservative mainstream newspapers. We can characterize such a phenomenon as "civil society vs. civil society." Cold War anti-communism continues to cast a shadow on the interests of labor, and the values of social welfare and redistribution of wealth, which are essential if workers are to enjoy social and economic benefits as full citizens in our society. The other dominant ruling ideology from the old regime, the development ideology of the authoritarian industrialization, has deftly grafted itself onto the neo-liberal ideologies of market efficiency and competition and has come back to us with a new face.

In short, despite its expansion in numbers and size, democratic civil society brought the paradoxical phenomenon of weakening, rather than strengthening, democratic and liberal foundations. This is because civil society in Korea was unable to develop the values of democracy and liberalism that could replace the ideological hegemony of the vested interests from the old regimes; furthermore, it thus embraced uncritically the anti-labor development ideology from the authoritarian era and the values and ideology of neo-liberalism. One can say that civil society contributed actively to spreading the neo-liberal principle of market efficiency and competition, as John Dunn said, promoting "a narrow egoist individualism at the expense of free, inventive and generous individuality,"[6] which is at the heart of neo-liberalism. In the meantime, civil society failed to broaden democratic citizenship and to create conditions that would strengthen the democratic social foundation through such an expansion. Thus, despite the fact that it was the social base of democratization, and the fact that it flourished under democracy, at least in numbers, civil society revealed clear limitations as it became absorbed and integrated into the hegemonic order of the old ideology. Accordingly, in organizing alternatives to solve the various problems that society faces, civil society cannot speak in one voice, representing homogeneous interests and

6 John Dunn, *Setting the People Free: The Story of Democracy* (Atlantic Books, 2005).

values. In a democracy, such a role is played by political parties. Thus, it is unrealistic and undesirable to mystify civil society as a non-political sphere that represents the universal values of society.

Civil Society without Labor

In Korean society, there is nothing that demonstrates the salient characteristics of civil society better than the status and role of the workers. Despite democratization, the worldwide end of the Cold War, and the great softening of the relations of hostility and confrontation between North and South Korea, the workers still cannot organize themselves politically in Korea. There is no relevant political party[7] that workers can vote for as a class, and their interests and perspectives are not recognized as important agenda items in the public sphere. The fact that labor is not politically represented is an important factor that weakens civil society, and this has a negative impact on the development of democracy. That is to say, although labor represents only one sector and only one special interest group among many in civil society, it is the most important collective body in modern capitalist society, in terms of its function and its number. Accordingly, political exclusion of labor interests and perspectives amounts to an exclusion of the most significant potential force for suggesting competitive ideologies for the creation of public goods, such as social integration, social welfare, and social justice. Also, this exclusion can only create negative impacts in terms of social class structure and the inequalities produced by the market, and in terms of checking the *chaebŏl*'s unilateral advantage of power in the economy and society.

The most direct result of the exclusion of labor is that after democratization it contributed decisively to the regionalized organization of political

---

7 Relevant party: A concept of Giovanni Sartori. Many party theories build a typology of a party system on the basis of counting the number of parties. In this case, a difficult question is raised as to how to count the party number. The questions include the following: are all parties within the system equally counted, or else are they counted according to certain important variables such as the proportion of votes obtained, the number of seats in the legislative body, being able to participate in forming a coalition, and durability of the party? Early studies of party systems often set a more or less arbitrary numerical threshold for being considered as relevant, say, 5 or 10 percent of popular votes. Sartori criticized such arbitrary counting rules and instead proposed the criterion of relevance: relevant parties had to have either coalition or blackmail potential (or both). In other words, a party is relevant if it "affects the tactics of party competition" by having "coalition potential" or having "blackmail potential" which is possessed by an anti-system party or one that can veto political arrangements. Giovanni Sartori, *Parties and Party Systems: A Framework for Analysis* (Colchester: ECPR, [1976] 2005).

parties in Korea. Ultimately, this party system based on regionalism brought the retrogressive result of strengthening the traditionalist, rightist, and private-interest elements in the confrontations of tradition vs. modernity, right vs. left, and private vs. public. It contributed to the organization of society into vertical layers of special interests and a network of connections among them. In other words, regionalism in the party system in Korea is more a result of weak civil society than the retrogressive behaviors of the political elite.

Non-political and Class-blind Civil Society

As can be observed in the political behaviors found among the post-democratization generation, the generational issue, including that of voting patterns, has emerged as one of the most important factors that could bring changes to politics in Korea. The structure of Korean civil society does not easily allow organization of alternative forces, and the generational issue illustrates the Korean phenomenon of how solidarity is created under such circumstances. Generational solidarity in Korea is an example of the fluidity and unpredictability of civil society, where an instantaneous eruption of collective passion may occur at any time. This example also reveals the frailty of the mass movement sector of civil society. The socially critical movement sector of civil society has its base in the educated urban middle class, and the issues around which it is mobilized are becoming overwhelmingly non- or anti-political. Accordingly, from the ideological perspective of this sector, it becomes increasingly more difficult to embrace labor and other class issues. Consequently, the movement sector of civil society has little or no interest in forming solidarity with the labor movement and is contributing to the isolation of the labor movement.

Can one say that civil society in Korea is strong today? Some say it is. To them, a strong civil society against a strong state is what characterizes Korea. Overall, that is a reasonable argument, and was particularly correct when Korea was going through the democratic transition period. Today, however, at a time when democracy should advance to a level higher, we cannot say that civil society is strong. There is significant weakness. Democratic institutions at the level of national politics have been established at a satisfactory level; however, at the sub-system level, which is controlled by civil society's central hegemony, a reversal of democratization is taking place. The vested rights and interests that had become unstable because of democratization are now being restored again and strengthened. Their influence was restored and strengthened not by the state as in the past, but by and within civil society. In the process, the role of the large conservative press was decisive. Buoyed by the fact that they played an overpowering role in the public sphere, the conservative press redoubled its emphasis on Cold War anti-communist ideology, appropriated public reason, and revealed that it is a bigoted conservative hegemonic power that does not allow "a diversity of reasonable comprehensive doctrines." Conversely, the movement sector of civil society revealed a major weakness. It failed to create reasonable alternative doctrines. As a movement led by the educated urban middle class, it has ideological limitations that are growing while on the other hand the labor movement is fast becoming weakened. The fact that the movement digs its heels in on non- or anti-political issues is another factor. The more important factor is that the movement sector of civil society has failed to create and institutionalize opportunities and channels for widespread pluralistic civil participation. It relies on the intermittently erupting passion of the public (as expressed through candlelight demonstrations) to sustain itself.

Part IV

Conclusion

8 Democratization of Democracy

Conservative Democratization

The aim of this book was to examine certain characteristic elements, i.e., certain structural characteristics that are continually reproduced even to this day, that run through the sixty years of modern Korean political history. If there is a single outstanding characteristic of Korean politics from liberation until today, more than anything else, it is the underdevelopment of the political representation system, or the party system. The underdevelopment of the party system is an asymmetrical phenomenon in comparison to the overdeveloped state that became very strong during the long period of the authoritarian political system. The underdevelopment of the system of representation, the system that organizes and speaks for the interests and demands of civil society, has transformed political society, the middle stratum between the state and civil society, into an autonomous sphere alienated from civil society. The fact that political society has existed independently of civil society signifies that the political society in Korea existed as a class unto itself, wanting to realize its own interests rather than representing and being accountable to the interests of the public at large.

What is interesting is that despite the limit of public participation, macroscopic changes have taken place from state formation to industrialization to democratization. In the sense that an elite-led reform took place without the participation of the masses, I have characterized Korean politics as manifesting a tendency exemplified by the phrases, "passive revolution," "revolution from above," and "conservative modernization," borrowing the concepts of Antonio Gramsci and Barrington Moore, Jr. Now, one more concept shall be added to the list, and that is "conservative democratization."

Korea achieved democratization against the odds presented by its Cold War anti-communist ideology, *chaebŏl*-controlled economic structure, and a social structure receptive to authoritarianism, including the massive state bureaucratic system. In earlier discussions, I have characterized this phenomenon by calling it "premature democracy," "democratization by popular movement," and "democratization by pact." At the beginning of democratization, the public was mobilized en masse as if civil society had exploded. In the "liberation space" of the post-liberation period, the bottom-up mobilization of the masses materialized in "premature democracy," and the June Struggle of 1987 resulted in "democratization by pact" that began with the June 29 Declaration. Today, however, "conservative democratization" is a term I use not to emphasize the democratic changes that have taken place but to highlight its unchanged aspects.

Cold War anti-communism and premature democracy formed a set in terms of social structure in Korea. It shaped a party system biased toward the conservatives, where two major political parties dominated politics based on an ideologically very narrow political representation system. In the past sixty years, the names of the political parties have changed over and over again, but the two-party system dominated by conservatives and molded under premature democracy has been unchanged. One of the two political parties was a derivative organization of the authoritarian state, while the other was the conservative party that had its roots in the KDP, which represented the interests of the landed class in the "liberation space." This conservative party with its roots in the KDP perpetually remained an opposition party under the authoritarian regimes, and thus many Koreans call it the "conservative opposition party."

The 1987 momentum for democratization also culminated in a conservative political order. What this signifies is that the democratic transition excluded widespread social demands and a reform agenda, and that it stopped at democratizing procedures for political competition only, based on a political pact signed by the elite. The conservative party system thus has not changed, even as the parties' names have changed. Furthermore, in this system of political representation, Korean society is deteriorating in many ways. Thus, the logical conclusion would be the emergence of a new party system. In the real world of politics, however, the old political forces are still dominant. Given that this situation continues, the possibility that reformist and progressive alternatives will emerge and break the conservative framework of democracy is weak.

Conservative democratization has given rise to the crisis of the party system. The system of political representation has failed to competitively represent widespread social change and demands. Having also failed to come up with an alternative, politics has become the target of public anger. It seems that it would be difficult to reduce the social dissatisfaction in Korea today without some fundamental changes. However, there is no political subject that detects such social dissatisfaction, recognizes it as a crisis, and responds to it accordingly. As long as this is the case, it would be difficult for politics to improve. Today, there are many basic problems that Korea faces, but the political parties and the party system that they comprise do not show a responsibility to meet social demands. When the political elite ignores society, society also knows how to ignore them. Society makes a mockery of politics and refuses to play the role of second fiddle to such politics. The decline of voter participation in Korea has to be understood as a desperate protest of the electorate against the repression of political alternatives.

The Repression of Conflicts and the Exclusion of Alternatives

A political party expresses and represents social conflicts and cleavages, and parties play the role of organizing various competitive arguments and issues regarding the public interest and the public good into policy alternatives. Indeed, a political party is an organization that mobilizes the masses. Depending on the result of the electoral competition, a political party can become the government or the opposition party, playing the role of the central actors in policy making or as organizers of critical alternatives, respectively. In a political process, the political parties are voluntary organizations that primarily express and represent social divisions and conflicts; however, they also embody the communal ties of society by providing hope for the future through the accomplishments of their policies or by presenting alternative policy visions.

In a democracy, "social consensus" does not mean a unanimous agreement; rather it refers to the process and its result in which the opinion of the majority is established through the competition of many alternatives. The authoritarian government in the past also frequently referred to "social consensus," by which it meant a unilateral government directive. Because of this, the authoritarian government tried in most cases to make up for a lack of legitimacy through macroscopic achievements, such as economic development, and sought to repress social conflicts in the process. Democracy is different from authoritarianism in that the former does not repress social conflicts. In other words, the difference is that democracy takes social conflicts and brings them into a political framework to build a social consensus. The role of a political party is to bring social conflicts into a political process where the conflicts are transformed into communal issues to be taken seriously by the entire society. In short, political parties express and represent conflicts and divisions, but their role is to organize alternatives based on those differences, compete in elections, and thus ultimately mitigate social conflicts for greater social unity. In this sense, political parties are the central political instruments of democracy. Accordingly, when political parties fail to properly carry out their role, democracy cannot develop, and it faces a crisis. This situation creates a stumbling block for the qualitative development of society. Ultimately, many problems faced by Korean society today have their cause in the underdevelopment of the party system. The problems of conservative democracy are clearly expressed in the crisis of the party system. The cause of this situation is found, more than anywhere else, in the fact that the party system in Korea is still tied up in the ideological framework of the past. The issues emerging from the post–Cold War neo-liberal era constantly require new perspectives and languages, while the framework and language of the Korean party system do not change. More than anything, political perspectives and methods must change.

As I have emphasized throughout this book, the party system based on Cold War anti-communism is characterized by its exclusion of the masses and labor. When the interests and demands of an important group in society are excluded, the narrowness of the party system is fortified. As a result, the gap between the party system and society inevitably widens; and at the same time, because politics cannot respond to central issues and conflicts of society, cynicism and indifference spread. Voter participation decreases, political parties become salons for the political class,[1] and it becomes the function of politics to guarantee the stable maintenance of vested interests. Such a party system, in turn, strengthens Cold War anti-communism, thus continuing the vicious cycle.

For democracy to function properly, the masses and labor—the groups that have not been socially integrated and politically represented—must enter into the political process. The political elite always speak of social integration, but to achieve it, cleavages and conflicts must be expressed and mobilized. In a democracy, integration refers to the expression and representation—through multiple competitive political parties—of social conflicts and cleavages. Only under these conditions can democracy function as an instrument that can mitigate and resolve social disharmony created by social conflicts.

1 Political class: A concept of the Italian political sociologist Gaetano Mosca. The concept was used to emphasize that even under representative democracy there exists a minority political elite who rule to pursue their own interests rather than those of the party members and supporters. Gaetano Mosca, *The Ruling Class* (New York: McGraw-Hill, 1939).

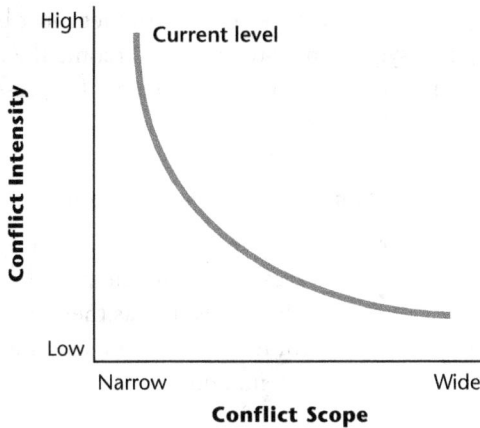

FIGURE 8.1 Inter-party Conflicts
Source: Author.

Generally, the scope of politically organized social conflicts can be mea-sured on a left-right ideological spectrum. However, in the case of Korea, where the ideological spectrum is very narrow, there can be little difference between the parties on the left-right spectrum. What Korea ends up with is politics based on regional sentiments. As long as there exists discrimination against a certain region and there is alienation associated with it, one can-not say that the politics of regional sentiment has no real basis. However, the politics of regional sentiment in Korea is fundamentally not a problem that came about because of regional differences or conflict. One must understand that it is a problem that has arisen out of the situation where important fac-tors of social cleavages could not become social issues or be raised as refer-ence points for political policies. In short, it is a problem that was created in the extremely narrow ideological spectrum caused by the strong influence of Cold War anti-communism. Accordingly, no amount of inter-regional reconciliation, official events promoting cooperation, and conscious-raising campaigns can change the party system based on regionalism as long as the conservative monopoly of the party system is not broken.

In the Korean party system, the scope of social cleavages represented by political parties is very narrow, as is the spectrum of their support base, while the intensity of inter-party conflicts runs very high. Paradoxically, the high degree of inter-party conflicts comes from the limited variety of con-flicts. The ideological foundations of the political parties are similar; the only way for the different parties to create differences among themselves is to emotionally incite the other and to mobilize hostile passion, which has little substance. In order to reduce excessive antagonism between political parties to an appropriate level, the scope of conflict must be expanded. In other words, the party system in Korea must overcome the closed structure of the conservative monopoly and open the system of representation so that it can widely reflect social demands.

Change in Voter Alignment and the Rigid Party System

Most voters in Korea show a desire for change. But election results do not reflect their preference because the existing political parties, being as conservative and intent on maintaining the status quo as they are, do not properly represent the desires of the electorate. The voters are thus alienated from the conservatively biased party system, and they do not vote. The following figure illustrates this phenomenon.

Figure 8.2 shows that the voter support market in Korea is divided in two. On the one side are voters who are leaning toward maintenance of the status quo; they are represented by the current conservative two-party system. Since this electorate market was developed in the authoritarian period, one could say that it is a backward-looking supporter market. It is in this voter market that the two conservative parties today have a monopoly. The other voter market is the one that is not represented by the existing party system. The voters in this market are critical of the existing party system and show a strong orientation toward change. As shown by the increasing number of non-voters in each successive election, this non-voting electorate market is becoming as big as the status-quo supporter market. The party system in Korea must be changed to represent their demands. That is to say, the scope of the conservatively biased system of political representation must be drastically expanded. If the existing political parties continue to be complacent, the instability of the party system will continue, and at the same time the rejection of the current party system by the voters will continue to expand.

The preference of the majority of the non-voters is largely leaning toward changing the status quo, but the specific changes and directions desired are unclear. It is the role of the political parties and leaders to define their demands and transform them into alternatives for public policy. Democracy is a political system where political parties and leaders competitively organize alternatives that the citizens then choose. How the parties and the leadership exercise authority depends on how conflicts are defined. Depending on how they define the conflicts and cleavages that are faced by Korean society today, the voter alignment and the scope of interested voters willing to participate in politics will change. When major conflicts in society and the interests and demands of the citizenry in general are not politically

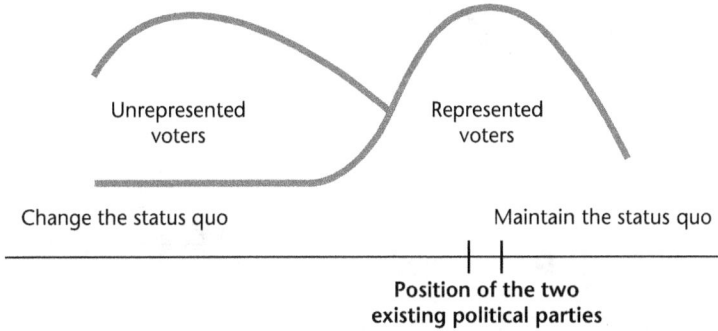

FIGURE 8.2 Party Competition, Voter Alignment, and the Conservative Party
Source: Author.

represented, democracy becomes biased toward serving the interests of the elite groups and the upper class, and thus the political participation of the public is minimized. The way to make the general public take interest in politics and participate is to politically mobilize and organize around conflicts that have impact on their interests, i.e. the central cleavages in our society. As has been emphasized by Schattschneider, democracy thrives on conflict.[2]

Today, the central factor of conflict in Korean society is the shock of post–Cold War and neo-liberal globalization. The conflict of Cold War vs. post–Cold War is not limited to the issue of North Korea policy. As mentioned earlier, the Cold War anti-communist political structure and social orders in Korea are deeply rooted. Everyday authoritarianism, the exclusion of labor, the system of discrimination and special privileges, the suppression of differences in opinion, and a great propensity for standardization are some aspects of Cold War anti-communism internalized in the Korean social structure and its sub-systems.

Although in a limited manner, the Cold War vs. post–Cold War conflict has been given an expression through public discussion of the "Sunshine Policy." On the other hand, the conflict brought on by neo-liberal globalization has hardly had any outlet for expression. The issue of neo-liberal globalization has imbedded in it the most classical and central question of modern capitalism, i.e. "How should the roles and functions of the state and market be divided in a democracy?" Unfortunately, among the political parties and the political elite in Korea, this is not an issue of social conflict. They are one and all sold on the idea of transforming Korea into a market economy and of excluding political discussion from the economy. This

2 E. E. Schattschneider, *The Semisovereign People: A Realist's View of Democracy in America* (Hinsdale, Ill.: The Dryden Press, 1975).

TABLE 8.1

Cleavage Structure in the Post–Cold War Neo-liberal Era

Post–Cold War

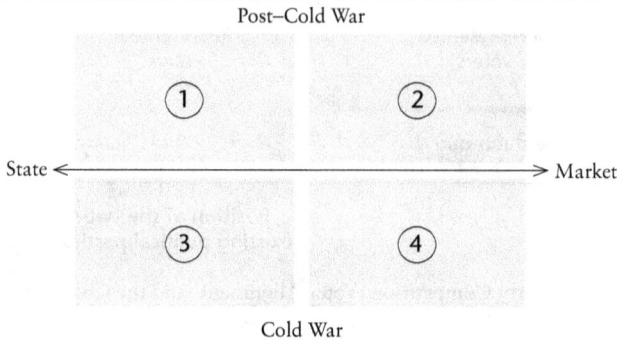

State ← → Market

Cold War

Source: Author.

market-oriented ideology is not only strongly advocated by *chaeböl* and the press, it is also the dominant argument in academia. Table 8.1 summarizes the discussion so far.

First of all, along the state vs. market cleavage line, differences between political parties cannot be found as of yet. Thus the only difference between parties is along the Cold War vs. post–Cold War cleavage line, or between quadrants (2) and (4). However, the Cold War vs. post–Cold War conflict debated by political parties remains narrow in scope, limited only to the North Korea policy issues. Quadrant (3), representing Cold War ideology and those who believe in state intervention in the market, signifies authoritarianism from the past. In reality this sphere does not exercise any significant influence. In quadrant (1), democratic values would be important, and discussions would take place on building national competence and resistance to neo-liberal globalization. In reality, this is unfortunately the space along the cleavage lines that is completely hollow. If we define today's society in Korea as a democracy, it is difficult to understand how quadrant (1) could be so hollow. It is the sphere where one would think about what a democratic state has to do in the post–Cold War and globalization era. As has been pointed out by the political scientist José María Marvell, when people realize that democracy brings social rights, is when democracy becomes consolidated.[3] Neo-liberal globalization has highlighted many social problems, including the income gap and job insecurity. As long as there is no faith that such problems will

3 José María Maravall, "Politics and Policy: Economic Reforms in Southern Europe," in *Economic Reforms in New Democracies: A Social-Democratic Approach,* ed. Luiz Carlos, Bresser Pereira, José María Maravall, and Adam Przeworski (New York: Cambridge University Press, 1993).

be addressed within democratic institutions—such as political parties, the National Assembly, and the government—the working class, although vulnerable in the labor market, will have little incentive to vote in elections.

The way to escape the government-led economy of the authoritarian past is not to minimize the scope of government's public policies and to transfer them to the market. Democracy is the power that mitigates the inequality effects of the market. Thus, in a democracy, politics must broaden its scope to include previously unattended issues, such as welfare and redistribution of wealth. The state is the only organization that could fully deal with the issues of the alienated, such as drop-outs from economic competition and the poor. When the state does not play this role, the class structure and discrimination under democratic government become more entrenched than ever. Today, in inter-party competition, the question of how the market and state should be reorganized in line with the principles of democracy is completely absent. Regardless of how strong the faith in democracy is on the part of the person occupying the Blue House, as long as this issue is not addressed, it would be difficult to expect changes in Korean society. The experience with the last two democratic governments in Korea amply illustrates this point. As long as the government does not have macroscopic alternatives and practical programs to simultaneously develop democracy and the market economy, it becomes difficult to escape from the *chaebŏl* and press hegemony that opposes every state intervention and from the conservative influence of the state bureaucracy that came of age under the authoritarian regime.

Moving into a Neo-liberal Democracy

The democratic governments that came to power after democratization in Korea have been more neo-liberal and more like market fundamentalists than the authoritarian governments before democratization. This is not to say that I would criticize them for having failed to wholly denounce neo-liberalism or to implement an alternative economic system that would be antithetical to neo-liberalism. I do not believe that a choice between neo-liberalism and a European-style welfare state is possible in Korea. It is also not true that a neo-liberal socio-economic path is the one and only viable path, nor is it true that nothing could be done about it.

As many studies have already corroborated, while it is true that neo-liberalism has had a dominant influence worldwide, there is a huge divergence from country to country on how it is practiced; even within a single country, its shape and content differ from one administration to another when it changes hands. What is salient about the results of these studies is not that economies of the world are converging on a single form of neo-liberalism, but that there is a considerable variety of neo-liberalism. Accordingly, I would like to emphasize that even within a neo-liberalist economic framework, it is possible to implement policy measures to curb its socially detrimental impact. In other policy areas such as labor and social welfare, too, it is possible to seek and develop alternatives that are more suitable for conditions in Korea.

It would be fitting to call the policy models pursued by the various administrations since the democratization of Korea a "Korean-style neo-liberal policy regime." That is because, and this point had been made earlier, the basic framework has been neo-liberalism, but it has at its core the growth-first ideology and values, the state-*chaeböl* alliance, and the exclusion of labor, all inherited from the development model of the historical authoritarian regime.

What is meant by "policy regime"[4] here is the basic framework of policy, or the structure and contents, adopted by a government to handle the economy. It encompasses the particular values and ideologies, the doctrine that theorizes and systematizes them, the policy measures to implement them, as well as the political and social consequences of these policies. Except during the inchoate period when such a policy regime emerges as an alternative to the dominant existing framework, the regime forges a far-reaching national consensus and, for that reason, lasts for a long time in most cases.

The formation of a policy regime is generally triggered by a specific political force challenging the incumbent, addressing the crisis of an existing policy direction. When it becomes a policy regime, however, it means that it has become a dominant regime that could galvanize support from an extensive base of the population or the electorate; accordingly, mainstream political parties come to accept and adopt them. In other words, the parties would not be fighting over whether or not to adopt the policy regime and its alternative policies but over how to more effectively and efficiently implement them.

Thus it is difficult to replace such a policy regime unless there is a widespread and growing popular sentiment—actually expressed in various public occasions—that the existing policy regime cannot address the socio-economic problems and crises of the time, unless such popular discontent leads to a spread of alternative economic theories and policy directions in

---

4 For more detailed discussion on the meaning of this term, its impact on competition between political parties, and theoretical importance, please see Adam Przeworski, "How Many Ways Can Be Third" in *Social Democracy in Neoliberal Times,* ed. Andrew Glyn (Oxford University Press, 2001), pp. 312–333.

public discussions, which a political party then adopts as its policy framework and uses to galvanize extensive support during an election, presidential or otherwise. This is precisely what the political parties have failed to do in Korea.

The nonsensical debate, in certain quarters, about the supposedly leftist policies of certain administrations apart, there is actually only one policy regime that is in operation in Korea; it is the combination of the worst of neo-liberalism and the historical growth-first policy. There is really no significant difference between major political parties, or between different administrations, in terms of socio-economic policies. This cannot but mean a weakened possibility for pioneering a different policy regime more in tune with democratic values.

Within the short period of less than ten years since the IMF bailout crisis, the underlying tone of policy has veered toward market fundamentalism, and all the more radically so in recent times. As a result, economy, politics, and social, cultural, and educational sectors in Korea have already been radically reorganized. If one were to say that Korea's radical pursuit of neo-liberalism does not mean that Korea is not a democracy, then one would have to redefine and recategorize this democracy as a "neo-liberal democracy."

What this means, in plain terms, is that economic democratization, or democracy in substance, has failed. Democracy after democratization in Korea did further develop in terms of institutional procedures. At the socio-economic level, however, democracy deteriorated after democratization, and the regression is still ongoing. This is the most salient characteristic of democracy after democratization in Korea; that is to say political democratization and economic democratization went counter to each other.

While the democratic governments in Korea pursued growth as their top policy priority and thus expanded market competition and the market-driven logic of efficiency to a far-reaching extent, the nation has been divided into two extreme poles, the haves and have-nots. Clearly democracy in Korea today has forsaken its role of mediating the ill effects of class inequality and social disintegration. What function, then, does democracy in Korea serve?

The Emergence of Super-*chaebŏl*

An examination of the issues surrounding the *chaebŏl* system more clearly enunciates the problems of the neo-liberal policy regime, which as I have said has been combined with the development model inherited from the historical authoritarian government to form the current "policy regime." Since the IMF bailout crisis, there have been much public debate and criticism in Korea surrounding the growth-first economic policy; the growing obesity of *chaebŏl* as the result of this policy; and the role of the top five to ten *chaebŏl* groups. There were talks about the concentration of the nation's corporate profit among them, as well as the concentration of their contribution to the nation's GDP, economic growth, and trade volume.

The rapid growth of Samsung after democratization is clearly a phenomenon that is distinct from the previous phenomenon of the familiar *chaebŏl* growth. Among the top ten *chaebŏl* groups, Samsung holds one-third of both the total revenue and profit; its contribution to exports is one-fifth of the national total; it generates 8 to 10 percent of the government's total tax revenue; and its shares makes up one-fourth of the total market capitalization of the Korea Exchange. It would be fitting to call this phenomenon the emergence of a "super-*chaebŏl*."

As of 2001, Samsung's share in terms of assets, liabilities, and other accounting categories among the top five *chaebŏl* was 30 to 40 percent. By 2004, the figure rose to over 50 percent in all categories. There is no other country in the world with the size of economy comparable to Korea in which a single business group is so dominant. This is indeed a new phenomenon. How did it come about? It would be nice if this phenomenal growth was the natural result of market competition, or the consequence of an efficient and rational corporate management, as the mainstream media or opinion leaders would like the public to believe. However, the reality is far from this claim. The role and the influence of this super-*chaebŏl* could not be put in check, even through the process of elections, the heart of any democracy, and certainly not in the policy decision and implementation process of the democratic governments thus elected.

What is important here is the fact that the emergence of a great economic power deforms democracy. From a macroscopic perspective, the productive system with a super-*chaebŏl* at the top of the pyramid interferes with the development of pluralism, a precondition for advancement of democracy. In other words, it makes the development of a decentralized and horizontal system of allocating the structural power of society difficult. Needless to say, hierarchical allocation of resources is not congruent with the pursuit of democracy.

Setting aside the socio-structural issues of pluralism, the growth of a super-*chaebŏl* also has a hugely negative impact on the economic system itself. When a business collaborates with a power outside of the economic sphere and enjoys a monopolistic position in the market, it naturally makes market competition and the creation of market efficiency difficult. It is well known throughout the world that *chaebŏl* ownership is hereditary and that key business decisions are often made at the whim of the reigning family tycoon.

This corporate governance structure is a system that is very different from not only the European "stakeholder capitalism" but also the U.S. system of division of ownership and management, accountability to shareholders, and transparency. (The European system is a decision-making structure and management principle in which not only the corporate managers and workers, but also public interest representatives of the community in which a business operates, participate.) The *chaebŏl* system is distinguished by the absolute power of the owner and the patriarchal, authoritarian, and paternalistic management style. Such a system is basically a legacy of authoritarianism from the era of developmental dictatorship; it is thus a system that is conducive to and inviting of authoritarian values and behaviors. What is even more problematic with this *chaebŏl* governance structure and its management style is that *chaebŏl* are being accepted as the symbol of the wealth created by the efficiency of market economy and that they are being benchmarked as a successful model of corporate organization.

The growth of a super-*chaebŏl*, the symbol of centralization of economic power in Korea, in many ways strangle and distort the operation of democracy. First of all, there is the power of money itself and the influence on election processes exercised by various media organizations that are the *chaebŏl* mouthpieces. Next, major policy decisions made by democratic governments are influenced by strong lobbying by mammoth corporations. There are three core public sectors in which the super-*chaebŏl* exercises its influence: the administrative, the legislative, and the judiciary branches of the government. The super-*chaebŏl* has systematically built up human networks in all three government branches. In other words, the super-*chaebŏl* has the ability to cross the line between public and private spheres of interests at will and to exercise osmotic influence. In this way, the boundary between government and private business, between public and private spheres have come crumbling down by the power resources of the super-*chaebŏl*.

The super-*chaebŏl* today is no longer the subordinate partner of the state as in the historical authoritarian period. Today the government not only accepts the values and policy programs proposed by *chaebŏl* but also actively utilizes and depends on the *chaebŏl* human networks; in other words, a new form of government-business relation is emerging. If necessary, the state would change a law, or allow it to be silent to give *chaebŏl* opportunities to realize profit, and the government thus becomes actively co-opted by the business. Equality before the law and the rule of law are prerequisites for any democracy, and as emphasized by the libertarian philosopher and economist F. A. Hayek, they are also prerequisites for the operation of market.

At least in relation to the super-*chaebŏl*, the governments that came to power since democratization in Korea have been unable to enforce the rule of law. Where the rule of law is strictly enforced is, in fact, extremely selective. The no-longer-new neologism, "the Republic of Samsung," is in fact an expression that emblemizes this alliance between the government and Samsung. There is probably no paradox more dramatic than the deformation of democracy in Korea brought on by the forging of an alliance between Samsung and the democratic governments which the people hoped and believed would deliver a substantive corporate reform. Again, the rise of the super-*chaebŏl* is the result of the policy regime in which the growth-first rational and the priority of market efficiency occupy a dominant position. It is no surprise then that this rise of super-*chaebŏl* was accompanied by the worst deterioration of the distribution of wealth in Korea since democratization.

Why Democracy Also Requires a Competent Government

The core problem of democracy after democratization in Korea that this book addresses is how to make a democratic government strong and competent. For this to happen, politics must play a central role in the democratic political process; since the central mechanism of that process is party politics, political parties and party system must be made sound and the social base strong. From this perspective, the development of the events so far has revealed many shortcomings. To understand why this happened, one needs to revisit the structure of the problem once more.

There are many differences between a modern representative democracy and the Athenian democracy of the classical period, the prototype of democracy. One difference, the subject of perennial debate and discussion, is the difference between representative democracy and direct democracy, a democracy where citizens with equal rights participate directly in the political process through a system of lottery. Another difference with the Athenian model is that in modern democracy, there is the problem of a state that is autonomous from society. As discussed in this book, the state is composed of a very large bureaucracy and a government that changes periodically through elections.

What would a competent democracy do specifically? It would run the state democratically and competently. During the period of the struggle to achieve democracy in Korea, the urgent issue was to shed the nation of authoritarianism; during such a stage, a dichotomous approach, of a democracy or no democracy at all, has its value. After democratization, however, such dichotomy is not helpful in understanding the problem. The important question is, how much democratization has been achieved, or how much actual advancement has been made in terms of resolving socio-economic

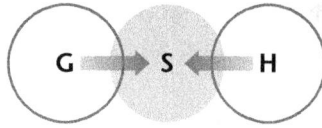

FIGURE 8.3 Structural Mechanics after Democratization
Source: Author.

demands and issues? In other words, democracy after democratization can be understood as a problem of degree within a spectrum.

The question is no longer whether Korea is democratic or not. The question now is about a democratically elected government running the nation effectively. In other words, it is about how much value we put on "competence." No matter how democratic the rules and institutions have become, elements of authoritarian legacy—the orientation, values, customs, and practices that founded and governed the nation under the old order; limited understanding about democracy; and the old-boy network—cannot automatically become democratized. Democratization of the state requires the competence of a democratic government; and while the state should represent the democratic government elected to power, the leadership and competence of its highest officer are also absolute requirements. In this regard, the question of whether a democracy is functioning well or not has a high correlation with whether or not the competence of a democratic leadership is demonstrated.

One can make a simple diagram of this issue, as in Figure 8.3. On the left of the diagram, "G" represents an elected government, while "S" represents the state with bureaucracy at its center, and "H" at the right represents the hegemony of the vested interests of civil society. Let us assume the force of democracy moves from left to right, while the force of vested interests moves from right to left. The state occupies the middle between these two forces. To make the state fully democratic, the force of the elected leadership must be strong. When that is not the case, the hegemonic force of the vested interests would greatly influence not only the state but also the elected government itself. The influence of the super-*chaebŏl* mentioned above is a case in point. What is important here is that there is a precondition for an elected government to be a competent government. It is the question of whether the elected government can mobilize democratic forces in society, how well it represents the democratic demands of society, and how it, thereby, establishes a firm and extensive support base.

It is not easy to address "competence" as one of the virtues a democratic government should have within a framework of democracy theory. There is not necessarily a cause-and-effect relation between a competent government and a democratic government; they are two different questions. A democratic government does not necessarily mean a competent one; conversely, a competent government does not necessarily mean a democratic one.

In theoretical discussions and in reality, democracy as a governing system has often been disparaged as a system of mob politics run by the ignorant and poor populace; and it has had challenges from the proponents of the "guardianship" theory, which gives more weight to the role of the elites who are supposed to have the expertise, wisdom, and experience more suitable to govern. Perhaps it is difficult to advance a democracy theory in which competence or excellence is recognized as an important virtue or value, but does not align itself with patricianism, elitism, or some form of management rationalism but with the grassroots elements, or the growth of grassroots power. Be that as it may, no one denies in reality that a competent leadership is decisive for the advancement of democracy.

A democratic government could perhaps competently run a macro-economy with little help from its support base by relying on the existing bureaucracy, expert groups, and the private sector. Or perhaps, a government that is incompetent in organizing human and intellectual resources to run the state could be competent enough to maintain its support base. Neither case would guarantee a progress of democracy. The best path would be for a democratic government to solidify its support base and at the same time successfully mobilize a wide network of human and intellectual resources and ultimately make sure that there is an extensive social base for democracy to firmly anchor itself. In other words, a cause-and-effect cycle has to be established in which what is democratic begets a competent system, and the competent system in turn strengthens the base of democracy.

Within the particular context of Korea, building a structure of such a cycle is all the more urgent. The reference point for measuring competence of the democratically elected governments in Korea has been the Park Chung-hee government. As is well known, this model is that of an authoritarian government that ruled at the expense of certain crucial democratic building blocks. Thus, whereas in advanced democracies the frame of reference for comparison is between democratic governments, in Korea the incompetence of a democratic government could very well, and directly, lead to the strengthening of the authoritarianism or elitism of the past model.

Modern representative democracy is a political system in which the idea of self-governance is realized through the principles of representation and accountability. Accordingly, as an elected representative, a democratic government bonds with its social base through the results of its governing behavior. This linkage between representation and accountability may be understood as having a dual function for and against an elected government. On the one hand, in terms of accountability, the system curbs the power and authority of an elected government so that it does not arbitrarily exercise them; on the other hand, in terms of representation, when the electorate supports the government and participates in democratic processes, the linkage can further strengthen the government's power and authority. That is to say, there is a direct relation between the advancement of the social content of democracy and the competence of a democratic government. What then would be the deciding factor that would make the competence of a democratic government supported not by elitism or expertism but by democratic forces in society and the government's support base?

It has been emphasized repeatedly in this book that the answer is a political system in which political parties are central. Democratic politics can be defined as a collective action in which, with a party system as a central mechanism, people mobilize the power of the masses by expressing and representing a wide spectrum of social conflicts and cleavages; they obtain power by winning elections and implement policy alternatives formed in this process; they then have to mobilize necessary social support to implement their policies.

One could say that the policy direction of an elected government is determined in the election process. The fact that a particular party and its candidate have won a majority vote means that the voters have given the winner a mandate to make their concerns and issues into concrete and viable policy programs and to implement them. This is how the linkage between representation and accountability, the core value of a representative democracy, is formed.

If "representation" means voters mandating a politician or a political party to represent their needs, then whoever is thus elected has the responsibility to meet and implement this mandate. Thus the minimum requirement to make any modern representative democracy a grassroots-oriented one is a government rooted in a party system. In advanced democracies outside of Korea, the ruling government is often referred to as a "labor" government, a "conservative" government, a "democratic" government, a "republican" government, or a "social democratic" government. In Korea too, governments should be party-based, not person-based. As a government, a good party would be a competent one; at the same time it would indeed be "a modern sovereign" and "an engine for democracy" that would strengthen the social base of democracy.

Index

abstentionism, 107, 107n
  accountability, 117, 117n, 137–138
  bureaucracy and, 126–127
  capitalism and, 199
  chaeböl and, 158
  delegative democracy and, 122–123,
    122–123n
  government incompetence and, 122–
    123
  horizontal, 126–127
  presidential, 133
  representation and, 202–203
  voter turnout and, 5
Ackerman, Bruce, 133
agenda setting, 15–17
Alavi, Hamza, 29
Almond, Gabriel, 96n
alternative government, 25, 25n
Althusser, Louis, 50n
Amsden, Alice, 64
anti-communism, 5–6
  centralization and, 59–60
  civil society and, 175–176, 181
  concentration of power and, 138
  constitution and, 48–49
  democratization and, 103
  expulsion of communists and, 30–31
  hegemony and, 118–119

  internalization of, 31–32
  nationalist movement and, 24–27
  polarization and, 49–51
  political parties and, 93
  premature democracy and, 43–44
  the press and, 177–179, 183–184
  regionalism and, 95–96
  repression of conflict and, 190–191
  structure of conflicts and, 14–19
Apollo Industrial Co., 153
April 3 Rebellion, 46, 46n
April 19 student revolution, 78, 89, 171
Arato, Andrew, 24n
Asiatic Research Center, 6–7
authoritarianism. *See also* Park Chung-hee
  bureaucracy and, 117, 126
  bureaucratic, 54, 55–57, 55–58, 87,
    146–147
  centralization and, 32–34, 138–139
  civil society and, 168–169, 172–174, 176
  Cold War and state-building and, 28–29
  constitutional process and, 46–49
  democratization and, 75, 85–86
  industrialization and, 53–72, 72–73, 82
  institutionalization of, 53–54
  Kwangju Uprising and, 105
  markets created by, 145–147, 150–156
  militarism and, 66–67n, 66–68

nostalgia for, 108–109, 163–164
political parties and, 94
presidential system and, 129–131,
    135–138
the press and, 78–80, 78n, 177–179
under Rhee, 39–41
social classes and, 73–74
social origins of, 54, 56–57
state-building and, 28–29, 113–114
autonomy, 128, 180. *See also*
    accountability

behavioral codes, 67–68
Berlin, Isaiah, 175n
Berman, Sheri, 170–171, 170n
bias, mobilization of, 95, 95n
Big Deal merger, 159
bureaucracy, 32–34
    accountability and, 117
    centralization and, 33–34
    civil society and, 179
    concentration of power and, 138
    corruption in, 127–128
    democratization and, 75
    executive branch and, 117
    incompetent, 125–128
    presidential system, 130, 133
    reforms of, 63
    the state and, 114–117
bureaucratic authoritarianism, 54, 55–58,
    87, 146–147

cadre parties, 7, 7n
Caesarism, 38–41, 40n
Capitalism, Socialism, and Democracy
    (Schumpeter), 51n
catch-all parties, 7, 7n, 36
Central Council for the Rapid Realization
    of Korean Independence (CRRKI),
    34
centralization, 32–34, 138–143
    dynamics of, 33–34
    easing, 142–143

industrialization and, 59–60
of power, democratization and,
    138–143
presidential system and, 130
CEO presidency, 131–132
chaebŏl, 53. *See also* economic
    development; industrialization
    Big Deal merger, 159, 159n
    bureaucratic elite and, 115
    business specialization and, 151, 151n
    centralization and, 138–140
    civil society and, 174, 180, 182–183
    conflict repression and, 193–194
    corporate elite and, 114
    corruption and, 147
    definition of, 8n
    democratization and, 150–151
    development of, 68–69
    globalization and, 149–150, 157, 158–159
    income inequality and, 8–9
    influence of, 74–75
    Kim Dae-jung and, 119–120
    labor and, 153–154
    liberalization of, 77
    market reform and, 148, 149–150
    markets created by, 145–147
    Park Chung-hee and, 68–69
    reforms, 62, 119–120, 150–151
    state power and, 163–165
    strengthening of, 160–163, 163–165,
        197–200
    super-, 197–200
chaeya movement, 85
Cheju Island Rebellion (1948), 46, 46n
Chŏnnodae, 152–153n
Chŏnnohyŏp, 152–153n
Cho Pong-Am, 35, 35n
Chosŏn dynasty, 29, 32
chronologies, 23, 53, 81
Chun Doo-hwan, 54, 77–80
    arrested, 133
    chaebŏl and, 151
    democratization and, 85–87, 105

elites and, 110
June 1987 Uprising and, 105–106
neo-liberal policy of, 149
opposition party and, 84
student movement and, 83, 85
civil service examinations, 10–11
civil society, 167–184
definition of, 167–168
democracy and, 170–173
democratization and changes in,
176–177
development of Korean, 167–171
labor and, 181, 182–183
liberalism and, 168, 169–170
political society vs., 174–176
the state vs., 178–180
strength of current, 183–184
vs. civil society thesis, 176–180
weakening of, 180–184
Western, 168–169
class. See social groups and
socioeconomic status
cleavages
definition of, 13n
globalization and, 157–160
IMF bailout and, 157–160
political parties and representation of,
137–138, 191–192
the press and, 17
regionalism and, 13–14, 95–96
social consensus and, 19
structure of conflicts and, 14–19
Cohen, Jean L., 24n
Cold War. See also anti-communism
advent of, 24–28
anti-communist ideology from, 5–6
civil society and, 175–176
ideological polarization and, 49–51
influence of in Korea vs. Japan, 38–43
overdeveloped state and, 28–29
premature democracy and, 43–44
collective action, 4–5, 17. See also mass
mobilization

colonial rule
authoritarianism in, 29
centralization and, 32–33
civil society and, 175
collapse of in Korea, 23–24
nationalism and, 24–27
overdeveloped state and, 29
Committee for the Preparation of Korean
Independence (CPKI), 27, 27n, 34
competition, 14–15. See also markets
centralization and, 140
for college admission, 9–12
conservatism and, 102
market reform and, 162
in markets, 146
newspaper market practices and, 17
conflict. See also regionalism
anti-communism and, 25–26, 49–51, 93
civil society and, 171, 178
consensus building and, 17–19
globalization and, 193–194
nationalist movement and, 24–27
political parties and, 136–138, 189–192
the press and, 178
representation of, 136–138, 189–192
role of the press in, 15–17
structure of, 14–19
Confucian culture, 32, 33, 138, 175
consensus building, 18–19, 42, 123, 136–
137, 189–192
conservatism
democratization and, 187–189
democratization by pact and, 100–110
economic reform and, 160–163
imperial presidency and, 131–132
modernization and, 89
nationalist movement and, 30
polarization and, 29–32
political parties and, 97–98
the press and, 16–17
reproduction of, 19
social consensus and, 18–19
social inequality and, 8

two-party system and, 34–38
voter turnout and, 5–6
Constitution
    amendments to, 41, 41n, 128–129
    democratization and, 100–101, 100n
    Park Chung-hee and, 71–72
    political party oppression and, 41
    on presidential authority, 128–129
    Round-Off Amendment, 41, 41n
    Selected Amendment, 41, 41n
    social reality and, 46–49
    three-term presidency and, 83n
corporatism, 154–155, 154–155n
    state, 172–173, 172n, 174
    supply-side, 155, 155n
corruption, 5, 121, 137
    bureaucracy and, 127–128
    chaeböl and, 147
    imperial presidency and, 131–132,
        134–135
    political parties and, 98
    social inequality and, 8
Council for Promoting Democratization,
    84n

Daalder, Hans, 104, 104n
Daewoo group, 151
Declaration of the Rights of Man and the
    Citizen (France), 47–48
delegative democracy, 122–123, 122–123n,
    134–135
democracy. See also democratization
    Caesarism and, 39–41
    centralization and, 140–142
    civil society and, 170–173, 179–180
    competition in, 102–103
    conservatism of Korean, 19
    consolidation of, 90, 90n, 193–194
    constitutional process and, 46–49
    continuous democratization of, 110
    definition of, 117
    delegative, 122–123, 122–123n, 134–135
    democratization of, 187–203

disenchantment with, 108–109
division of Korea and, 44
effects of industrialization on, 55–63
industrialization and, 63
institutionalization of, 98–100
market reform and, 160–163
militarism and, 66–68
minimalist conception of, 51, 51n, 129
national unity and, 44
neo-liberal, 194–197
opening spaces for, 72–80
under Park Chung-hee, 53–80
participation rates in, 3–7
pluralization and, 12
premature, effects of, 43–49, 188
presidential leadership in, 135–138
presidential system and, 129–131
the press and, 16–17, 78
representation in, 3–7
social consensus and, 18–19
social origins of, 54, 56–57
sustainable, 117–118
transition to, 53–54, 98–100, 108, 108n,
    118
value associated with, 71–72
Democratic Justice Party, 97, 100n, 118,
    118n
Democratic Korean Party, 84, 84n
Democratic Liberal Party, 97, 118, 118n
Democratic Nationalist Party, 94
Democratic Republican Party (DRP), 94
democratization, 59
    bureaucracy and, 124–128
    characteristics of Korean, 81–92
    chronology of, 81
    civil society after, 167–184
    concentration of power and, 138–143
    conservatism in, 100–110, 103, 187–189
    continuous, 110
    cost of, 108–109
    of democracy, 187–203
    economic significance of, 147
    as freedom from authoritarianism, 180

globalization and, 148–150
government incompetence after,
    117–121
industrialization and, 63, 74–77
labor and, 151–156
market reform and, 145–165
by pact, 92–103, 92n, 187–189
by popular movement, 188
deregulation, 149
desencanto, 108, 108n
developmental state theory, 64–68
di Palma, Giuseppe, 43, 43n
discourse alliance, 134
divide and rule strategy, 105–106, 106n
Downs, Anthony, 121–122, 121n
Dunn, John, 181
Duverger, Maurice, 7n

economic development, 56. *See also*
    industrialization
    centralization and, 138–140
    chaebŏl and, 69, 198–200
    democratization and, 103–104, 147, 197
    failure to reform, 163–165
    five-year plans for, 61, 63
    growth-first, 76–77
    growth-first strategy in, 76–77, 147,
        197–200
    imperial presidency and, 131–132
    interest groups and, 172–173
    in Japan, 64–68
    Korean War and, 62
    labor and, 154–156
    market creation and, 145–147
    militarism and, 66–67n, 66–68
    under Park Chung-hee, 61
Economic Planning Board (EPB), 63, 66
education, 9–12, 30, 56, 140
    centralization of, 141, 143
    elites and, 143
elections, 203. *See also* voting and voting
    rights
    1967 and 1971, 70–72

abstentionism and, 107, 107n
founding, 3–7, 36–38, 99, 102
low voter turnout for, 3–7
presidential system and, 129
electoral-professional parties, 7, 7n
elites
    authoritarianism and homogenous,
        114
    bureaucratic, 114–117, 124–128
    civil society and, 178
    concentric, 32–33, 138–140
    decentralization of, 142–143
    in democratization, 99
    divide and rule by, 105–106, 106n
    military, 61–63
    mobilization of bias and, 95, 95n
    pisŏn organizations and, 120–121
    political parties and, 97–98
    the press and, 17
    reform from above and, 93–94
    reform mandate and, 116
    regionalism and, 95–96, 109
    representation and, 109–110
    student movements and, 89
emergency decrees, 85, 86–87, 131
Emergency Order on Real-Name
        Financial Transactions and
        Confidentiality, 148, 148n
ethics, 173
executive branch, 117

factionalism, 106, 107
Fair Trade Act, 151n
Federation of All Hyundai Group Trade
        Unions, 153
Federation of Korean Industries, 172
Federation of Korean Trade Unions, 172
Ferguson, Adam, 169
founding elections, 3–7, 36–38, 99, 102
freedom of speech, 17, 78, 78n
freedom of the press, 16
freezing effect, 37–38, 37n
French Revolution, 33, 47–48

Gandhi, Mohandas K., 25n, 27
general strike of 1996, 153, 153n
generational issues, 4–5, 183
Gerschenkron, Alexander, 66
Giddens, Anthony, 16, 110
Gini coefficient, 8–9, 8n
globalization, 124–125. *See also*
    liberalism/liberalization
    cleavage from, 157–160
    conflict over, 193–194
    International Monetary Fund and,
      157–165
    labor and, 153–154
    market reform and, 148–150, 162
goals, national, 126
government. *See also* presidential system
    alternative, 25, 25n
    centralization and, 142–143
    competent, 200–203
    democracy and competent, 200–203
    incompetence of, 5, 71–72, 117–121,
      128–129
    opposition party and, 121–123
    state as, 54
government-circle organizations, 172–173
government examinations, 10–11
Gramsci, Antonio, 14n, 24n, 93n
Grand National Party, 97
grassroots mobilization, 17
growth-first strategy, 76–77, 147, 197–200
guardianship theory, 202

Habermas, Jürgen, 51n
haebang konggan. See liberation space
hagwŏn, 10, 10n
Hampshire, Stuart, 18
Han Pae-ho, 54
Hayek, F. A., 199
hegemony
    anti-communism and, 50–51
    of *chaebŏl*, 74–77, 165
    civil society and, 178–179
    definition of, 14n

government incompetence and, 117–
    121
the press and, 177–179
strong state and, 103–104
structure of conflicts and, 14–19
of vested interests, 14
Henderson, Gregory, 12, 33
Hirschman, Albert, 66, 67, 67n
Ho Chi Minh, 25n
Honam issues, 94–95, 97–98, 103, 105–
    106. *See also* regionalism
housing, 9
Hume, David, 169
Hyangbodan (Homeland Protection
    Group), 46, 46n
Hynix Semiconductor Inc., 159n
Hyŏnch'ongnyon, 153
hyper-centralization, 32–33
Hyundai group, 153, 159n

Ichiro, Hatoyama, 43
ideological interpellation, 50, 50n
ideology, narrow base of. *See also* anti-
    communism
    anti-communism and, 31–32, 49–51
    centralization and, 32–34, 143
    civil society and, 177–180
    Constitution and, 48–49
    democratization and, 188–189
    development of, 34–38
    government incompetence and, 121–
      123
    hegemony and, 118–119
    polarization of, 29–32
    political discourse and, 18, 50–51, 93
    political parties and, 36, 96–98
    the press and, 15–17
    regionalism and, 14
    structure of conflicts and, 14–19
    voter turnout and, 5–6
IMF. *See* International Monetary Fund
    (IMF)
imperial presidency, 131–135, 131n

import substitution, 55, 68–69
income
    civil society and, 181
    education and, 9–12
    increased inequality in, 8–14, 8n, 165, 181
    labor and, 154
    social consensus and, 17–19
    voter turnout and, 6–7
incompetence, government, 5, 71–72, 117–121, 128–129
    democracy and, 200–203
    voter turnout and, 5
Independence Alliance, 25
independence movement, 24–27
Indian National Congress, 25n, 27
indicative planning, 61–62, 61n
individualism, 181
industrialization. *See also chaebŏl*
    authoritarian, 74–77
    centralization and, 33, 138–139
    civil society and, 173–174
    democratization and, 63, 74–77
    developmental state theory and, 64–68
    elites and, 114
    growth-first strategy in, 76–77, 147, 197–200
    import substitution, 55
    in Japan, 64–68
    markets created by, 145–147
    media conglomerates and, 16–17
    middle class and, 69
    militarism and, 66–67n, 66–68
    under Park Chung-hee, 53–73, 82
    political systems and, 54–57
    regionalism and, 13
    social groups and, 69–70, 72
    timing of, 58–59, 66, 77
infrastructure, 54, 114–117, 125–128
interest groups, 50–51, 167, 171, 172–173. *See also* civil society
inter-Korean relations, 18–19, 30–31. *See also* reunification movement

internationalization policy, 149
International Monetary Fund (IMF), 157–165
    bureacratic elite and, 124
    chaebŏl reform and, 161–163
    civil society and, 180–181
    education and, 11
    labor and, 153–154, 156
    market reform and, 148–149
    reforms after bailout by, 119
    structural adjustment program, 161, 162
interventionism, 146–147

Japan
    1955 system in, 41–43
    authoritarianism under, 29
    colonial rule by, 23–24
    developmental state model of, 64–68
    normalization of relations with, 83, 83n, 84
    reverse course policy in, 42–43, 42n
    state-building in, 38–43
    vested property, 68, 69n
Johnson, Chalmers, 64
Joong Ang Ilbo (newspaper), 15
June 29 Declaration (1987), 81–82, 105–106
June 1987 Uprising, 24, 84, 104, 105–106, 129
    civil society and, 171
    democratization by pact and, 92–103, 92n, 188
    market reform and, 148
    by mass mobilization, 72–74, 82
    minjung movement and, 85–87
    Park Chung-hee and, 72–80
    pattern of, 88–89
    political, 90–91
    political parties and, 107–110
    presidential system and, 128–138
    social class and, 91–92
    the state after, 113–143

student movement and, 82, 83–85,
88–92
two-step, 103–106
weakness of movement for, 106–107

Karl, Terry L., 117
Keane, John, 16
Kia Motors, 151
Kim Dae-jung, 71, 77
abduction of, 83n
bureaucracy under, 126
chaebŏl reform under, 62, 151, 159,
160–163
civil society under, 178, 180
democratic movement and, 97
democratization of the state and,
115–117
elites and, 110, 124–125
hegemony and, 118–120
imperial presidency and, 133–134
labor issues and, 154–156
political parties and, 103
regionalism and, 94
student movement and, 84n
support for, 108
Kim Il Sung, 25
Kim Jong-pil, 118, 118n
Kim Ku, 25, 34
Kim Kyong-suk, 79n
Kim Kyu-sik, 34
Kim Sŏng-su, 25, 27, 34
Kim Yak-su, 40–41n
Kim Young-sam, 77
bureaucracy under, 126
chaebŏl reform under, 150–151
civil society under, 178
democratic movement and, 97
democratization of the state and,
115–117
elites and, 110, 124
expulsion of, 79n
globalization policy under, 149, 157
hegemony and, 118–119

imperial presidency and, 133–134
labor and, 152–153, 156
market reform under, 148, 160
student movement and, 84n
support for, 108
three-party merger and, 118, 118n
Kirchheimer, Otto, 7n
Korea Development Institute, 9
Korea Employers Federation, 172
Korean Central Intelligence Agency
(KCIA), 63, 126
Korean Communist Party (KCP), 27, 27n,
34
Korean Confederation of Trade Unions
(KCTU), 155
Korean Democratic Party (KDP), 30,
35–36, 59, 94
Korean Educational Development
Institute, 10
Korean Federation of Teachers'
Associations, 172
Korean People's Party, 27n
Korean Provisional Government (KPG),
34
Korean War, 62, 175
Korea Tripartite Commission, 154–155,
154n, 156
Kungmin undong ponbu, 100
Kwangju Uprising, 83, 84, 94–96, 104–
105, 171
Kyonghang Daily Newspaper, 78

labor and labor movements
anti-communism and, 49, 55–56
authoritarianism and, 75–76
civil society and, 181, 182–183
democratization and, 75–76, 82, 86–87,
91–92, 151–156
disdain for, 15
exclusion of from markets, 146–147
globalization and, 158–159
industrialization and, 55–56
market reform and, 148, 163

Park Chung-hee and, 69–70
presidential system and, 132
the press and, 79, 164
representation of, 6–7, 76
repression of conflict and, 190–191
social consensus and, 17–19
student movement and, 91–92
unemployment and, 9
Labor People's Party, 34
Ancien Régime et la Révolution
    (Tocqueville), 33–34
land reform, 31, 31n, 59–60, 60–61, 93–94
Latin America, 67, 82, 87, 117–118,
    122–123, 168
legislative branch, 134
legitimacy, 61, 113, 175
LG Semiconductor Company, 159, 159n
Liberal Democratic Party (Japan), 41–43
liberalism/liberalization, 36–37, 36n. *See
    also* globalization
    bureaucracy and, 124–125
    civil society and, 168–169, 169–170,
        174–175
    market reform and, 148–150
    student movement and, 85
Liberal Party, 35–36, 39
liberation space, 23–24, 25, 28, 188
liberty, negative and positive, 175, 175n
Limongi, Ferdinando, 56, 56n
Linz, Juan J., 24n
Lipset, Seymour, 13n, 37n, 54, 56, 137–
    138
Locke, John, 169, 174, 175
Loveman, Brian, 82n

"mad cow" candlelight vigils, 4
mandate to reform, 116, 116n
Maravall, José María, 193–194, 193n
March First Independence Movement
    (1919), 29–30
markets
    authoritarian industrialization and,
        145–147

democratization and, 145–165
    failure to reform, 160–163
    globalization and, 148–150
    inequality effects of, 194
    parallel development of democracy
        and, 124–125
    reform of, 145–150
    regulation of, 8
    social inequality and, 8
    super-*chaebŏl* and, 198–200
martial law, 87
Marx, Karl, 60
mass mobilization, 23–29, 50–51, 72–74,
    82
mass movements, 167–168, 169, 176–177,
    183–184, 188. *See also* civil society
McAdam, Doug, 84–85, 84n
media conglomerates, 16–17
median voters, 122, 122n
militarism, 66–67, 66–67n, 75
    bureaucratic elite and, 114–117
    democratization and, 85–86
    minjung movement and, 85–87
    the press and, 79–80
military elite, 62–63
military guardianship, 82, 82n
Miller, John, 169
Minbodan (People's Protection Group),
    46, 46n
Ministry of International Trade and
    Industry (MITI), 64–65, 66
Minjok t'ongil yonnmaeng (National
    Unification Alliance), 91
minjung movement, 82, 85–87, 139, 174,
    176–177
MITI and the Japanese Miracle
    (Johnson), 64
mobilization
    of bias, 95, 95n
    bottom-up mass, 23–24
    mass, 23–29, 50–51, 72–74, 188
    top-down, 38
modernization, 40

conservative, 89
democratization and, 85–87
under Park Chung-hee, 53–54, 63
the press and, 78
unavoidability of, 72
modernization theory, 54, 56, 58
monopolies, 16–17, 146. *See also chaebŏl*
Moore, Barrington, Jr., 54, 56–57, 56n,
    58, 66–67n, 72, 74, 93n
Mosca, Gaetano, 190n

Nasser, Gamel Abdel, 63
National Agricultural Cooperative
    Federation, 172
National Assembly "spy infiltration"
    incident, 40–41, 40n
National Campaign Headquarters
    for Democratic Constitutional
    Amendment, 100, 100n
National Congress for New Politics, 97
National Election Commission, 4
National Independence Alliance, 34, 34n
nationalism, 24–27, 29–30, 49
national judiciary examination, 11
National Security Agency, 126
National Security Law, 41n, 49
National Society for the Rapid
    Realization of Korean Independence
    (NSRRKI), 38, 38n
National Unification Alliance, 91, 91n
nature, state of, 169, 174–175
Nazi regime, 170–171, 170n
Nehru, Jawaharlal, 25n, 27
neo-liberalism
    bureaucratic elites and, 124–125
    CEO presidency and, 131–132
    civil society and, 180–181
    conflict over, 193–194
    definition of, 11n
    democracy and, 194–197
    labor and, 156
    market reform and, 149, 162–163,
        163–164

neo-modernization theory, 56, 56n
Nettl, Peter, 113
New Democratic Party, 70–71, 83–84,
    83n, 94
    minjung movement and, 87
    in three-party merger, 118, 118n
New Democratic Republican Party, 118,
    118n
new economic policy, 152, 152n
New Korean Democratic Party, 84, 84n
New Korea Party, 97
New Millennium Democratic Party, 97
newspaper subscription trade practices,
    17
New Village Movement, 70
Nixon, Richard, 133
non-governmental organizations, 167. *See
    also* civil society

October Uprisings of 1946, 28, 28n
O'Donnell, Guillermo A., 3n, 36, 54, 55,
    92n, 99
    on corporatism, 172n
    on delegative democracy, 122–123,
        122n, 134–135
    on horizontal accountability, 126–127,
        126n
overdeveloped states, 28–29, 33–34, 55

pact, democratization by, 92–103, 92n,
    187–189
Pak Hŏn-yŏng, 25, 27n, 34
Panebianco, Angelo, 7n
Park Chung-hee
    bureaucracy under, 125–126
    chronology of events under, 53
    coup by, 83
    democratization and, 72–80
    developmental state theory and, 64–68
    development model of, 125, 163–164
    economic policy under, 66
    elections of 1967 and 1971, 70–72
    emergency decrees by, 85

government competence under, 202
industrialization under, 13, 61–68
militarism under, 66–67
the press and, 77–80
regime characteristics of, 53–68
social support base for, 68–72
support for, 61–63
parliamentary system, 129
parochialism, 95–96, 96n
Party for Peace and Democracy, 97
passive revolution, 89
path-dependency, 99
patriarchy, 130
pisŏn organizations, 120–121, 120n, 136
plastic surgery, 15
Plato, 130
pluralism, 12
    chaebŏl and, 198
    civil society and, 173, 180–182
    corporatism compared with, 154–155n
    decentralization and, 138–140, 142–143
    presidential system and, 130
polarization, 8–9, 29–32, 34–36, 49–51.
    See also ideology, narrow base of
policy-making, 66
policy of sharing the burden, 152
policy regimes, 196–197
political classes, 190–191, 190n
political discourse, 18. *See also* conflict
    anti-communism and, 50–51, 93
    desire for change and, 193–195
Political Man: The Social Bases of Politics
    (Lipset), 137–138
Political Meeting of Eight Representatives,
    100n
political opportunity structure, 84–85
political parties
    after independence, 26
    boss system in, 36
    cadre, 7, 7n
    catch-all, 7, 7n, 36
    characteristics of Korean, 36
    civil society and, 175, 176
competent government and, 202–203
conservatism of, 34–38, 188–192
democratization and, 104–105, 107–
    110, 109, 187–189, 188–189
electoral-professional, 7, 7n
freezing effect in, 37–38, 37n
government incompetence and, 121–
    123
imperial presidency and, 131, 134–135
inclusion of, 42–43
interest groups and, 171
Japan 1955 system of, 41–43
labor excluded from, 182–183
lack of alternatives in, 189–192
movements and, 97
opposition, 36, 93–94
    democratization and, 107–110
    oppression of, 40–41, 40n
    social base for, 121–123
origin and characteristics of Korean,
    92–94
regionalism and, 14, 94–98
rejection of current, 19
relevant, 182, 182n
representation by, 3–7
under Rhee, 39–40
social foundations of, 94–96, 136–138
strong state and, 103–104
structure of, 96–98, 102–103
suppression of, 27
two-party system and, 34–38
voter alignment and, 192–195
Political Parties and Political Development
    (LaPalombara & Weiner, eds.), 7n
Political Parties: Organization and Power
    (Panebianco), 7n
political society, 24, 24n
politics of vortex, 33
poverty, 9, 67. *See also* income
presidential system, 48, 128–138
    authoritarianism and, 129–131
    bureaucracy and, 117, 126–127
    constitutional amendments on, 128–129

democratic leadership and, 135–138
imperial presidency and, 131–135
three-term amendment and, 71–72, 83n
press, role of, 15–17, 77–80
    anti-communism and, 177–179,
        183–184
    civil society and, 177–179, 183–184
    imperial presidency and, 134
    Kim Dae-jung and, 119–120
    labor movement and, 79, 164
    vested interests and, 102
private sphere, 51, 51n, 168, 169–170, 199
privatization, 149, 151
Progressive Party, 35–36, 35n, 40–41
propaganda, 131
Przeworski, Adam, 36n, 54, 56, 90n, 92,
    99, 117–118
public accountants' examination, 11
public sphere, 51, 51n, 169–170, 173–174,
    199
Pusan/Kyongnam faction, 110
Pusan-Masan Uprising (1979), 79n
Pusan Political Upheaval, 41, 41n

Reagan, Ronald, 11n
real-name financial transactions law, 148,
    148n
Red Devils, 4
reform from above, 93–94, 93n, 146–147
régime censitaire, 44–45, 45n
regionalism, 12–14
    anti-communism and, 15
    civil society and, 182–183
    conflict repression and, 191
    democratization and, 103, 104–105
    elites and, 95–96, 109
    pisŏn organizations and, 121
    political parties and, 14, 94–98
relevant party, 182, 182n
rent-seeking, 6, 6n, 121
representation
    accountability and, 202–203
    bureaucracy and, 34

of conflict, 136–138
conservative democratization and,
    100–103
democratization and, 187–189
elites and, 109–110
ideological narrowness and, 5–6
of labor, 182–183
labor and, 6–7, 76
opposition party and, 121–123
polarization of, 34–36
presidential system and, 134–135
the press and, 17
voter turnout and, 3–7
Republican Party, 70–71
Reunification Democratic Party, 97, 100n,
    118, 118n
reunification movement, 91, 91n, 98–99,
    119–120
reverse course, 42–43, 42n
Rhee, Syngman, 25, 27, 30
    Caesarism under, 39–41
    centralization under, 59–60
    Constitutional amendments and, 41,
        41n
    constitutional power of, 48
    democratization after fall of, 59
    division of Korea and, 35
    elites and, 109
    military elites and, 62
    political parties and, 34, 40–41, 40–41n,
        93
    the press and, 78, 78n
    student movement and, 88–89, 91
    support for, 60–61
Roh Moo-hyun, 118, 124, 126, 156, 180
Roh Tae-woo, 110, 115, 124
    arrested, 133
    internationalization policy of, 149
    labor and, 152, 156
Rokkan, Stein, 13n, 37n
Rousseau, Jean-Jacques, 130
rule of law, 199–200
Rustow, Dankwart A., 18, 44

Sabuk Mining Town incident (1980), 87, 87n
Samsung, 8, 151, 198, 200
Sangdo-dong, 84n
Sartori, Giovanni, 182n
Schattschneider, E. E., 13n, 95, 95n, 171
Schlesinger, Arthur, Jr., 131, 131n, 133
Schmitter, Philippe C., 3n, 36, 92n, 99, 108n, 117, 155n
Schumpeter, Joseph A., 51n
secret-line organizations, 120–121, 120n, 136
Seoul
    centralization and, 32–33, 140–142
    urban concentration in, 12
Seoul Spring (1980), 83, 87, 104, 105, 171
September General Strike of 1946, 28n
"Seven Principles of the Way to Peaceful Reunification," 40–41n
Shefter, Martin, 104, 104n
Shigeru, Yoshida, 43
Shonfield, Andrew, 61n
Smith, Adam, 169
social consensus, 189
social groups and socioeconomic status
    after Korean War, 62–63
    anti-communism and, 49, 50–51
    authoritarianism and, 56–57
    chaebŏl and, 69
    civil society and, 168–169
    conflict repression and, 190–192
    constitutional process and, 46–49
    democratization and, 73–74, 90–91, 101, 106–107, 160–163
    educational status and, 9–12
    farmers, 69–70
    globalization and, 157–160
    industrialization and, 56, 57–58
    inequality increased in, 8–14
    market reform and, 147, 160–163, 165
    militarism and, 66–68
    minjung movement, 85–87
    Park Chung-hee support base and, 68–72

political discourse and, 50–51
political parties and, 36, 121–123, 136–138
premature democracy and, 45–46
presidential system and, 132
regionalism and, 12–14
representation and, 6–7
Rhee supporters, 60–61
student movements and, 89
universal suffrage and, 45–46
voter turnout and, 6–7
Socialist Party (Japan), 41–43
social justice, 6, 17–19
social mobility, 10–11, 147
social movements, 84–85
social welfare, 181
Song Chin-u, 27, 34
South Korean New Democratic Party, 27n
South Korean Workers' Party (SKWP), 27n, 34
spatial model of voting, 121–122, 121n
Special Committee for Constitutional Amendments, 100n
specialization of business activities, 151, 151n
stakeholder capitalism, 199
state, the
    after democratization, 113–143
    authoritarianism and, 28–29, 114
    building, 23–51
    bureaucracy and, 125–128
    centralization of power and, 32–34
    chaebŏl power and, 163–165
    chronology of, 23
    civil society and, 168–169, 171–180
    Cold War and, 24–27
    corporatism of, 172–173, 172n, 174
    definition of, 114
    ideological polarization and, 29–32
    interventionism by, 146–147
    Korean and Japanese compared, 38–43
    levels of, 114–117
    markets and, 125, 145–147

overdeveloped, 28–29, 33–34, 55
    strong, 23–29, 103–104
state of nature, 169, 174–175
Stepan, Alfred, 24n
strategic ambiguity, 122
student movements, 62–63, 73–74
    civil society and, 173–174
    democracy movement and, 89–92
    in democratization, 82, 83–85, 88–89
    the press on, 78
    radical, 98–99
success orientation, 14–15
Sunshine Policy, 119, 178, 193
supply-side corporatism, 155, 155n
Sustainable Democracy (Przeworski et
    al.), 117–118

Taegu/Kyongbuk faction, 110
Tarrow, Sidney, 84–85, 84n
technocratic managerialism, 75, 75n
Thatcher, Margaret, 11n
*Structural Transformation of the Public
    Sphere* (Habermas), 51n
three-party merger, 118, 118n, 148, 152
three whites industry, 68, 68n
Tilly, Charles, 84–85, 84n
Tocqueville, Alexis de, 24n, 33–34, 60, 77,
    113, 170, 179, 179n
Tonggyo-dong, 84n
"The Trajectory of Poverty in Korea
    and Analysis of Its Factors" (Korea
    Development Institute), 9
*Transitions from Authoritarian Rule:
    Tentative Conclusions about
    Uncertain Democracies* (O'Donnell
    & Schmitter), 3n
transparency
    chaebŏl and, 150, 158
    globalization and, 158–159
    in markets, 146
trasformismo, 98, 98n
Traxler, Franz, 155n
trusteeship issue, 28

uncertainty, institutionalization of, 101, 102
unemployment, 9, 17–18, 193–194
United Liberal Democrats (ULD), 163
urban concentration, 12
USAMGIK (United States Army Military
    Government in Korea), 27
U.S.-USSR Joint Committee, 28, 28n

values, civil society and, 173
Verba, Sidney, 96n
vested interests, 14
    centralization and, 139
    civil society and, 183–184
    democratization and, 102
    globalization and, 157
    Kim Dae-jung and, 119–120
    the press, 80
vested property, 68, 69n
voluntary associations, 170–171, 181
voter turnout, 3–7, 46, 189
voting and voting rights
    civil society strength and, 183–184
    elections of 1967 and 1971, 70–72
    low turnout and, 3–7
    Park Chung-hee and, 70
    party system and, 19
    political parties and freezing effect in,
        37–38
    premature democracy and, 44–46
    Rhee and, 60–61
    spatial model on, 121–122, 121n
    universal suffrage, 44–46
    voter alignment and, 192–195
    voter mobilization and, 6

War on Terror, 133
Washington consensus, 149, 149n
Weber, Max, 64, 75n, 115
welfare states, 154–155
Williamson, John, 149n
winner-take-all systems, 39
Woo-Cumings, Meredith, 64
World Cup, 4, 24

YH Trading Company incident, 79, 79n,
    87
Young Turks, 63
Yŏ Un-hyŏng, 25, 27, 27n, 34–35
youth, 4–5

Yushin system, 55–56, 73–74
    democratization and, 85–87
    opposition to, 83, 83n
    press autonomy and, 78–79
    regionalism in, 94–96

The authorized representative in the EU for product safety and compliance is:
Mare Nostrum Group
B.V Doelen 72
4831 GR Breda
The Netherlands

www.ingramcontent.com/pod-product-compliance
Lightning Source LLC
Chambersburg PA
CBHW070407270326
41926CB00014B/2738